Dussich   New Perspectives in Control Theory:
         Social Coping of Youth under Supervision

Interdisziplinäre Beiträge zur kriminologischen Forschung

Herausgegeben vom
Kriminologischen Forschungsinstitut
Niedersachsen e. V.
Direktor Dr. Helmut Kury

Band 11

Carl Heymanns Verlag KG · Köln · Berlin · Bonn · München

New Perspectives in Control Theory: Social Coping of Youth under Supervision

Von John P. J. Dussich

Carl Heymanns Verlag KG · Köln · Berlin · Bonn · München

CIP-Kurztitelaufnahme der Deutschen Bibliothek

Dussich, John P. J.:
New perspectives in control theory : social coping of youth under supervision /
von John P. J. Dussich. – Köln ; Berlin ; Bonn ; München : Heymann, 1985.
 (Interdisziplinäre Beiträge zur kriminologischen Forschung ; Bd. 11)
 ISBN 3-452-20282-8
NE: GT

Das Werk ist urheberrechtlich geschützt. Die dadurch begründeten Rechte, insbesondere die der Übersetzung, des Nachdruckes, der Entnahme von Abbildungen, der Funksendung, der Wiedergabe auf photomechanischem oder ähnlichem Wege und der Speicherung in Datenverarbeitungsanlagen, bleiben, auch bei nur auszugsweiser Verwertung, vorbehalten.

»Gefördert aus Mitteln der Stiftung Volkswagenwerk«

© Carl Heymanns Verlag KG · Köln · Berlin · Bonn · München 1985

1985   ISBN 3-452-20282-8
Gedruckt von MVR Druck Köln GmbH

> "... no more important task faces the social sciences today than to determine by which 'image of man' they are to be led."
>
> Reinhard Bendix

Acknowledgements

In spite of the fact that only one name appears on the cover of this final report, many persons, named and not named, participated in this two and a half year research project.

First and foremost was H.-Folke Jacobsen who was my constant companion, through theory and methods, through administravia and analysis, gleefully playing the "devil's advocate", yet always constructive and supportive. He continually made personal sacrifices beyond the call of duty. I am honored to call him my friend.

No research project functions without assistants: those poor souls who are offered up for the cause and who spend their time ungloriously "in the trenches", fighting the boredom of seemingly endless numbers and plagued by doubts about the sanity of it all. My debt of gratitude goes out to Brigitta Köhler, Udo Iwannek, Helga Hattendorf, Bettina Greffrath, Helgard Heim, Uwe Bartels, Michael Gernke, Susanne Müller, Axel Schöpf, Ingo Briel, Jens Thompson, and John Kiedrowski.

Perhaps the most unobtrusive support a research project receives is from that cadre of people known as "administrative support". These are persons who unfortunately don't have the opportunity to directly participate in the research decisions, yet play a vital role in its eventual outcome. To Helmut Kury, Eva Zimmermann, Arno Oestreich, Johanna Mietzner, Maria

Burghardt, Gunter Link, Annemarie Kirmst, Petra Effinghausen, Doris Habenicht, Heinz Barth, and Susan Eckenberg, many thanks.

Also of significant assistance was the advice given by the KFN Kuratorium and the cooperation of the judges and parole supervisors throughout Lower Saxony. I also wish to say thanks to all my colleagues at the Institute for their suggestions, friendship and patience with my "holprig" German.

A special note of gratitude goes to that special group of friend-colleagues who, during the course of this project, provided valuable input, criticism, feedback and support: Friedhelm Berckhauer, Richard Blath, Peter Dillig, Paul C. Friday, Wolfgang Gottschalk, Burkhard Hasenpusch, Hans-Jürgen Kerner, Gerd F. Kirchhoff, Heinz W. Krohne, Wolf Nowack, Klaus Sessar, Gernot Steinhilper, Magdalena Stemmer-Lück, Josine Junger-Tas, Kurt Weiss, Elmar Weitekamp, and Catrin Wenzel.

Final thanks go to my family, Edda, Edward and George, who have always been the real victims of my professional aspirations; to them go my deepest gratitude.

I wish to dedicate this work to my parents Manlio and Maria who habe always supported me in my diverse endeavors, encouraged me to excell an taught me how to cope.

Table of Contents

	Acknowledgements	5
	Table of Contents	7
	Figures	9
1	General Perspectives	13
1.1	Abstract	13
1.2	The Purpose and Value of this Research	15
1.3	Main Research Questions	18
2	Parole	19
2.1	Background Issues in Parole Research	19
2.2	Comments on Parole Decision-Making	26
2.3	An Overview of Parole Practices in Lower Saxony	29
2.4	The Parole Process in Lower Saxony, Germany	38
2.5	The Youthful Parolee File-card Pre-study for Hannover	43
2.6	The Staff/Client Interaction (According to American Studies)	53
2.7	Interaction with Others	56
2.8	Parole Problem Pre-study	59
3	Theory	81
3.1	Coping Theory	83
3.1.1	A Survey of Coping	83
3.1.2	Comments on Real-life Coping	87
3.2	Control Theory	89
3.2.1	Hirschi's Control Theory	90
3.2.2	Friday's Control Theory	94
3.2.3	Further Remarks on Control Theory	98
3.3	Spaceround Integration	99
3.4	The Social Coping Model	108
4	General Methodological Information	121
4.1	Instruments	121
4.1.1	Development of the Coping Instrument	121
4.1.2	Development of the Coping Dimensions Scale	127
4.1.3	Development of Control Theory Questionnaire	128
4.1.4	Development of the Integration Instrument	130
4.1.5	The Problem Moment Continua System (PMCS)	131
4.1.6	Classification Method for Social Class	132
4.2	Obtaining Access to Subjects	134
5	The Coping/Supervision Study	137
5.1	Data Collection	138
5.2	Data Reduction	143
5.3	Findings	144
5.4	Conclusions	155

6		The Success/Failure Study	159
6.1		Data Collection	161
6.2		Data Reduction	165
6.3		Findings	166
6.4		Conclusions	199
7		Implications for Policy, Practice, and Research	211
7.1		Policy	211
7.2		Research	213

Summary 217

    Social Coping of Youth under Supervison 217

    Junge Erwachsene, die unter Bewährung stehen und ihr Social Coping 247

General Bibliography 281

Appendix

    Text of skits III
    Examples of the Interview Interaction According to Spacerounds XVII
    Coping Dimensions XXIII
    Interview Questionnaire XXVII
    The Integration Instrument IL

Figures

1.	Comparison of the Supervision Research Since 1954 According to Age, Groups, and Category	17
2.	Comparison of the Number of Persons under Supervision and Those Imprisoned in Lower Saxony	30
3.	Client Caseload for each Supervisor in Lower Saxony	31
4.	Youthful Parolees in the State of Lower Saxony	34
5.	Drug Criminality in the State of Lower Saxony	34
6.	Unemployed Persons in the Region of Hannover	34
7.	The Parole Process - formal and informal - as seen by a House leader at JVA Hameln, Lower Saxony	39
8.	The Parole Process as seen by Parole Supervisors in Lower Saxony	42
9.	Information File Card	44
10.	The Age of Youthful Parolees in the State Court District of Hannover 1981	46
11.	Marital Status of the Parolee	48
12.	Status of Parents	48
13.	Number of Persons convicted as Youth and Adults	49
14.	The Offense Breakdown for this Group	50
15.	Time Remaining on Original Sentence at Release - Parolees -	51
16.	Length of Parole as of 1.1.1982	52
17.	Results of the Parole Problems Pre-Study	62
18.	Problem Spaceround Prioritization: Comparisons between Parolees and Nonparolees	69
19.	Problem Spaceround Prioritization: Comparisons between Parolees and Supervisors	70

20.	Problem Spaceround Prioritization: Comparisons between Parolees and Adult Prisoners	71
21.	Problem Spaceround Prioritization: Comparisons between Parolees and Studies	72
22.	Problem Spaceround Prioritization: Comparisons between Supervisors and Studies	74
23.	Problem Spaceround Prioritization: Comparisons between Supervisors and Adult Prisoners	75
24.	Problem Spaceround Prioritization: Comparisons between Adult Prisoners and Parole Studies	76
25.	Problem Spaceround Prioritization: Comparisons between Nonparolees and Supervisors	77
26.	Problem Spaceround Prioritization: Comparisons between Nonparolees and Adult Prisoners	78
27.	Problem Spaceround Prioritization: Comparisons between Nonparolees and Studies	79
28.	Causes of Delinquency	92
29.	Significant Role-Relationships	95
30.	Spacerounds	100
31.	The Coping Milieu	110
32.	Individual Resources	111
33.	Problem Moment Continua	113
34.	The Four Phases of the Problem Response Process	115
35.	Spaceround Coping Milieu	119
36.	Skit: "Argument at the Dinner Table" (see Appendix)	
37.	Skit: "The Neighbor Lady" (see Appendix)	
38.	Skit: "Poor Work" (see Appendix)	
39.	Skit: "At the Employment Office" (see Appendix)	
40.	Examples of the Interview Interaction According to Spacerounds: Family, Neighbor, Employment Office, and Work (see Appendix)	

41.	Coping Dimensions (see Appendix)	
42.	Rater Mean Values for all 13 Coping Dimensions	129
43.	Interview Questionnaire (see Appendix)	
44.	The Integration Instrument (see Appendix)	
45.	Spaceround: The Family Skit 1: Argument at Supper	146
46.	Spaceround: Community/at the Apartment Skit 2: The Friendly Neighbor	148
47.	Spaceround: Community/Civil Servant Skit 3: Disappointment at the Employment Office	149
48.	Spaceround: Workplace Skit 4: Argument with the Boss	150
49.	Factor Analysis Using Four Separate Skit Responses	152
50.	Coping Dimensions Across all 4 Skits Correlated with Word Count	154
51.	The Percentage of Success/Failure with Regard to Extent of Spaceround Importance	167
52.	The Relative Spaceround Importance for Successful Subjects	170
53.	The Relative Spaceround Importance for Failure Subjects	172
54.	Success and Failure Financial Dependency in the Family of Orientation	173
55.	Success and Failure Frequency of Contact in the Family of Orientation	173
56.	Success and Failure Frequency of Contact in the Family of Procreation	175
57.	Success and Failure Emotional Dependency in the Family of Procreation	176
58.	Success and Failure Norm Similarity at Work	176
59.	Success and Failure Cognitive Dependency at Work	178
60.	Success and Failure Emotional Dependency at Work	178

61.	Success and Failure Cognitive Dependency in the Community	179
62.	Success and Failure Emotional Dependency in the Community	179
63.	Success and Failure Frequency of Contact with Peers	180
64.	Success and Failure Norm Similarity with Peers	180
65.	Success and Failure Frequency of Contact with Civil Servants	182
66.	Success and Failure Extent of Meaningful Relationships with Civil Servants	182
67.	Success and Failure Extent of Meaningful Relationships with the Community	186
68.	Success and Failure Extent of Meaningful Relationships with Peers	186
69.	Success and Failure Extent of Meaningful Relationships at Work	187
70.	Success and Failure Importance of Family of Orientation	187
71.	Success and Failure Extent of Meaningful Relationships with the Family of Procreation	188
72.	Success and Failure Extent of Meaningful Relationships with the Family of Orientation	188
73.	Elementary School Education	193
74.	Vocational School Education	194
75.	Success and Failure Differences on 13 Coping Dimensions for Skit 1	205
76.	Success and Failure Differences on 13 Coping Dimensions for Skit 2	206
77.	Success and Failure Differences on 13 Coping Dimensions for Skit 3	207
78.	Success and Failure Differences on 13 Coping Dimensions for Skit 4	208
79.	Success and Failure Differences on 13 Coping Dimensions over all four Skits	209

1 General Perspectives

> "Action is built up in coping with the world instead of merely being released from a preexisting psychological structure by factors playing upon that structure. By making indications to himself and by interpreting what he indicates, the human being has to forge or piece together a line of action."
>
> Herbert Blumer

1.1 Abstract

With the publication of his book Causes of Delinquency, Travis Hirschi launched Control Theory on a new course. His focal point was the bond. Subsequently, Paul Friday extended Control Theory and his focal point was role relationships. Spaceround Integration Theory is an attempt to synthesize the micro-sociological aspects of Hirschi's control model with the macro-sociological aspects of Friday's control model and then, to develop a broader dynamic extention which would more fully explain the social control mechanisms of all human behavior not just those of delinquents. Spaceround is a concept that embodies five dimensions: place, objects, people, ideas and time. It provides an interactive backdrop for explaining the milieu within which social control takes place. The main focal point in this model is meaningful relationships which are principally influenced by the conjugate conditions of frequency, duration, self-disclosure, cathexis, dependency, norm similarity, and overlap. These relationships determine to what degree an individual becomes integrated into a given spaceround.

An extension of control theory is made by taking a sociopsychological approach to explain the dynamics of how people deal with problems in their changing environments using the state of the art of psychological coping research, and it tries to explain why some people succeed and others fail. It takes into account the macroprocesses of social structures and how they influence individual behavior through significant spacerounds and, it takes into account the microprocesses of cognition and how they influence individual behavior through the Coping Process. Herein Social Coping will mean the successful application of a person's behavioral repertoire in overcoming problems.

Prior to using this theoretical model, two pre-studies were conducted, one to provide basic information on the research subjects, and one to identify the major problem areas and situations of young parolees. The social coping model was empirically applied to eighty-one young male offenders who were under supervision. The subjects watched four video skits, were then measured in terms of thirteen coping dimensions, and finally given a questionnaire based primarily on control theory items. From this data collection effort, two studies emerged: first was a methodological analysis that dealt with 81 subjects under community supervision (Bewährung) and which focused on coping skills; second was a study that used 35 parole subjects who had either succeeded or failed.

In the analysis of coping dimensions it was found that three basic factors could be distinguished. Each of these three factors were identified by unique clusters of dimensions with heavy loadings. The dimensions in these three dominant clusters produced a unique character for each factor: I - Normative (accounting for 22.7 % of the variance), II - Outcome (accounting for 6.3 % of the variance), III - Coping (accounting for 47.7 % of the variance). These findings would suggest that the subjects in this study responded to coping situations in three basic ways: in concern with normative expectations, with a focus toward behavioral outcomes, and with a special orientation to coping skills.

The success/failure substudy showed that subjects who succeeded and those who failed could be distinguished on the basis of their total coping score ($t = 2.17$; $p = .038$). This suggested that those parolees who succeeded obtained significantly better coping scores than did those who failed. It was also found that successful subjects had significantly higher levels of interaction frequency over all spacerounds than did the failure subjects ($t = 4.56$; $p = .0001$), and that those who succeeded had higher degrees of individual integration than those who failed ($t = 2.01$; $p = .053$).

While this research project was not conducted to specifically test the Spaceround Integration model or the Social Coping model (as they evolved during the course of the research), the findings, none-the-less, lend considerable support to the validity of these theoretical models.

1.2 The Purpose and Value of this Research

The purpose of this research was to gather information about the ability of youthful parolees in the Hannover area to cope with their lives in the period immediately following their release from prison. More specifically, this research was interested in finding out about the techniques used to achieve success in specific problem areas such as in the family, place of work, with neighbors, among friends, and with civil servants.

The value of this research would be realized in applying its findings to the various agencies which either prepare or assist parolees to succeed as well as to those agencies that make decisions as to whether a sentenced offender will receive parole and whether a parolee is to remain under parole or be released. If this research is able to expand our current knowledge of parolees' use of coping skills, the information could become an important asset to all decisions made with regard to the parole process.

Another important dimension of this research's potential value is in focusing on success. According to the 1979 statistics in Lower Saxony on youthful offenders who were placed on parole after serving time in prison, 59 % succeeded (see Rechtspflege, Fachserie 10, Reihe 5: Bewährungshilfe, 1979, 36-37. Statistisches Bundesamt Wiesbaden (Ed.)). Why they succeeded and how they succeeded is a relative mystery. In the Federal Republic of Germany, this area of concern has been almost totally neglected. Much of what has been studied thus far, has been concerned with describing the characteristics of failure.

In the last twenty years about 82 % of the probation and parole research has dealt with adults and only 18.0 % with youth (see Figure 1). When comparing the extent of research conducted between parole and probation, one finds that only 27.9 % has dealt with parole and 72.1 % with probation. This means that the most over-researched client is the adult on probation (57.3 %), and the least researched client is the youth on parole (3.3 %). Thus, this research focused on an under-researched client (the youth parolee), with a relatively under-researched concern (success).

In an effort to focus on success, this researcher decided to investigate the process of overcoming problems and difficulties by youth on parole. This process of dealing with problematic situations is referred to as coping. Coping, however, is too general a concept to use in a small focused research project. A person attempts to cope with every problem, large or small. Hypothetically, one would be confronted with the totality of youth parolee problem solving. Therefore, another aspect of the coping phenomena was needed.

Figure 1: COMPARISON OF THE SUPERVISION RESEARCH SINCE
1954 ACCORDING TO AGE, GROUPS, AND CATEGORY

		AGE GROUPS		totals
		Youth	Adults	
S U P E R V I S I O N C A T E G O R Y	P R O B A T I O N	4^1 5^2 9 (14.8 %)	21^1 14^2 35 (57.3 %)	44 (72.1 %)
	P A R O L E	1^1 1^2 2 (3.3 %)	10^1 5^2 15 (24.6 %)	17 (27.9 %)
totals		11 (18.0 %)	50 (82.0 %)	61 (100.0 %)

Sources: [1] Journal "Bewährungshilfe", Juli 1954 - September 1980
[2] Library of the "Deutschen Bewährungshilfe e.V.",
Bonn 1981

The logical next step was to consider patterns of coping. The principle question then became what types of coping behaviors could be discernable as patterns. Were these patterns meaningful? Did they distinguish between those parolees who were successful and those who were not? Were these patterns influenced by the socialization process and/or by current relationships? How did these patterns cluster and become part of individual coping repertoires? Were coping repertoires different for parolees and probationers, and between those who succeeded and those who failed on supervision?

This line of thought evolved from a concern for how parolees achieve success, to a more focused inquiry on coping repertoires and their relationships to other variables.

1.3 Main Research Questions

- Do coping patterns exist that differentiate between youth parolees who fulfill their parole periods successfully, and those who are returned to prison because they failed on parole.

- Do the number of meaningful relationships have an effect on coping patterns.

- Does the intensity of relationships have an effect on coping patterns.

- How are coping patterns effected by other variables such as: age, education, socioeconomic status, family situation, work situation, relationship to peers, etc.

- What is the inter-relationship between coping, social integration and other social phenomena.

- What is the relationship of coping to individual resources.

2 Parole

> "It would seem that a series of relatively limited studies on the environmental correlates of successful and unsuccessful transitions to community life could be of some more direct utility and could also serve as building blocks in a general theory of adoptation."
>
> Marc William Renzema

2.1 Background Issues in Parole Research

Parole, as it is currently known, is the result of the development of measures to better control criminals within the criminal justice process. It has three basic concepts (see Giardini, 1959, 5-6):

1. a conditional remission of part of the sentence or its commutation,
2. a contract or agreement between the recipient of parole and the authority granting it, and,
3. a provision for the supervision of the parolee under ordinary social conditions.

These concepts can be traced to such practices as the conditional pardon, the indenturing of servants and apprentices, the transportation of criminals to the New World, and the Australian system of conditional liberation later to be called the ticket-of-leave (pp. 6-7).

A number of these concepts were first introduced in the penal codes of the 16th and 17th centuries. Commutation was first used as a type of pardon and later as an incentive for good behavior in prisons. The "good-time" concept came from this origin. In France in 1832 this form of conditional release was used with juvenile offenders. Spain used it in the Cadiz code of 1805. The concept of the indeterminate sentence has its roots in the Middle Ages as a device to control habitual offenders. Its first appearance was in the code of 1532 under Charles V of Germany and later in the code of 1768 of Maria Theresia. It is interesting to note that this practice of the indeterminate sentence gained widespread use in Europe and particularly in Germany. One of the major developers of this concept was Obermaier in Germany from 1830 to 1862 who expanded it, especially to include helping inmates in vocational trades (p. 8).

It can be seen that the concept of parole, as we know it today, is the result of numerous contributions, primarily in Europe. However, the word "parole" was first used in America by the writer S.G. Howe of Boston, Massachusetts in 1846 (p. 9).

In the face of severe criticism by reformers, Americans were searching for new answers to the problems created by prisons. In England, Spain, and Germany, systems of reformation in prison with conditional release had received much international praise. Thus, in Michigan in 1869 the first indeterminate sentence law was passed, primarily due to the efforts of Zebulon R. Brockway. However, this law was later declared unconstitutional. In spite of this setback, in 1876 as Brockway took charge of the Elmira Reformatory, he was successful in having the same basic law passed in New York, thereby allowing him the opportunity to establish a complete system.

This first parole system had a method for grading inmates, providing compulsory education, and establishing a careful process for parole selection. The first parole supervisors were volunteers, called "guardians", and the parolee had to report to their guardians on the first day of each month. Today all 50 American states have parole laws on their statute books (see Giardini, 1959, 11-12).

Because parole was established separately in each of the states, each one developed a different brand from the same basic concept. While recent attempts have been made to standardize these different systems through the use of national standards and goals, they remain none-the-less a somewhat complex array of different structures, functions and practices (American Correctional Association, 1966; National Advisory Commission on Criminal Justice Standards and Goals, 1973).

According to Paul Hahn, today there are four main reasons for the use of parole (1976, 149):

1. it is cheaper to keep someone on parole than in prison,
2. it is considered a more humane practice than prison,
3. it fulfills the community's expectation that an offender be punished since it is an extension of the prison term and usually has punitive aspects to it, and,
4. research seems to indicate that recidivism is lower if a period of incarceration is followed by parole rather than the offender being abruptly released into society.

While it may surprise the average reader, it is nevertheless true that the majority of parolees in the USA successfully complete their parole.

In 1972, 19,540 male felons were paroled and at the end of a three year period 74 % were either still on parole or had successfully completed it. The most successful parolee by crime category is usually the homicide offender, with other offenders being less successful. Women are slightly more successful over men. Unfortunately there is <u>almost no research on juvenile parole</u> (see Shover, 1979, 195-196).

It has been known that:

> "Younger parolees are more likely to fail than older parolees, that persons who were involved in crime for longer periods of time are more likely to fail than individuals with short records, that those who begin early are more likely to continue, that individuals more heavily involved in crime are most likely to fail than those not so heavily involved, that persons frequently confined are more likely to fail than those who have not been confined, and that crimes against property offenders fail more often than violent offenders" (Bartollas and Miller, 1978, 378).

The Youthful Parolee

Research in the area of the youth parolee is one of the major voids in the parole literature today. The paucity of knowledge on younger parolees comes primarily from isolated studies and minor extensions from major adult studies. Some of what is known revolves around their poor success rates when compared to older parolees (see Glaser, 1969, 249). A number of studies have shown that about 50 % of all youthful parolees return to confinement (see Glaser, 1969, 12; Jamison et al., 1966; Van Couvering, 1966).

Summarizing the research on the subject of youth parole (which includes juvenile after-care) together, Lipton et al. (1975) drew the following conclusions:

> "1. No convincing evidence exists that assigning juveniles to parole officers with small case loads contributes significantly to lowering juvenile recidivism;
> 2. Adequate supervision does appear to increase the chances of success to juveniles on parole;
> 3. Some parolees do better on aftercare if they have been institutionalized, but the majority do better if they are left in the community;
> 4. Some evidence exists that the type of institutions in which youths are confined does make a difference in how they respond to parole; and
> 5. Some evidence also exists that early release does not increase recidivism and, indeed, actually reduces it for the majority of youthful offenders."

What appears to be the single major study dealing with youth parole was published by W.R. Arnold in 1970. His study focused on community social factors affecting juveniles after they left the institutions. With regard to the family, he found that the earlier problem of the family's controlling the juvenile appeared again after the juvenile was released. However, these attempts to exercise control over their child, was usually in vain and rarely were these parents effective (94-131). He also found that peer groups had the greatest impact on the attitudes and behavior of the parolee. Most youth went back to their old groups within a day or so of their return to the community. If the old groups were no longer there - new ones were sought. When the family moved, then new friends in the new area broke the influence of former antisocial friendships. Arnold's study indicated that youth generally return to the original delinquency producing environment and that peer expectations were more influencial than parents. Another interesting finding was that newly released parolees were initially shunned by practically all friends and acquaintances and they did not automatically become the "returning hero" when they came back. This information lends support to the information obtained by Glaser (1969) in that the younger the releasee, the more contact he had with others who had also been in prison with them. This in turn seems to support his thesis that "social cohesion is uniquely charactistic of youthful offenders" (255).

As a result of studying youth, W.R. Arnold has attempted to formulate a theory of delinquency. He indicates that delinquency and crime are on-again, off-again affairs. He further points out that juveniles become involved in crime only on occasion in provocative situations. Getting caught is a risk weighed against the prospect of obtaining peer status. His main point here is that delinquency results from peer approval. With regard to parole, Arnold believes that the same mechanisms are operating. He feels that those on parole return to peer groups that have experience with crime. Additionally, there are no other persons, adults or youth, in these peer groups who would disapprove of delinquent behavior. Thus the parolee returns to a social milieu which supports further criminal activity and offers little in the way of inhibiting it. Finally, W.R. Arnold feels that juveniles who recidivate experience four specific problems (1970, 141):

1. They have more difficulty adjusting to their peers than do nonrecidivists;
2. They are more likely than nonrecidivists to be in groups to which it is difficult to adjust;
3. They are more likely than nonrecidivists to maintain interactions with older groups that have a history of delinquency; and
4. They receive less effective antidelinquent teaching than do nonrecidivists.

From research conducted by Irwin (1970, 112) and Glaser (1969, 332) it appeared that prior to release from prison most offenders had good intensions and were optimistic about leading a crime-free life. These prerelease attitudes were about equally distributed among those who complete their parole periods and those who were revoked. The question that begs asking is, if most released offenders had such positive attitudes and intentions, were there other significant differences which distinguished between those who failed and those who succeeded. This theme has been the subject of countless research projects since the Burgess study in the 1920's (see Vold 1931, 14-19), and the seminal work by Gottfredson in the 1960's (1970, 807-813). These and other studies have only been able to show that those who would probably fail and return to prison were usually men who were young, men who were already recidivists, those convicted of property offenses and those who were drug addicts (see Gough et al., 1965, 432-441). While this information has some value in predicting successes and failures, it is primarily focused on the individual and virtually excludes the influences of the released offender's environment. Recent writers of the parole phenomena have stressed the importance of interactive environmental factors which influence behavior, and hence the decisions of parolees (see Irwin, 1970; Jenkins and Sanford, 1972; and Waller, 1974).

In spite of these studies, empirical work concerned with the parolee's interactive processes dealing with his or her problems have been scarce. One of the first studies to look directly at the coping process during parole was done by Petraglia (1965). In 1960 to 1961 she retrospectively studied the parole coping experiences of recently released female offenders. Even though Petraglia's study had a number of methodological weaknesses (systematic sampling error, subjective description of problems, unclear explanation of her findings), it was one of the first clear attempts to look at the parole coping phenomena in the broadest sense. Since Petraglia's pioneer work, others have also dealt with parolee's problem responses to the environment (see Johnson, 1962; Diwitt et al., 1966; Glaser, 1969; Irwin, 1970; Stuart, 1972; Erickson et al., 1973; and Waller, 1974); however, the only recent work that has again directly dealt with coping during parole is Marc W. Renzema's 1980 work entitled "Coping With Freedom: A Study of Psychological Stress and Support in the Prison-to-Parole Transition".

With the exception of Renzema's study most of the previous parole studies were limited to studying the person and/or his or her contact with the parole authority, and largely excluded the influences of the remaining environment. Another frequently found general weakness has been the emphasis on parole outcome (success or failure) rather than including the dynamics of the parole process as well. Renzema tried to avoid these weaknesses in his study. He not only looked at the problems of release as perceived by the parolee himself, but also focused on such factors as the environment, the dynamics of adapting, and intrapsychic adaptations as well. This environmental psychological approach allowed him to consider the parolee's coping world from a wider perspective than any of his predecessors.

Renzema (1980, 98) found that his 53 parolees indentified seven major problem ("concern") areas in descending order of importance: employment, money, family, parole, stigmatization, interpersonal, and self-management. As will be seen later in this book, these seven areas are somewhat similar to those found by me using a younger population in the Federal Republic of Germany. Renzema's interview produced seven "major strategies of adaptation": environmental construction; activity; limited catharsis; converting conviction to an asset; selective attention to the positive; temporary disengagement; and direct action (1980, 188-206).

While Renzema did not address the possible causes of the various strategies, or whether a particular strategy was more or less effective, or whether specific problems and resources could be correlated with specific strategies, he did note that as the problem "issues become more complex and the threats less clearly defined, the defenses seem to become less clearcut" (1980, 243, 480). His point here is that one cannot use a simplistic model and vocabulary derived from studies of extreme stress for describing coping management of abstract, complex and mildly stressful problems.

Of all the previous research done with parolee's problems and coping Renzema's is the most similar to the interests of this research.

2.2 Comments on Parole Decision-Making

One of the major areas of interest in parole throughout its evolution has been with the parole authority's decision-making process. The basic assumption that underlies the parole process is that informed diagnosis will result in the right treatment for the offender. Research, however, indicates this cannot be done accurately. Much research has been conducted by psychologists who question what parole decision makers can do without benefit of psychological knowledge. The ability of clinicians with extensive psychological training cannot insure the reliability of their diagnosis. This problem also calls into serious question the use of statistical prediction devices.

Traditionally the main objective of parole prediction research has been the development of prediction tables that could be of use to parole decision-makers and help insure a greater degree of accuracy in the determination of who would be a safe risk in the community and who would not commit any new crimes. Rather than producing a perfect prediction instrument, prediction research has given a device that helps to eliminate extreme guesses (if the tables are used). Furthermore, it points out certain information on how parole decisions could fare. According to Shover (1979) parole prediction research has also shown that two generalizations are true:

1. "parole success decreases as the length of a releasee's previous criminal record increases (the longer the previous criminal record, the lower the success rate)".

2. "parole success increases with the age of prison releasees" (1979, 197).

The main problem with these types of predictions is that they apply primarily to groups of offenders and not to individuals (Shover, 1979, 198). In the broader context of parole decision-making, which unfortunately has only a minute concern with parole prediction tables, many variables were found by Dawson to have nothing to do with the offender's condition or the likelihood of recidivating. In any case, they were used in deciding to release persons on parole (1966, 244-300). O'Leary and Glaser stated, ... "no matter how one designates or tabulates it, the leading preoccupation of most parole board members in their decision to grant or deny parole, was their judgement on whether or not the prisoner was likely to commit a serious crime if paroled" (1972, 138).

Schmidt found the following reasons why parole was denied to female inmates:

1. "poor institutional adjustment;
2. a perceived obligation to protect the public from those who have shown themselves capable of assaultive behavior;
3. the belief that a convict may have served too little time for the institution to 'get to know her' and her case;
4. to give the convict time to benefit from prison programs;
5. the belief that the convict has not served enough time for the type of crime committed;
6. to avoid criticism of the parole system should the convict commit a new crime - especially one that is widely publicized" (1977, 123).

Schmidt also found three variables that, in combination, had the strongest effect on the decision to parole female inmates, these were:

1. "the amount of time the convict had served;
2. her prison custody classification, and
3. the length of her sentence" (1977, 34).

In spite of the lofty ideals and aspirations for parole which have existed for the past 100 years or so, research has shown that the parole process is not the rational procedure it was once hoped to be. As a valid process to be continued, parole in the USA is suffering. Parole boards as discretionary decision-making entities are more vulnerable to being abolished (primarily due to their poor track record) than is parole supervision (see Hussey and Duffee, 1980, 99).

Because much of what is new in parole policy has come from liberal political convictions, parole has been somewhat over idealized as being mainly rehabilitative and not punitive. Consequently parole research has dealt primarily with administrative problems. Only recently have researchers begun to look at traditional convictions and assumptions (see Shover, 1979, 196).

2.3 An Overview of Parole Practices in Lower Saxony

Detailed information concerning the parole and probation practices in Lower Saxony is found in a report, written by the Commission (Bericht der Planungskommission für den Sozialdienst in der Niedersächsischen Strafrechtspflege, herausgegeben vom Niedersächsischen Ministerium für Justiz, Hannover, 1979) for Social Workers, Lawyers, and Higher Officials within Criminal Justice. The Commission was given the task of providing advice for the further development of probation and parole. The results of the Commission's work brought together a widespread collection of probation and parole data from Lower Saxony.

The main purpose of probation or parole in Lower Saxony is to help integrate individuals back into society and to prevent them from serving long sentences. Thus, the Commission was established to address these two purposes. The Commission set a maximum quota of 35 offenders per supervision officer. However, because of the increase in youthful criminality and in case management, the officers are now handling more than 35 clients (see Figures 2 and 3). This increase in case management is not only stressful for the supervising officers, it also limits the time needed to deal with each client.

The Commission pointed out that:

> "A temporary strain of overwork for the supervising officer can not only lead to an irreparable loss of confidence for the offender, but in certain circumstances it can destroy the whole area of care and control. The concern with working stress is therefore of eminent importance."

Figure 2: COMPARISON OF THE NUMBER OF PERSONS UNDER SUPERVISION AND THOSE IMPRISONED IN LOWER SAXONY

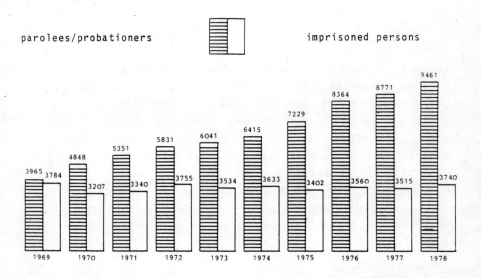

Source: Ministery of Justice for Lower Saxony (Ed.): Empfehlungen zur Bewährungshilfe, Führungsaufsicht, Gerichtshilfe. Bericht der Planungskommission für den Sozialdienst in der niedersächsischen Strafrechtspflege. Hannover, 1979, Anhang 2.

Figure 3: CLIENT CASELOAD FOR EACH SUPERVISOR IN LOWER SAXONY

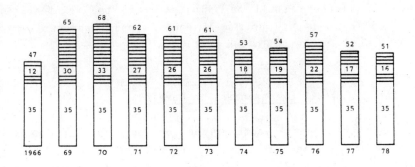

Explanation:
1. The lower part of each column shows the recommended case-load for each supervisor (35 clients).
2. The upper part of each column shows the higher actual case-load für each supervisor.
3. The total column shows the average number of clients, that have been added to each supervisor as of the 31st of December.

Source: Ministery of Justice for Lower Saxony (Ed.): Empfehlungen zur Bewährungshilfe, Führungsaufsicht, Gerichtshilfe. Bericht der Planungskommission für den Sozialdienst in der niedersächsischen Strafrechtspflege. Hannover, 1979, Anhang 9.

To overcome this working stress among supervising officers, the commission proposed the concept of a team-office which involves three to seven officers per team. This team concept was established in 1974 five years before the Commission's proposal. The fundamental idea is to have closer contact and cooperation with voluntary probation and parole assistants. The positive influence of this voluntary social work with youthful offenders shall be illustrated by the reintegration practice in the youth prison of Hameln (near Hannover) which is discussed in the following section.

Treatment of youthful offenders in Hameln

Hameln is the central youth prison for young male offenders in the region of Hannover. In an information booklet for the treatment of youthful offenders (Richtlinien und Orientierungshilfen, Dr. Gerhard Bulczak, Hameln, 1979) the director of the prison stated: "Young people who are sent to prison are in danger, their contact to other people is immensely disturbed and hindered ... Therefore, the relationship of the youth to their relatives, friends, employers, probation officers, and offices is to be maintained and to built up or to consolidate ..." (58-59).

At Hameln, great importance is attached to sporting, cultural, political and religious events. Inmates are able to make regular visits outside the prison, for instance being a member of different clubs, social, religious or political groups. This type of encouragement is provided by the staff (148). The prison also offers activities provided for by volunteer assistants. These volunteers help with educational, cultural, political, sporting, and leisure activities, both inside and outside the prison. They also provide companionship to the inmates and assist in the preparation of their releases.

External volunteers are of primary importance to the reintegration of inmates at the Hameln youth prison. They also assist in helping the inmates to cope with problematic situations once released from prison. This is done to neutralize the institutional influence and to create independent social relations. Besides volunteers, social, political, religious, and cultural groups also play an important role at the institution, because they enable the inmates to build up social contacts, which gives them social experience even after their release. These contacts with volunteers and social groups are claimed to be also important for the inmate's parole prognosis. The measured efforts of these external volunteers compared to other youth prisons not using this approach suggests the importance of beginning early in the reintegration process. Finally, social workers, priests, and volunteers in 1971 founded a local association in order to initiate and encourage these outside contacts.

Probation practices for youthful clients in Lower Saxony

The material published by the Federal Office of Statistics (Fachserie 10, Reihe 5: Bewährungshilfe) gives the following information on youthful offenders on parole (acc. §§ 88, 89 JGG) in Lower Saxony (see Figure 4). Besides an increase in case management, supervisors must also deal with a broad variety of youth crimes. For example drug-related crime has increased between 1973 and 1977 as a "typical youth offense" (see Uwe Dörmann, 1977), in Lower Saxony (see Figure 5).

The probation/parole officer must also deal with the increasing crime among foreigners. The Commission's report of Lower Saxony on crime amongst labor-emigrants states: "It is important to note a distinct rise of young foreigners. Social circumstances, especially for these people, are poor, because of the unfamiliar surrounding and their lack of apprenticeship, or profession; their future is extremely problematic." The

Figure 4: YOUTHFUL PAROLEES IN THE STATE OF LOWER SAXONY

1976	1977	1978	1979	1980
835	883	853	891	819

Figure 5: DRUG CRIMINALITY IN THE STATE OF LOWER SAXONY
(RECOGNIZED ADDICTS)

1973	1974	1975	1976	1977
1412	1464	1929	2595	3258

Figure 6: UNEMPLOYED PERSONS IN THE REGION OF HANNOVER
(ENPLOYMENT OFFICE DISTRICT)

	under 18 years old	under 20 years old	under 25 years old
September 1980	144 (100 %)	764 (100 %)	2.958 (100 %)
September 1981	407 (283 %)	1.638 (214 %)	5.350 (181 %)
September 1982	495 (344 %)	2.088 (273 %)	∿ 6.000 (203 %)

Commission recommends that probation/parole officers, especially in these areas with immense social changes get sociological and pedagogical training.

Dörmann (1977) has also pointed out the special connection between leisure-activities and problematic future-prognosis: "For a part of this youth, the growing leisure and the difficulty to do something significant, according to society, has become a main problem. This is even more difficult with the situation on the labor market ..."

Especially this part of the examination by Schünemann(1971) clearly showed defective probation/parole practices with young offenders: The probation officers have placed minimal emphasis on leisure time activities for offenders. ... Concerning success, those intensively cared for, show, of course, distinctly better results than those with average and than the not so well (without leisure-activities) cared for (p. 248).

Leisure and Work-Therapy Services in Hannover and the Surrounding Regions

Since the beginning of the 1970's there have been several attempts in the Hannover region to improve the leisure situation and apprenticeship for youth. Centers, cafés, communes, and workshops have been developed for these youths. Supporters of these services besides the state "Jugendhilfe" were churches, unions, societies, and private initiatives. The significance of these services are shown in interviews with those youths who frequent Hannover's old village pubs. When asked: "Do you know, where one can speak about personal problems?" the following tabulations represent the responses given:

Youth Counseling Service (Hinterhaus)	(29.16 %)
Youth and Drug Counseling (Jugend- und Drogenberatung)	(16.20 %)
Family Counseling Service (Pro Familia)	(4.86 %)
Youth Center (Jugendzentrum)	(4.05 %)
Outreach Program (Jugendcafé)	(2.43 %)
Hotline (Telefonseelsorge)	(2.43 %)
Miscellaneous	(40.87%)

The five first named institutions are all run by independent organizations, partly with government funds. Here only a small portion of the unofficial services were mentioned which can be of help for probation/parole officer's work. Due to the growing economical crisis and generally tight budgets for the state, the subsidies for independent organizations are reduced. To make this situation clearer, it may be pointed out that funds determine the financial planning of Hannover's Civil Services. Compared to the budget from 1973, the expenses for social/education/leisure from 1982-1985 were 34.38 %, the budget from 1982, reduced these expenses for 1983 to 12.56 % and for 1986 will be only 8.79 % of the entire budget.

Because of this reduction of funds, many services must close down. Additionally, probation/parole work for youth will become more difficult because of the rising number of youth under 20 who are unemployed.

According to the Commission's report, a fourth of the offenders are unemployed and only a third have school diplomas and vocational certificates. The work-therapy services of the independent "Jugendhilfe" are also concerned with the budget of the state Lower Saxony and the Hannover civil services. The work-therapy workshop of Hannover is also threatened by the shut down, because the hitherto existing subsidy will end and the civil services are not prepared to support further costs of this project alone.

Altogether it can be stated that work for youth offenders on parole is minimally available even for the concerned probation/parole officers. Added to this, the average number of clients in Hannover and region had risen to 50 per probation/ parole officer. Besides this, the courts are turning more to probation and parole even if an offence has been comitted during the probation or parole period. Consequently, multiple care from a variety of services is on the increase. The actual numbers give too positive an impression of the real amount of working stress on the probation/parole officers.

That portion of youthful offenders who are concerned with unemployment are roughly a third of the entire clientel. This is a bigger concern especially when the number of persons unemployed in the Hannover region are very high (see Figure 6). This level of concern is then reflected in the employment oriented tasks of most officers. That is why the participation in professional training courses for Hannover's probation/parole officers, as was proposed by the Commission, is nearly impossible. All training activities (either dealing with leisure or role playing of typical release conflicts) apart from the administrative control-function can only be accomplished after duty hours without pay and therefore rarely takes place.

Hannover's probation/parole officers regret that volunteer work is only done for inmates but not for youth offenders on parole/probation. The reason for this is seen in the fact that the clientel in prison is easily available and the volunteer can make contact more easily.

To insure that the number of offenders is lowered to 35, even through political means, no support seems in sight unless an appeal is made by the state government in Lower Saxony to the Federal Minister of Justice. Setting a limit for clients by law, as in Austria, has only recently been discussed.

On the whole, it can be stated that the parole/probation situation for youthful offenders seems to be getting worse.

2.4 The Parole Process in Lower Saxony, Germany

The parole process, formal and informal, as seen by a house leader at the Youth Prison (JVA) in Hameln, Lower Saxony

A young offender who is sentenced to the youth prison in Lower Saxony has four preconditions with regard to parole (see Figure 7):

1. determinate sentence,
2. indeterminate sentence,
3. either explicit or implicit sentence justification, and
4. the "rule of thumb" (which assumes parole eligibility at two thirds of the sentence).

These preconditions, play an immediate role in the identification of parole eligibility for an inmate entering the system. If the offender is judged not eligible for parole it is due to either 1). technically not qualified, or, 2). the inmate refuses parole (this is usually the result of prior experiences on parole or the influence of other inmates). If the offender is eligible for parole, his eligibility is automatically based on a minimum sentence (indeterminate sentence or six months minimum for all other determinate sentences).

In response to the inmate's eligibility for parole, the parole authority informally counsels them with regards to the different options of parole. This informal counselling can result in the inmate's decision not to seek parole further, or it can result in an informal agreement with the paroling authority. The informal agreement is ultimately developed into a formal statement of parole conditions.

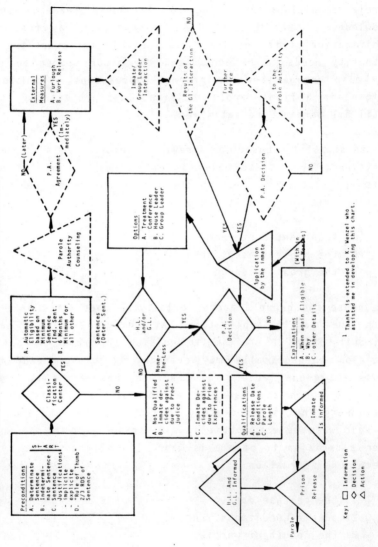

Figure 7: THE PAROLE PROCESS - FORMAL AND INFORMAL - AS SEEN BY A HOUSE LEADER AT JVA HAMELN, LOWER SAXONY[1]

[1] Thanks is extended to K. Wenzel who assisted me in developing this chart.

This formal statement is then discussed between the house leader and the inmate. This informal discussion is made to help insure that the inmate will be able to cope with the parole conditions according to the house leader's specific knowledge of the inmate. These discussions may result in a modification of the parole conditions. In the event the parole authority needs to be consulted, the group leader and inmate may also engage them in informal discussions, ultimately resulting in a final parole decision. This process may continue until all parties are satisfied.

At this point, based on previous informal discussions and decisions, the inmate makes a formal application for parole. This application is sent to the parole authority and to three sections within the institution:

1. treatment conference,
2. the house leader, and
3. the group leader.

The house and group leaders formally, either agree or disagree with the parole application. At this point, the paroling authority makes the ultimate decision to parole or not. This decision theoretically may overide the disagreement of the house and group leaders. In practice, however, this is rarely the case. When the paroling authority decides not to parole the inmate, he is immediately provided with an explanation and is told when he could be eligible again (within six months). When a decision to parole is made, it is accompanied by three pieces of information:

1. the release date,
2. parole conditions, and
3. the length of parole.

This information is formally sent to the inmate as well as to the house and group leaders. Upon receipt of this information all parties concerned make final arrangements for the release date and the parole process.

The Parole process as seen by a parole supervisor in Lower Saxony

From the view of the parole supervisors (see Figure 8), the parole process begins with three basic documents:

1. the parole application,
2. the parole statement from the warden to the parole authority, and
3. a copy of the parole statement to the parole supervisors.

This statement is received by the parole supervisors approximately two months prior to release. In response to this notification the parole supervisor is expected to visit the client at the institution to establish a working relationship with him. However, in practice this does not always occur. In ideal situations, the parole supervisors will use their visits to the institution as an opportunity to clarify the parole conditions and technicalities. The supervisor's main purpose is to begin making arrangements for employment, for housing and for the establishment or re-establishment of community ties. Upon being released, the inmate may be met at the gate by his parole supervisor. Again, this is the exception rather than the rule. Either way, the first required meeting between the parolee and his supervisor takes place at the supervisor's office. Here final arrangements are made as to the parole conditions and their limitations. In the event the inmate fails to show up, the supervisor must visit him at this home and finalize the aforementioned conditions. Subsequently the parolee is expected to fulfill his parole conditions. If this does not occur, the parolee and supervisor make new parole conditions (assuming no new crimes have been committed). If

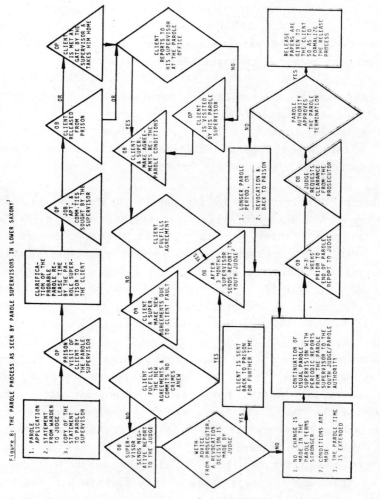

Figure 8: THE PAROLE PROCESS AS SEEN BY PAROLE SUPERVISORS IN LOWER SAXONY[1]

Key: OP OPTIONAL; OB OBLIGATORY; ☐ Information; ◇ Decision; △ Action

[1] Thanks is extended to B. Köhler who assisted me
[2] Parole Authority & youth judge are the same person
[3] or any time super, may submit a positive report to shorten the parole

the lack of compliance persists, the supervisor is required to inform the paroling authority, who, in conjunction with the counsel, prosecutor's makes a revocation.

In some cases, when the paroling authority decides against revocation, the judge may make no changes, strengthen the terms of the parole conditions, or extend the parole period. When revocation is decided upon the parolee is returned back to the institution. On the other hand, when the parolee fulfills the parole agreement to the satisfaction of the supervisor, a report may be sent to the paroling authority as early as three months after release. In response to the positive report the parole authority may decide to either shorten the parole period or continue with the original parole conditions. If the parole authority seeks to have the parole period terminated it must obtain clearance from the prosecutor. Upon receipt of the prosecutor's clearance, release papers are drawn up and sent to the client informing him of the decision. If the parole authority does not approve of the parole termination, the parolee would either be expected to remain on parole or may be sent back to prison.

2.5 The Youthful Parolee File-card Pre-study for Hannover

This pre-study focused exclusively on information taken from official information file cards (see Figure 9) filled out on each parolee by the respective parole supervisors. The information was collected for 1981, computerized and analyzed. The data were based on a total population and provided the following parolee profile.

During the year 1981, Hannover had 197 (100 %) males on parole who were sentenced in accordance to the German Youth Laws. Of the 197 youths, 186 (94.4 %) were German and 11 (5.6 %) were foreigners. The average age of the youths in this sample was 22.6 (see Figure 10). There were 182 (92.4 %) youths who were

Figure 9: INFORMATION FILE CARD

Land _____ | Abgangs-Zählkarte |

Bewährungshilfestatistik

Zählkarte

für nach Jugendstrafrecht verurteilte Probanden

1. Kennzahl des Landgerichts: |4| |3| KA
2. Kennzahl der Dienststelle: | |4| |5| |6|
3. Kennzahl des Bewährungshelfers: | | | |8|
4. Lfd. Nr. des Dienstregisters: | | | |9| Nr. | Jahr |13|
5. Beginn der Bewährungsaufsicht: | | | |14| Tag | Monat | Jahr |19|

6. Personalien des Probanden
Name (auch Geburtsname): _____

Vorname: _____

Geschlecht: männlich .... |1|
weiblich .... |2|

Geburtsdatum: .... | | | | Tag | Monat | Jahr

Staatsangehörigkeit: deutsch .... |1|
nicht deutsch .... |2|

Familienstand bei Unterstellung: ledig .... |1|
verheiratet, verwitwet, geschieden |2|

Eltern bei Unterstellung: geschieden oder getrennt lebend |1|
ein Elternteil tot .... |2|
beide Eltern tot .... |3|

7. Urteil/Gesamtstrafenbeschluß des _____
-gerichts _____
vom _____ Gz.: _____
Strafe und/oder Maßregel: _____

Straftaten (Vorschriften nach Paragraphen, Absatz, Nummer, Buchstabe und Bezeichnung des Gesetzes):

nicht ausfüllen
			30
			32
			33
			36

Bei §§ 222, 230, 330a, StGB: in Verbindung mit einem Verkehrsunfall? ja .... |1|
nein .... |2|

Verurteilt als: Jugendlicher .... |1|
Heranwachsender .... |2|

Vermindert schuldfähig (§ 21 StGB)? ja .... |1|
nein .... |2|

8. Bewährungsaufsicht angeordnet
durch Entscheidung des _____ -gerichts/
Vollstreckungsleiters
vom _____ Gz.: _____
Bewährungszeit bis zum: _____

Es ist darauf zu achten, daß die Ordnungsangaben (Lfd. Nrn. 1 bis 5) in der Zugangs- und in der Abgangs-Zählkarte übereinstimmen. Bei Abweichungen ist das Statistische Amt gehalten, die Abgangs-Zählkarte zur Korrektur zurückzusenden.

(Das Statistische Amt führt die jeweiligen Zugangs- und Abgangsbelege maschinell über diese Ordnungsangaben zusammen.)

|1|
|2|
|3|
|4|
|5|
|6|
|7|
|8|

|1|
|2|
|3|
|4|

|1|
|2|
|1|
|2|
|1|
|2|

Bei Beendigung der Bewährungsaufsicht, bei Abgabe an einen anderen Bewährungshelfer oder bei einem Wechsel der Dienststelle durch den Bewährungshelfer ohne Abgabe der Bewährungsaufsicht bitte die nachfolgenden Nummern ausfüllen und diese Abgangs-Zählkarte gem. Geschäftsanweisung an das zuständige Statistische Amt einsenden.

|1|
|2|
|1|
|2|
|1|
|2|

13. Abgabe an einen anderen Bewährungshelfer ..... |1|20|

14. Wechsel der Dienststelle durch den Bewährungshelfer ohne Abgabe der Bewährungsaufsicht .... |2|20|

15. Beendigung der Bewährungsaufsicht
15.1 Tag der Beendigung: .... | | | |21| Tag | Monat | Jahr |26|

15.2 Grund der Beendigung
Erlaß der Jugendstrafe .... |1|
Tilgung des Schuldspruchs (§ 30 Abs. 2 JGG) .... |2|
Verhängung der Jugendstrafe (§ 30 Abs. 1 JGG)
nur oder auch wegen neuer Straftat .... |3|
aus sonstigen Gründen .... |4| |27|
Widerruf   nur oder auch wegen neuer Straftat .... |5|
aus sonstigen Gründen .... |6|
Beendigung aus anderen Gründen (z.B. Tod) ..... |7|
Grund: _____

BwH 13a – Gen. 11.76
JVA Willich

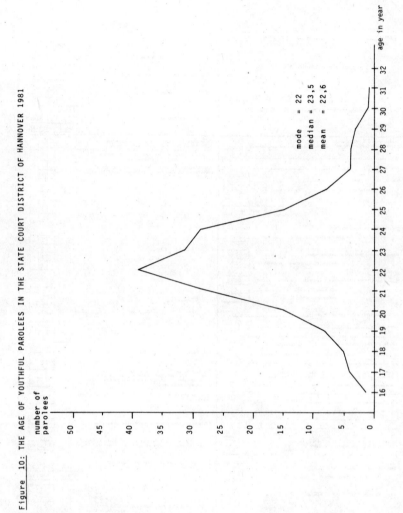

Figure 10: THE AGE OF YOUTHFUL PAROLEES IN THE STATE COURT DISTRICT OF HANNOVER 1981

single and 15 (7.6 %) were either married, widowed or divorced (see Figure 11). There were 67 (34.0 %) of the youths who had parents separated or divorced, while 18 (9.1 %) of the youths had only a mother or a father and 111 (56.3 %) of the youths had both parents residing with each other (see Figure 12).

Of the 197 individuals, 60 (30.5 %) were convicted as youths and 137 (69.5 %) were convicted as adults (see Figure 13).

In terms of how long the youths had been on parole, 11 (5.6 %) had been on parole since 1978 (3 years); 43 (21.8 %) had been on parole since 1979 (2 years); 68 (34.5 %) had been on parole since 1980 (1 year), and 75 (38.1 %) were placed on parole during 1981. Finally, the majority of offences committed were thefts, while robbery was the second highest offence committed (see Figure 14).

At the time of release for the 197 parolees, 31 % had less than 6 months of time remaining on their original sentence. However, it was found that the majority of parolees (39.6 %) had from six months to one year of time remaining on their sentences. A much smaller number (8.3 % and 7.6 %) had between one to two years and more than two years, respectively, remaining at the time of their release (see Figure 15).

In terms of the length of parole for the offenders, 27 % had a parole time ranging between zero to six months. Seven to twelve months of time for parole shows only 13 % of the parolees to be categorized here. A slight increase is shown for the thirteen to eighteen month time period with 19 % of the parolees here. The percentages decrease from this point as the length of time for parole increases as is illustrated by Figure 16.

Thus, the dominant profile in 1981 for young parolees in the state of Lower Saxony was: a single German male, who's parents lived together, convicted of theft, had been on parole about one year and was 22.6 years of age.

Figure 11: MARITAL STATUS OF THE PAROLEE

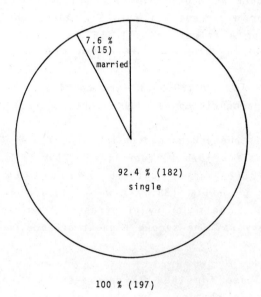

Figure 12: STATUS OF PARENTS

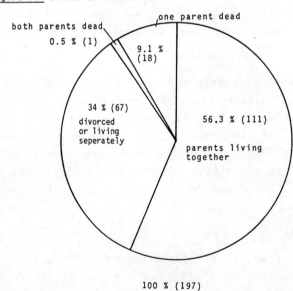

Figure 13: NUMBER OF PERSONS CONVICTED AS YOUTH AND ADULTS

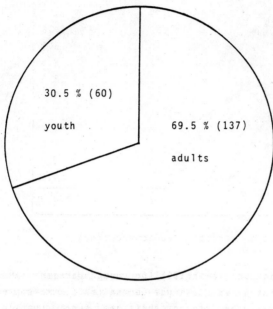

Figure 14: THE OFFENSE BREAKDOWN FOR THIS GROUP is as follows:

	f	%
Robbers	29	14.7
Thieves	108	54.8
Swindlers	10	5.1
Drug Offenders	7	3.6
Murderers	5	2.5
Assaulters	18	9.1
Traffic Offenders	2	1.0
Alcoholics	2	1.0
Dangerous Persons	2	1.0
Sexual Offenders	6	3.0
Miscellaneous	8	4.1
	197	100*

*numbers don't add up correctly due to rounding

Thus, the dominant profile in 1981 for young parolees in the state of Lower Saxony was: a single German male, whose parents lived together, was convicted of theft, had been on parole about one year and was 22.6 years of age.

Figure 15: TIME REMAINING ON ORIGINAL SENTENCE AT RELEASE
- PAROLEES -

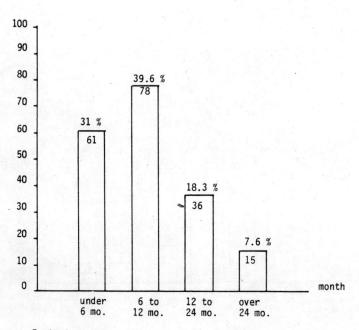

7 missing cases

Figure 16: LENGTH OF PAROLE AS OF 1.1.1982

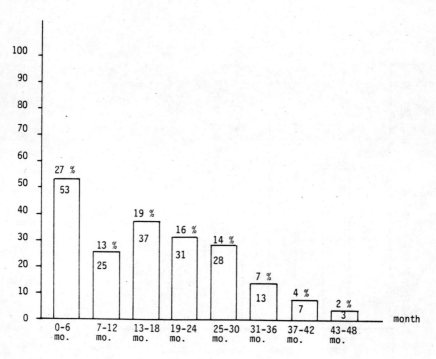

2.6 The Staff/Client Interaction (According to American Studies)

American studies conducted in the mid 1960's, showed that while the client is still in prison awaiting to be released on parole, a number of significant attitudes are operating which affect the staff/client interaction. First, looking at the inmate's social relationships, one notes an irony. During the incarceration period most of his friendships have been lost but the ties with family have become stronger (see Glaser, 1969, 240). The loss of friends also includes criminal acquaintances, and this is especially pronounced if they were co-conspirators in the crime for which the inmate is now serving time. This actually creates an "alienation from criminal" phenomena in spite of the physical vicinity of other criminals in prison. The result of this process is an increased identification with anti-criminal persons (1969, 243).

With these two seemingly positive developments it would appear that the state is set for good family support and good staff/client interaction. The realities of these relationships, however, are much more complicated and fraught with many hazards.

The structure of the correctional process, be it probation, prison or parole, creates conflicts of interest between staff and clients. Knowing that the "correctors" are making decisions based on their perception of the offender, a logical response is to try to accentuate those characteristics that are being sought by the correctors. Recognizing this overacting, the correctors, on the other hand, are continually afraid of being conned. Thus, recognizing this "fear-of-being-conned" syndrome, the offender is never certain whether to be overly contrite (and appear as false) or to be completely honest (thereby running the risk of divulging potentially harmful information that could be used against him). Consequently distrust and uncertainty clouds the relationship from both sides of the staff/client diad (see Shover, 1979, 222).

A second problem of the staff/client interaction is that most offenders do not wish to accept the correctional staff relationships as their primary means of identification. The result of this conflict is to keep interaction with staff to a minimum, and also to minimize as much as possible the influence of their status as supervised offenders on the rest of their lives. Obviously the correctional system is so structured as to greatly hinder an accomodation to these aims (see Hussey and Duffee, 1980, 294).

A third conflict area between staff and client is their social orientations. The difference in the social worlds of staff and client is usually extreme. On the one hand the staff usually comes from a conforming orientation. On the other hand the client usually comes from a deviant nonconforming orientation. Yet these two people are thrown together in a somewhat intense interaction that is significantly meaningful for both. An interaction that is based on behavioral expectations and binding commitments. The client is continually placed in a position of trying to conform to a set of middle-class norms he is mostly not aware of, or if he is, he does not subscribe to them. The staff must try to understand a person usually of another socialcultural orientation. Consequently, the nature of the staff/client relationship is one of minimal contact, little understanding, and rarely of any major concern for each other. Clearly it does not or cannot (given these hindrances) effectively deal with fundamental problems or concerns of the parolee (see Shover, 1979, 224-225).

The fourth conflict arises from the differing views about the worth of correctional services. Obviously the staff feels what they are doing is important and useful; while the client sees no sense in it at all. Actually, clients see it as a way to perpetuate the system's harassment. It is also viewed by the offender as a way of justifying the existence of the system and to perpetuate the status quo to the benefit of the staff. The result is for the offender to avoid staff at all costs.

After all, nothing positive can possibly result, so the inmate's thinking goes. The result of this avoidance is a serious deficit in the communication between staff and client, thereby blocking the possibilities for positive exchange (see Shover, 1979, 223-224).

An issue for theorists and social planners alike, and perhaps less articulated by practitioners or clients but clearly related to the client/staff interactive process, is the question of voluntary treatment versus coercive treatment. The research concerning the planned change process shows that it is important for the person being changed to enter into the process willingly if the effects of that change are to be long-lasting. Hussey and Duffee write "Volunteerism increases the commitment to the change process and reduces the threat of self-concept" (1980, 298). In spite of the demonstrated relevance of the voluntary prerequisite, this is an often difficult condition to achieve. Before the offender can feel comfortable enough to volunteer for the change, he or she must trust that the change process will not be a threat to their already battered self-images. One of the main limitations to trusting, is perceiving the worth of the helpers and understanding the helping system. Consequently, those in a low socio-economic status trust less and those in a high socio-economic status trust more (1980, 299).

There is often an accompanying psychosocial dilemma which occurs with parolees in their interaction with their supervisors. If they cooperate with their supervisors, it means they must accept the negative self-image imputed to them by virtue of the parolee/supervisor relationship. The staff maintains a "coercive superiority" over the offender. If the parolee cooperates within that identity, he or she can get help and services from the parole supervisor, and continues enjoying the freedom his "good behavior" allows. On the other hand, if the parolee is not willing to suffer the threat to his self-concept, he or she can stay away from the parole officer, but then runs the risk of not getting services or of not being in the good graces of the supervisors, thereby jeopardizing his or her freedom (see Hussey and Duffee, 1980, 297).

2.7 Interaction with Others

The process of changing an offender's status from inmate to parolee requires them to go through one status to another. These changes often result in "change-traumas" which may produce depression, confusion and threats to the self-concept. One way of coping with these traumas is to find familiar surroundings and people (not unlike the remedy for culture shock when in a foreign country). Thus, when offenders are released from prison, whether they are in a parole status or not, they usually seek their old group associations (see Hussey and Duffee, 1980, 300). The point of change from inmate status to parolee status has important relevance in terms of self-image.

The parole supervisor is unfortunately a continual reminder of an inmate's negative past. This relationship can be a threat to a parolee's self-image. This is why one of the more positive change agents in this type of setting is the use of self-help groups. These are groups made up of other parolees who have been through similar experiences and can understand one another much better. This shared-experiences perception usually reduces the severity of the threat to self-image which accompanies the change process (see Hussey and Duffee, 1980, 297). This may very well explain why the larger percentage of juvenile parolees go back to their deviant gang when they get out of prison. Evidently their self-image is safe in the gang even if it often means a risk to their parole status.

A somewhat related, and equally problematic situation is the dilemma of a parolee's family. Having access to a home can be both positive and negative. While it is critical, especially where the inmate has little funds, for him to have a place to stay and food to eat, it is often problematic to return to family, friends or relatives that may have played a major role in the onset of the criminal activities for which he or she is being punished (see Glaser, 1969, 244).

The issues of home and family is somewhat different for adults than it is for youths. In his classic research with adult male parolees, Glaser found that after release, 29 % lived with their parents, 32 % lived with their wives (and other family members), 24 % lived with other relatives, 3 % lived with friends, and 12 % lived alone (1969, 249). This type of information is almost unavailable for juveniles. Glaser also found that men whose first place of residence is with their wives had the highest rate of success and those living alone had the least amount of success. The higher than average failure rate among those living alone was a consistent finding and not a function of age. However, the high success rate of married releasees is in large part a function of age, as the married releasees produce better success rates than younger parolees. The only type of residential association Glaser found to be consistently unfavorable in making prognosis, is living alone (1969, 249). Thus, based on Glaser's findings, it would seem appropriate to say that, at least for males, the postprison success rates are very much "related to the way in which the releasee interacts with those with whom he resides" (1969, 250).

Contact with the police represents another source of hazardous interaction for the parolee. While the issues of police harassment is frequently heard of among inmate groups, the expectations of harassment are greater than the reality (see Glaser, 1969, 262). None-the-less, the fears of police harassment are real. Some police agencies do in fact have policies of harassing known ex-convicts, especially to keep them away from so-called respectable areas of the community (see Glaser, 1969, 260). It is interesting to note that when police contact with an ex-prisoner involved possible arrest for a felony charge, it was usually a good index of the parolee's subsequent failure on parole (see Glaser, 1969, 261).

Dealing with a community's negative response is also an often heard fear among inmates preparing to reenter society on parole. So pervasive is this myth that this author has observed inmates turn down parole for fear of the con stigma and what it would do to his or her chances of survival in the community. However, Glaser (1969) found very little change in success rates after a change in residence had taken place among federal adult parolees. He thus concluded that "for the releasees studied, the handicap of a criminal record in the community of release appears to have been more than compensated for by benefits from resources in the old community" (248-249).

The positive benefits of one's own community's resources is a dimension infrequently heard of in parole research. It would appear of major importance to know how those who do good on parole differ from those whose parole is revoked in terms of utilizing the community's other (non criminal justice) resources. It is relevant to mention that Glaser found that parolees who did not recidivate could generally be differentiated by their "achievement of economic self-sufficiency, and by satisfaction in primary group relationships" (where these primary groups did not support criminal activity) (1969, 331).

Not only is the influence of the parole supervisor, the family and the community critical in understanding the parolee's situation, but what specific efforts he puts forth are also of major importance. This is especially true when considering the world of work. In spite of the "futility myth" which espouses that much of what happens on parole is negative and in vain, research indicates that over 90 % of the releasees seek noncriminal careers for about one month and that about 65 % continually seek employment that are predominantly free of serious criminal involvement (see Glaser, 1969, 331). It must be kept in mind that these figures represent some very valient efforts on the part of the parolee as the majority of offenders have minimal skills, education, prestige or class association that give them the chances to achieve many of the goals most people achieve in solving their individual problems or in becoming successful members of their communities (see Hussey and Duffee, 1980, 295).

As this author sees the interaction dilemma, the parolee wishing to sucessfully reintegrate into society must associate with societal norms that are strange and unfamiliar to him and consequently a threat to his self-image. If he is to make the transition he is forced into the dilemma of success with pain, or no success with comfort (see Hussey and Duffee, 1980, 301).

2.8 Parole Problem Pre-study

Overview

This pre-study focused directly on typical parolee problems. It was conducted by using exploratory interviews of <u>parolees</u>, <u>non-parolees</u> of the same age, parole <u>supervisors</u>, analyzing data from a prerelease study of <u>adults</u> in Nürnberg, FRG and studies reported in American and German parole <u>literature</u> (see Figure 1). From each of these data sources a list of problems emerged which were collapsed into five areas: family, civil servants, community, work, and peers.

Based on the frequency with which problems were mentioned, these areas were prioritized according to data source. Since this was only used in the development of the coping instrument, small samples were used. Consequently, inferences beyond simple comparisons were not made.

Comparing each data source with each other produced a different ranking of problems. For each of these problem comparisons three statistical tests were used: Chi-squared, Tau, and Contingency Coefficient. Chi-squared is a test of significance usually used for nominal data to indicate whether our observations differ from what would be expected by chance. Tau is referred to as Kendall's rank correlation coefficient. It is used when at least ordinal data is achieved and a measure of association between two sets of attributes are nominal in character. The Contingency Coefficient is a measure of association between two sets of attributes which are nominal in character.

Conducting the Interviews

Contact with parolees and parole supervisors were obtained with the help of two parole centers in Lower Saxony. The interviews took place in the parole supervisor's offices. During the parolees' interviews, the supervisors were absent. With regard to parolees, efforts were taken to create a non threatening interview; however, some parolees were inhibited and presented themselves as having no problems. In these cases, through the use of encouragement and persistent questioning, the interviewer was able to get the parolees to mention some of their problems. In contrast to these parolees, most showed less reluctance and spoke more openly. The duration of the parolees' interviews ranged from about 30 to 60 minutes and for the supervisors it ranged from about 45 to 60 minutes.

The Analysis of the Interviews

The purpose of evaluating the interviews was to discover what problems the subjects had with regard to the categories: Family, School, Work, Peers, Community, and Civil Servants. The evaluation of the interviews was done as follows. Each interview was recorded on tape and then had to be transcribed. Subsequently each transcript was read through once in order to obtain a general impression. Next, the problem area or categories were analyzed. An additional concern at this point was whether the problems mentioned, were in fact, the existing ones. In some cases, it appeared that the parolees were responding to their perceptions of the interviewer's expectations. In selecting appropriate problem categories, the above issues were resolved by discussions with the research team. Next, each parolee's problems were organized into the above mentioned six problem areas. Finally, the results of these evaluations were validated by having three outside raters independently organize the problems into these same categories.

Analyzing the Data in Detail

Some of the 16 parolees who were interviewed, obviously showed the urge to justify their statements, as if they had to convince the interviewer how successful their parole was. Perhaps this was due to the fact that the parole supervisors organized these interviews. Other parolees tended to speak freely about problems they had overcome, but made very few remarks about current problems which provided further difficulties.

Figure 17 shows the tabular results of this pre-study. The following paragraphs discuss the categories according to the five data sources: youthful parolees, youthful non-parolees, parole supervisors, adult inmates just prior to release, and parole literature.

The category Family proved to be the most problematic (27.3 %) for parolees. They expressed their feelings in detail and spoke about their problems openly ("Yes, home was shit!"). This manner of speaking openly was especially noticable with parolees who no longer lived with their parents. A lot of parolees felt that these family conflicts caused their criminal behavior ("From time to time, my parents weren't always faultless"). In this context, the father's authoritarian behavior was often mentioned.

Figure 17: RESULTS OF THE PAROLE PROBLEMS PRE-STUDY *

Spacerounds	Adult Inmates Just Prior to Release			Youthful Parolees			Youthful Non Parolees			Parole Supervisors			Parole Literature		
	N_{1i}	A_i	(%)	N_{1i}	A_i	(%)	N_{1i}	A_i	(%)	N_{1i}	A_i	(%)	N_{1i}	A_i	(%)
Family	7	0.2	8.8	42	2.6	27.3	17	1.4	21.8	48	3.7	21.5	12	1.1	11.5
Work	15	0.4	18.7	27	1.7	17.5	21	1.8	26.9	57	4.4	25.6	29	2.6	27.9
Peers	14	0.4	17.5	21	1.3	13.6	16	1.3	20.5	40	3.1	17.9	12	1.1	11.5
Community	17	0.5	21.3	28	1.8	18.2	10	0.8	12.8	37	2.8	16.6	26	2.4	25.0
Civil Servants	27	0.7	33.7	36	2.3	23.4	14	1.2	18.0	41	3.2	18.4	25	2.3	24.1
Σ	80	2.2	100.0	154	9.7	100.0	78	6.5	100.0	223	17.2	100.0	104	9.5	100.0
N_2	37			16			12			13			11		

i — Spacerounds
N_1 — Absolute frequency of Problems identified
N_2 — Number of Sources

$A_i = \frac{N_{1i}}{N_2}$ — Ratio of Problems identified per Source

$\Sigma_A = \frac{\Sigma N_1}{N_2}$ — Sum of the Ratio of Problems identified per Source

% — Relative frequency

* H.-F. Jacobsen, Udo Iwannek and Helga Hattendorf assisted me in the development of this chart.

The second highest scored category was <u>Civil Servants</u> (23.4 %). Negative experiences were acute, especially the ones experienced with the criminal justice system and the results of post-release problems with finding a place to stay, work, and money. For example: "I think everything is a big mess, because nobody seems to see things clearly." "I hate it like the plague!" Only a few supervisors showed concern about the parolees' visits to civil servants. Some supervisors claimed they let the parolees find their own way in order to encourage their independence. The parolees, therefore had a lot of criticism about this category: problems with parole and the parole supervisors were especially taken into consideration. The problems that surfaced here, were mainly based on the fact that there was not enough understanding between the two groups and also little trust. ("It's difficult for me to go there every 6 weeks ... and it's pretty nerve-racking, too; he asks me if everything is O.K. and I tell him: I told you already before. Didn't you believe me?")

The categories <u>Community</u> and <u>Work</u> (18.2 %, 17.5 % respectively) reflected objective problems of society such as mass-unemployment and housing shortages. For the parolees, these are big problems, as it especially effects them since they largely belong to the underprivileged class. ("Work and a place to stay, there're the most important things when you get out"). Parolees with a steady job were often afraid that their peers or bosses would find out that they were previously convicted. ("Well, I'd be out of the woods, unless after working there already six months or so and they would find out. That would be something else, but otherwise...!")

The category <u>School</u> was only mentioned by parolees who still went to school or who could remember their school days. Parolees who had been previously punished during their school years, reported about problems with teachers who were not capable of dealing with their delinquency. ("They teased me, I shouldn't think that because of this, I couldn't do that and that. You couldn't talk to them, either.") Because this category proved to be unimportant in this part of the study, it was left out of further discussions.

In the category Close Friends (9.7 %) only faint remarks were made about problems. It appeared that most of these had to do with intimacy. In the following discussions, these problems were combined with those in the category Peers (13.6 %).

Only few problems were found in the category Peers (3.9 %). This might be explained by two reasons: firstly, the parolees might try to keep their distance from them, at least that is what they said, since these friends often had something to do with their criminal past; secondly, and also more convincing, is the explanation that Peers by nature are a relative "unproblematic" group (see Hirschi, 1979; Friday, 1980b; Dussich and Jacobsen, 1982).

Problems from the View of the Probation Supervisors

As a result of the extra social science training that all supervisors received, the difference in supervisor sensitivity for client psycho-social problems was shown in their interviews. Furthermore, it can be noted that the supervisors, being professional interviewers, often reflected scientific terminology in describing their work with clients and how the clients dealt with their problems.

In contrast to the parolees, the category Work was on the top of the problem list mentioned by these parole supervisors (25.6 %). This resulted because on the one hand, many supervisors continually advised their clients to reintegrate into a regular working life. They would say "Work is very important" or "it's our duty to focus on our parolees' Work" and in this regard the supervisors had a high degree of knowledge concerning their clients' Work experience. On the other hand, with regard to these experiences, supervisors claimed they would recognize problems which were not clear to their clients.

Nearly all parole supervisors felt that the category Family (21.5 %) had a major impact on the parolees' criminal behavior. ("Family, in my opinion, is the main reason for several disturbances.")

In the category Civil Servants (18.4 % of the mentioned problems), the supervisors viewed the lack of independence as being the major problem of their clients. Also, with regard to parole and probation, the supervisors stated that the clients act like consumers, expecting care and help without contributing toward their own welfare themselves ("They expect everything to be done for them as soon as possible").

In the category Community (16.6 %), besides the difficulty of finding an apartment, the stigmatization of neighbors was also frequently mentioned by supervisors as an important problem.

The category Close Friends (9.4 %) was mentioned as a source of additional problems ("These problems are a big headache"); however, for the most part this sort of relationship was mentioned as being a stabilizing factor.

The category Peers (8.5 %) was at the bottom of the list; Peers have been rarely viewed as an asset for working with the clients. Furthermore, supervisors explained that they would purposely stay out of this area so as to grant their clients at least some privacy. In this regard, the supervisors had rather little knowledge about problems with peers.

School was a rather unimportant category, as many clients no longer attended school.

Problems of Non-Criminal Young Adults

This group was more heterogeneous than were the parolees: it consisted of 4 pupils, 5 apprentices, and 3 employees. Unusual, yet easy to explain was the greater awareness of the category Work and School (added together 26.9 %) compared to the other group's problems. Difficulties with different school subjects and conflicts with teachers were the most often mentioned problems for the category School; stress and trouble with the boss were the major problems in the category Work.

Following these two categories, which were the most dominant in this group's everyday life, came the categories Family (21.8 %) and Civil Servants (18.0 %). The majority of the members of this group lived with their parents and yet had also had numerous experiences with civil servants. The father's authoritarian behavior and problems due to the parents being divorced, were most frequently mentioned with reference to the running of the Family. With reference to Civil Servants, trouble with the police was a major problem (usually concerning traffic and minor rule violations). Furthermore, complaints about the constant presence of the bureaucracy were made. In this regard, special mention was made of problems at the employment office and at the housing office.

In the category of Community, the problems mentioned (12.8 %) were limited to occasional neighborhood troubles caused by music being played too loud or the lack of possibilities to play soccer and complaints about isolated living on the city's periphery.

Parolees' Problems Found in the Literature

Two dilemmas should be mentioned at the onset: firstly, most of the literature on youthful parolee problems, with few exceptions, came from the U.S.A., and Canada. Whether these findings are transferable to German conditions is questionable. Unfortunately, comparable German literature in this field is seriously lacking. The second problem was that the various studies had different theoretical and/or methodological dispositions and therefore could not always be compared to each other. None-the-less, we tried to compare them.

The most problematic category which was mentioned by all authors was Work (27.9 %). Work was claimed to be especially important for successful parole. Several times the problem of "job-finding" was mentioned. "Finding and keeping a job is a major problem" (Hirsch and Hanrahan, 1979, 76; see also Erickson et al., 1973, 98; Glaser, 1964, 358-359; Fairweather, 1980, 46-50; Irwin, 1970, 134; Stanley, 1976, 149-155).

The category Community was the second highest problem area mentioned (25.0 %). "The parolee's return to the community is an enormous change that involves all kinds of emotional and practical problems" (Stanley, 1976, 137; see also Glaser, 1964, 400-401; Hirsch and Hanrahan, 1979, 73-75).

Peers were seldom evaluated as a problem for young parolees: only 11.5 % mentioned problems with youths of the same age with a similar social background as the parolees. Contact with former inmates was often stressed as being a related problem (see Waller, 1974, 6).

Comparison of Spaceround* Prioritization

Figures 18 to 27 are graphically separated from Figure 17 which shows all the numerical values.

---

*See section 3.3 for an explanation of the term spaceround.

Contrasting youthful parolees with non-parole youth from the general population indicates that for parolees Family (27.3 %) was most often mentioned and Peers (13.6 %) least often; with non-parole youth Work (26.9 %) as the least mentioned (see Figure 18). There was no significant relationship between youthful parolees and non-parole youth (x^2 = 5.969; tau = 0; p = .20).

Comparing youthful parolees with parole supervisors, it is clear that each group has a different perception as to where the problems are: the supervisors feel the area of Work (25.6 %) is where most parolee problems are, while the parolees place Work (17.5 %) problems almost at the bottom of their list (see Figure 19). There was no significant relationship between the two groups (x^2 = 6.182; tau = .20; p = .19).

Looking at the problem perceptions of youth parolees and adult prisoners, one notes the ranking of problematic spacerounds is almost the same except that for youth, Family (27.3 %) is the number one problem area, and for adults it is at the bottom of the list (8.8 %) (see Figure 20). The difference in spaceround problem prioritization was very significant between the two groups (x^2 = 11.557; tau = .20; p = .02).

When comparing youth parolees with the findings of parole studies, Family is at the bottom of the list for the studies (11.5 %), and at the top for parolees (27.3 %) (see Figure 21). The comparison between youthful parolee and parole studies was also very significant (x^2 = 12.012; tau = -.30; p = .02).

When comparing findings of parole studies with parole supervisors, one notes a difference in prioritization of problems: the parole studies tell us the main problem area is Work (27.9 %) and the least problematic spacerounds are Family (11.5 %) and Peers (11.5 %). Parole supervisors identified Work as the most important problem spaceround (25.6 %); how-

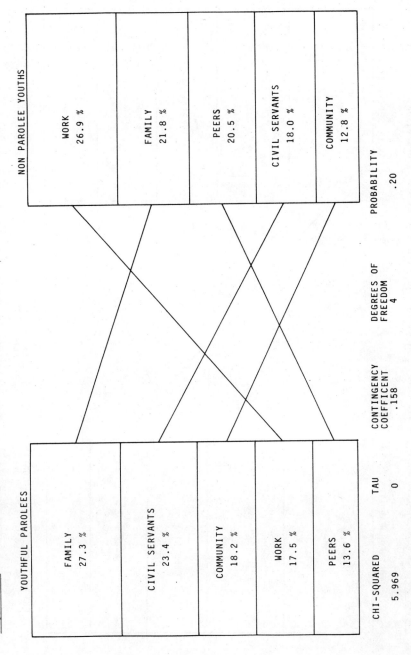

Figure 18: PROBLEM SPACEGROUND PRIORITIZATION: COMPARISONS BETWEEN PAROLEES AND NONPAROLEES

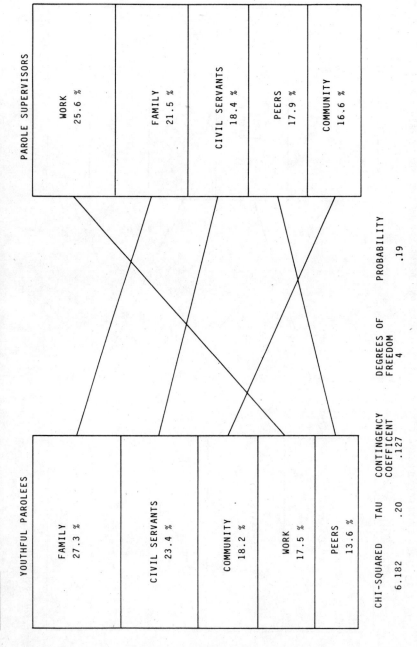

Figure 19: PROBLEM SPACEROUND PRIORITIZATION: COMPARISONS BETWEEN PAROLEES AND SUPERVISORS

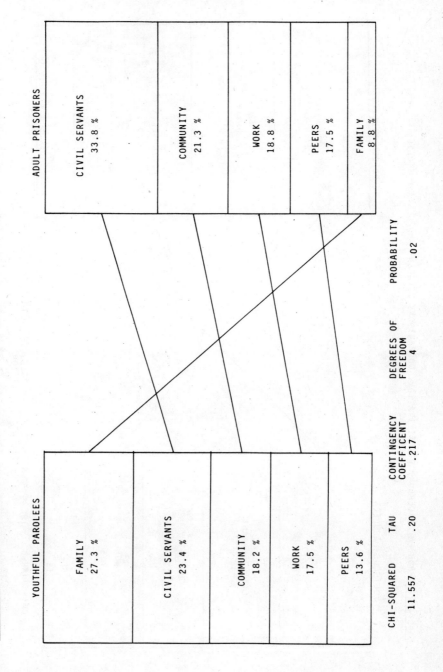

Figure 20: PROBLEM SPACEROUND PRIORITIZATION: COMPARISONS BETWEEN PAROLEES AND ADULT PRISONERS

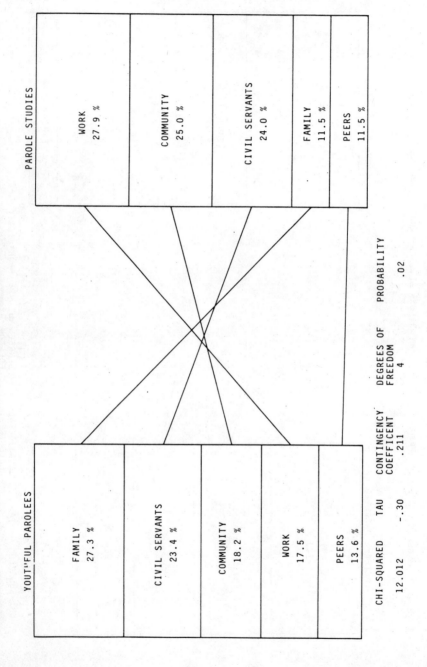

Figure 21: PROBLEM SPACEROUND PRIORITIZATION: COMPARISONS BETWEEN PAROLEES AND STUDIES

ever, they gave Family (21.5 %) a high ranking among possible problem spacerounds (see Figure 22). The difference between parole supervisors and parole studies were somewhat significant (X^2 = 9.552; tau = -.30; p < 05).

When comparing parole supervisors with adult prisoners just prior to release it appears that a very different list of problem prioritization exists (see Figure 23). The difference between parole supervisors and adult prisoners was very significant (X^2 = 13.359; tau = -.20; p < .01).

When comparing parole studies and adult prisoners one finds agreement only in identifying Family and Peers as low problem areas (see Figure 24). There was no significant relationship between adult prisoners and parole studies (X^2 = 4.837; tau = -.10; p = .30).

A striking similarity was found in the comparison between nonparole youths and parole supervisors (see Figure 25). There was no significant relationship between nonparole youths and parole supervisors (X^2 = .782; tau = .80; p = .94).

A very different perspective of problem spacerounds is reflected in the comparison between nonparole youths, and adult prisoners just prior to release. The youths identify Work (26.9 %) as the most problematic area, while the adults picked dealing with Civil Servants (33.8 %) as the most problematic area (see Figure 26). There was a significant relationship between nonparole youths and adult prisoners (X^2 = 11.213; tau = -.40; p < .02).

Finally in comparing nonparole youths with parole studies, there seems to be concordance with the spaceround Work as being most problematic. However, with the other areas there is no agreement (see Figure 27). There was, however, a very significant relationship between nonparole youths and adult prisoners (X^2 = 9.405; tau = -.30; p < .05).

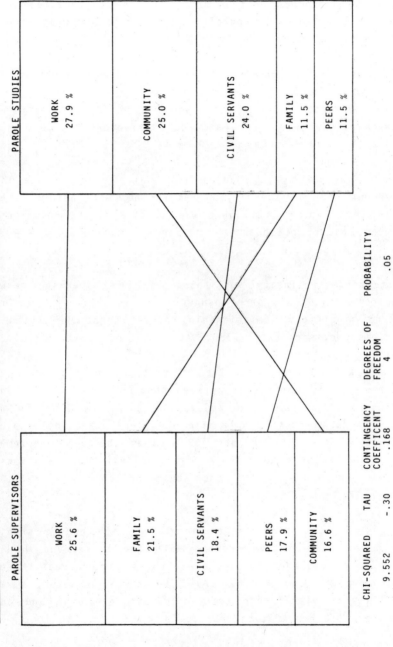

Figure 22: PROBLEM SPACEROUND PRIORITIZATION: COMPARISONS BETWEEN SUPERVISORS AND STUDIES

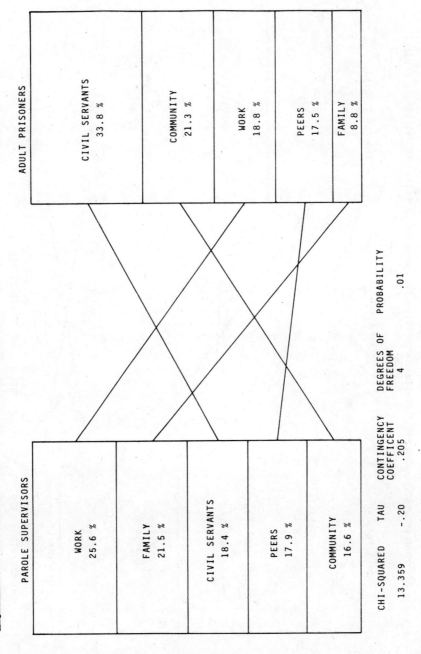

Figure 23: PROBLEM SPACEROUND PRIORITIZATION: COMPARISONS BETWEEN SUPERVISORS AND ADULT PRISONERS

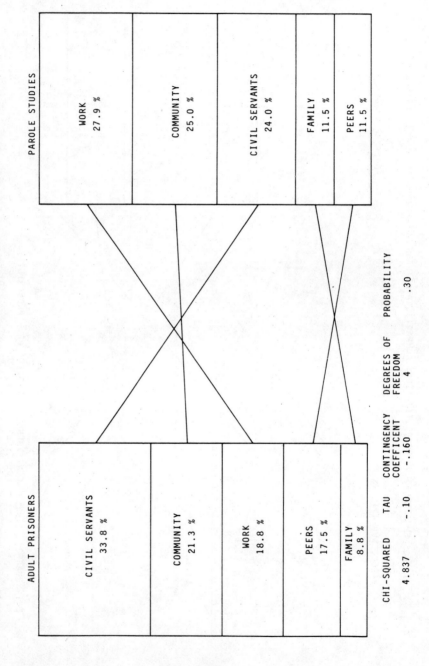

Figure 24: PROBLEM SPACEROUND PRIORITIZATION: COMPARISONS BETWEEN ADULT PRISONERS AND PAROLE STUDIES

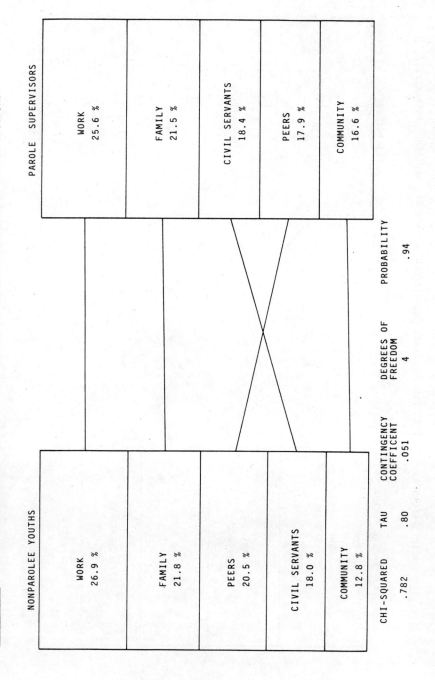

Figure 25: PROBLEM SPACEROUND PRIORITIZATION: COMPARISONS BETWEEN NONPAROLEES AND SUPERVISORS

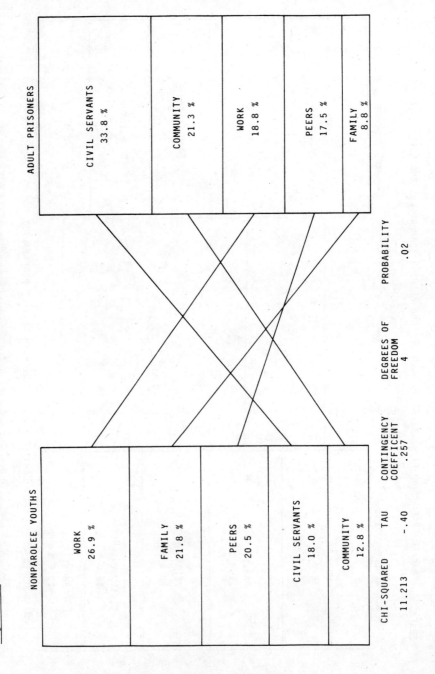

Figure 26: PROBLEM SPACEROUND PRIORITIZATION: COMPARISONS BETWEEN NONPAROLEES AND ADULT PRISONERS

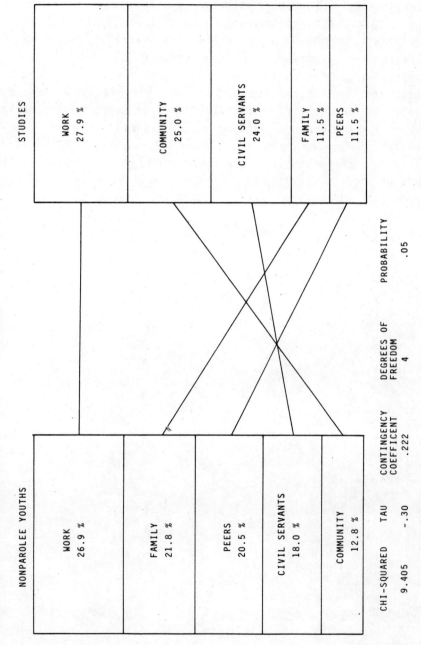

Figure 27: PROBLEM SPACEROUND PRIORITIZATION: COMPARISONS BETWEEN NONPAROLEES AND STUDIES

As a result of this Parole Problem Pre-study, the four problematic spaceround situations most frequently mentioned were developed into four separate skits. These four typical problem situation skits where play-acted by professional actors and recorded on video cassettes. This provided an opportunity to show each research subject the same four skits (see section 4.4.2). The purpose of this procedure was to be able to present a standardized set of empirically derived typical parolee problems to all subjects equally so as to elicit solution responses to each separate skit. These solution responses (or coping attempt responses) were then measured by a series of criteria (validated by a panel of professional experts) which focused on a broad range of coping attempts.

3 Theory

> "Society exists in my mind as the contact and reciprocal influence of certain ideas named 'I', Thomas, Henry, Susan, Bridget, and so on."
>
> Charles Horton Cooley

The Theoretical Overview

The <u>theoretical overview</u> of this research is based on a mixture of predominantly experimental psychological research on coping techniques mostly at the cognitive level and sociological theories of social control. The most relevant theoretical points of this research are:

a. <u>Coping</u> is subject to the principles of <u>learning</u>. These are specific empirically derived principles that explain the general nature of learning or the functional relationships between "certain antecedant conditions and changes in performance of a task" (English a. English, 1958). Since this research is in large part dealing with an analysis of what people do (as oppose to only what they think), and is concerned with the conditions under which they perform (i.e. the response to environmental stimuli) this approach partially falls within the realm of neobehaviorism (see Bandura and Walters, 1959; Hastorf, 1965, 268-284; Henker, 1964).

b. By using a list of <u>coping dimensions</u> (for a further discussion, see sections 4.4.3 and 4.4.4) an attempt was made to identify those specific patterns that are applicable in many situations. They may more accurately be referred to as coping principles which may be either preparatory or response acts; and, they may be cognitive or behavioral in nature.

c. Coping repertoire is a concept developed to represent a person's constellation of coping techniques. It is herein contended that these repertoires can be identified, measured and classified; and, that they vary widely among the general population. Also of primary interest is the size of these repertoires, the way coping techniques are prioritized within them, and to what extent these repertoires are influenced by other social phenomena.

d. Meaningful relationships are clearly a sociological concept that came from the roots of modern sociological thought, especially from the traditions of symbolic interactionism, behaviorism, the concepts of primary groups, the looking-glass self, and the significant other (see Cooley, 1902; Dewey, 1930; Mead, 1934; Blumer, 1969). The current use of this concept of meaningful relationships comes from the recent work of Friday and Hage (1976). They used the term "intimate role relationships" (borrowed from Marwell and Hage, 1970). This concept of significance or intimacy is discussed by them in terms of "saliency", "meaningfulness", "integration" and "number of activities", in an attempt to characterize the nature of role relationships. In this author's opinion, the term meaningful relationships better captures the sense of symbolic interaction.

e. Social integration, as mentioned earlier, is a broad sociological concept (originating with Durkheim in 1951) applicable to youth crime throughout the world and relating to how people are socialized to the dominant norms of society. The principle spacerounds of socializing activity are, family, school, work, community, and peers. This orientation is used because it is postulated that learning coping techniques is part of the socialization process (see Friday, 1981a; Thibaut and Kelly, 1959).

f. What is important (in terms of its influence) to an individual in a spaceround depends on the meaning of its major <u>interactive components</u>: people, objects, place, ideas and time. The way a person's repertoire of meanings evolve is through the process of interaction with these five basic components. In the arena of interactions (spacerounds), one is continously confronted with options concerning how to cope. The motivation and the forces which influence this selection process is of major interest to this study.

3.1 Coping Theory

> "The task before us, then, is to specify the appropriate patterns of alternative coping strategies that do not violate the recognition that coping strategies are always conducted in a historical-cultural as well as in a situational context."
>
> Aaron Antonovsky

3.1.1 A Survey of Coping

Coping refers to "things that people do to avoid being harmed by life-strains" (Pearlin and Schooler, 1978, 2). The term coping has a number of closely related concepts such as mastery, defense and adaptation (see White, 1974). This protective function is activated in three primary ways: by altering the conditions that cause the problems; by cognitively controlling the definitions of the problem so that the resultant stress is neutralized; and, by placing comfortable limits on the emotional response to problems (see Pearlin and Schooler, 1978, 2).

Research on coping has been steadily increasing in the last two decades, especially since the early work by Lois Murphy (1962) titled 'The Widening World of Childhood'. Murphy studied children's reaction to threat. She identified three basic steps that characterize the coping process: preparation, coping, and secondary coping. Four years later, Richard S. Lazarus (1966), in his book 'Psychological Stress and the Coping Process', identified similar patterns for adult coping.

Pearlin and Schooler (1978) point out that while the social sciences have not dealt with coping, per se, they have been extensively concerned with situations that disrupt the well-being of people. They cite such classic examples as "the discontinuities between early socialization and the demands confronted later in life (see Benedict, 1938); the contradictions among the norms that define situations and actions (see Stouffer, 1949); the disparaties between different dimensions of status (see Lenski, 1954; Jackson, 1962); and the motivations toward culturally prized goals that are frustrated by limited opportunity structures" (see Merton, 1957).

Today coping is at the center of stress research. One of the first major considerations in studying coping is the importance of developing "taxonomies of life-stressors". In so doing, the specific means of controlling "biological, ecological, psychological and social conditions of stress reactions" would be facilitated (Prystav, 1979, 297).

For the most part, the coping literature has dealt with coping in response to various forms of stress. It has been dominated by psychology and has mostly focused on coping at the cognitive level. Some examples of cognitive activities often mentioned in the literature are: intellectualization; isolation; denial; rationalization; reversal of affect; supplementary projection; complementary projection; active mastery; resignation; avoidant thinking; search for strategy; worry; and lack of strategy (see Houston, 1977a, 208). The bulk of the studies have been done in laboratories using finite measures of physiological and psychological activity.

The sociological dimensions of coping have been considered only to a very limited extent (see Blath, Dillig, and Frey, 1980; Pearlin and Schooler, 1978). These kinds of considerations have gone from a behavioral perspective and in response to broader social phenomena (situations). Work in the social and behavior areas of coping have been recognized as being seriously underdeveloped (see Prystav, 1979, 297; Pearlin and Schooler, 1978, 2).

Prior to discussing the techniques or characteristics of coping it is imperative to recognize that socio/psychological environments within which coping techniques function are the two basic givens: <u>social resources</u>, and <u>psychological resources</u>. These two terms refer to what is available that can be drawn upon in the development of coping techniques/repertoires. <u>Social resources</u> are reflected in the "interpersonal networks" of which people are part and which represent a potential for social support: family, friends (peers), school mates, fellow workers, organizations and acquaintances (see Pearlin and Schooler, 1978, 5). <u>Psychological resources</u> are reflected in the personal chacteristics people use to deal with problems in their environment: self-concept, self-esteem, assertiveness, self-denigration, mastery, intelligence, etc. (see Pearlin and Schooler, 1978, 5). In distinguishing between psychological resources and coping responses, Pearlin and Schooler (1978) state that psychological resources represent some of the things people <u>are</u>, aside from their particular roles, while coping responses represent some of the things people <u>do</u> to deal realistically with their life-strains (problems). One might take this discussion one step further by saying that social resources represent some of the things that people <u>have</u> in terms of their social roles and relationships.

Perhaps the most logical way to organize the literature on coping is to use the three basic steps that Murphy (1962), Lazarus (1966), and others (see Janis, 1958; Mandler, 1962; Ax, 1964; Schachter, 1966; Arnold, 1970; Glass and Singer, 1972) have generally used to describe the coping process as mentioned above.

In the preparation phase Meichenbaum et al. (1975) stated that "Much of the coping process is anticipatory in nature and is initiated before a confrontation with a threat or stressor". The results of most of these type studies have pointed to the enormous variability in the ability and style that people use in coping with stress. Preparing or rehearsing for stress is what Janis (1965) called "The Work of Worrying". This worrying process then gives way to coping or self derived reassurances. Meichenbaum (1973) referred to this process as "learned resourcefulness".

When there is an absence of cognitive preparation or rehearsal a person fails to cope and the result is helplessness, disappointment in protective authorities, and increased expectation of vulnerability (Meichenbaum et al., 1975, 339). Seligman (1973) called this process "learned helplessness".

In the coping phase an almost unlimited number of possible acts exist. Lazarus et al. (1974) differentiated between two coping modes: direct action and intra psychic. These may be liberally translated into behavioral modes and cognitive modes, or as Meichenbaum et al. (1975, 345) stated, "a) the physical acts one can engage in to prepare for stressors, and the physical manipulation of the environment (e.g. building physical defenses, and arranging escape routes), and b) cognitive manipulation to create an impression of safety, security or gratification, which includes what the person attends to, how he interprets both the external and internal environments, and how he assesses his own capabilities of coping."

In the <u>secondary coping phase</u>, an attempt is made to focus on the <u>feed-back</u> one gets as a result of trying the vast number of possibilities that could be used to deal with stress ("threat or challenge") and which suggests four general guidelines for training adaptive coping mechanisms:

> First, since coping devices are complex they need to be flexible. Murphy (1962) suggested that coping flexibility is important for adaptation. Coping techniques used successfully in one situation may be unsuccessful in another or even in the same situation another time.
>
> Second, in any training, one must be sensitive to individual, cultural, and situational differences, well illustrated in the research on cultural differences in emotion and on the "meaning" of painful experiences (see Zborowski, 1969).
>
> Third coping involves strategies for dealing with the environment. It incorporates potentially threatening events into cognitive plans which reduce anxiety and lead to more adaptive responses. Information that causes the work of worrying (mental rehearsal) may reduce stress or its after effects.
>
> Fourth, exposure to similar less threatening stressful events has a beneficial effect and can be used in training (see Meichenbaum et al., 1975, 348).

Based on this available information on coping, it is clear that the anticipation to or response after stress can be positive or negative. One can survive the stress or suffer psychic and/or physical set-backs, depending on the nature of coping technique used.

3.1.2 Comments on Real-life Coping

The literature on coping has evolved for the most part from psychology and has primarily dealt with the cognitive responses to various forms of stress. White (1974), for example, used the concepts of mastery, defense, and adaption. Houston used finite measures of physiological and psychological activities to describe coping in terms of intellectualization, isolation, denial, rationalization, reversal of effect, supplementary projection, complementary projection, active mastery, resignation, avoidant thinking, search for strategy, worry, and lack of strategy (1977a, 208).

The term coping has thus far been defined primarily to include psychological and physiological variables. Since this research deals with a broader form of coping, a more comprehensive definition was selected. Thus, for the purpose of this research, coping refers to "things that people do to avoid being harmed by life-strains" (Pearlin and Schooler, 1978, 2). In other words, coping should be understood as any reaction towards externally caused disturbances of both the cognitive and emotional equilibrium. Furthermore, coping refers to the interdependent levels of tension which are caused by an individual's interaction with fellow human beings as individuals and as groups not only in these relationships, but also within their own emotional state.

The general assumption of this concept implies that people react to specific information that is of direct concern to their well-being. In real-life situations a large part of this information is social in nature. That is, it originates in interaction with other persons; the other part of this information comes from non-person origins. Kurt Lewin (1948), the well-known Field Theorist, tried to simplify the relationship between behavior (B), people (P), and environment (E) by proposing the formula $B = f(P,E)$. This formula recognizes the simple reality that all behavior is a function of both people and environment.

A necessary precondition for the comprehension of coping or problem solving, is an understanding of the total environment's influence upon individual response patterns. This model tries to take into account the totality of a person's coping milieu, but more specifically, the main concern is with the social influences on individual behavior. It is my contention that any theory of coping can only be intelligible when coping is viewed as a fundamental adaptive phenomena of individual <u>and</u> social behavior within a dynamic interactive milieu. This dimension has not been adequately considered in the coping literature. By including the social component, one can go beyond the cognitive and emotional forms of coping and consider coping within the broader context (see Pearlin and Schooler, 1978; Blath et al., 1980).

In an attempt to understand how people cope or more specifically, how and why some male parolees seem able to overcome life's problems and some not, a theoretical model was needed that would comprehensively deal with psychic, social, and physical variables. Thus, the Social Coping Model was proposed.

3.2 Control Theory

> Social Control brings the "act of the individual into relation with this social object".
>
> George Herbert Mead

Control Theory

The four dominant sociological traditions developed in the U.S. for delinquency have been Strain Theories, Cultural Deviance Theories, Labeling Theories, and Control Theories. Strain Theories (also called Anomie Theories) claim that a person is forced into delinquency in order to satisfy legitimate desires that are not provided through conformity to society. Perhaps the best example of a Strain Theory is that of Robert K. Merton esoused in his book 'Social Theory and Social Structure' (1957). Cultural Deviance Theories claim that delinquency is a middle class perspective which views deviance as conformity to another set of norms. One of the classic Cultural Deviance Theories was propounded by Edwin H. Sutherland and is known as Differential Association (1939). The Labeling Perspective declares that a behavior is deviant only if society labels it so. One of the recent major statements of the Labeling Theory was developed from Lemert's work by Howard Becker titled 'Outsiders: Studies in the Sociology of Deviance' (1963). Control Theories claim that delinquents are amoral beeings whose bond to society is broken. The most explicit statement of this theoretical tradition was made bei Travis Hirschi (1969) with the publication of his book 'Causes of Delinquency'. Of the four above mentioned approaches, Control Theory seems to best capture the social reality of delinquent behavior. For additional discussions of control theories one should see Kornhauser (1973), Caplan (1978), Becker (1980), Friday (1980a), Weitekamp (1980), and Dussich and Jacobsen (1982).

This next section represents an attempt at describing two recent developments in control theory, culminating in a proposed theoretical extension. In my opinion this extension provides control theory with a more dynamic character which encompasses and postulates from social-psychology and sociology. This theory attempts to explain how individuals, through their interactions, become integrated into their respective normative spaces.

3.2.1 Hirschi's Control Theory

The pattern for explaining conforming behavior can be found in the continuation of the traditional concept of social integration (see Durkheim, 1938) in criminological control theories (see Hirschi, 1969). In explaining deviant behavior,

Hirschi was the first one to develop the concept of nonconformity without falling into the rut of etiological theory, as happened partly with Nye who attempted to explain delinquency as a function of family based causes (1958, 3-4). Although Hirschi was able to describe, and empirically research factors of conventional attitudes, he strongly stressed the affective level: "delinquent acts result when an individual's bond to society is weak or broken" (Hirschi, 1969, 16).

According to Hirschi, behavior is a product of an individual's bond to society, for which there are four important elements: attachment, commitment, involvement, and belief (see Figure 28).

<u>Attachment</u> is a person's affective bond to individuals, institutions and the world of work, marriage and peers (see Hirschi, 1969, 16, 110, 135). A person violating the norms, acts contrary to the wishes and expectations of most members of a society; consequently his or her scope in displaying deviant behavior is enlarged, thereby weakening the bond.

<u>Commitment</u> refers to the process of assessing the "costs" of deviant behavior compared to those of conformity. In this process the person decides whether to risk the investments in conventional aims or purposes (see Hirschi, 1969, 20). This element is the rational component of conformity.

<u>Involvement</u> is a consequence of commitment. It refers to the all consuming occupation with conventional activities which results in a lack of opportunities to commit deviant acts (see Hirschi, 1969, 22).

<u>Belief</u> implies that within a society there exists an acceptance of mutual values. Somebody accepting this system of values, and with it the prohibition of deviant behavior, conforms more with the conventional rules of society and commits less delinquent acts (see Hirschi, 1969, 26, 198).

Figure 28: CAUSES OF DELINQUENCY
        - A Control Theory - *(Hirschi 1969)*

INSTITUTIONS

- family
- school
- peers
- bonds

ELEMENTS OF THE BOND
(Hirschi 1969, 16)

- attachment
- commitment
- involvement
- belief

Result

- conformity

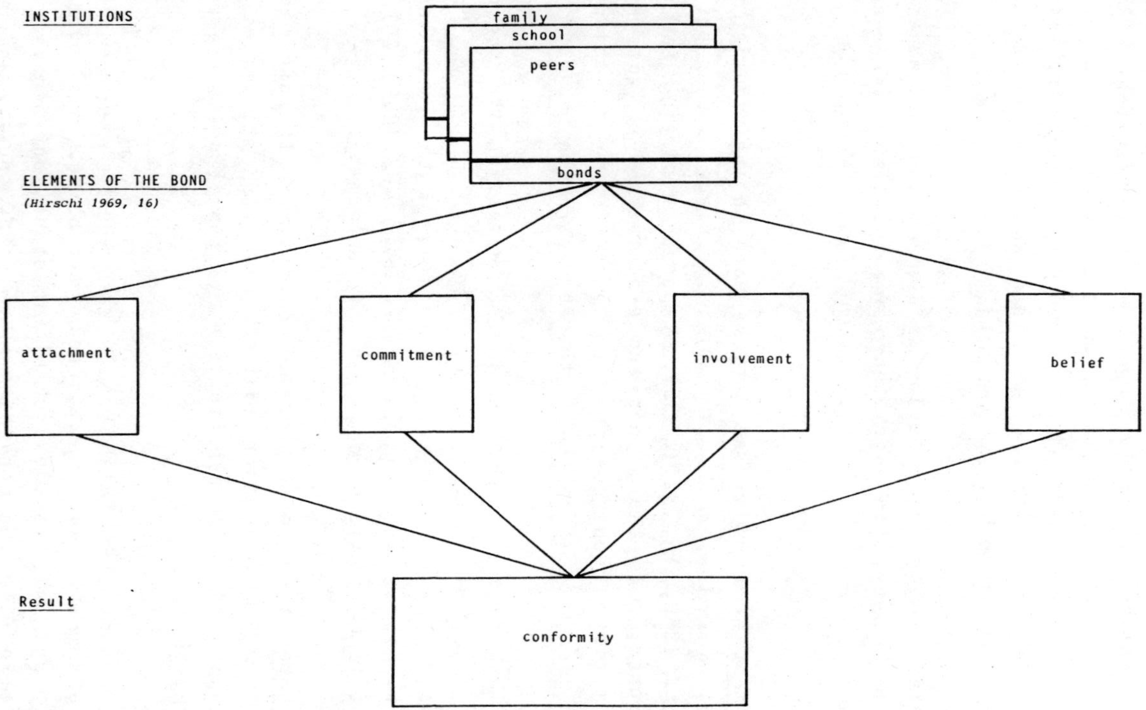

As Hirschi's concept of control theory indicates (see Figure 28), the four elements of the individual's bond to conventional society function within the social institutions of the family, the school, and peers. These institutions show characteristics which determine elements of the bond. Thus, the <u>family</u>, for example, may structurally and functionally be disturbed, exhibit a certain socio-economical status, offer the youth the possibility of exchanging his or her thoughts and feelings; and, thereby create a certain degree of intimacy or realize its function of leadership and control. Conventional parents can accept a non-conforming position towards the existing norms and can also exhibit emotional mutuality with their youth's peers (see Hirschi, 1969, 96).

In the area of the <u>school</u>, youth may hope to acquire certain diplomas, which are threatened by deviant behavior. In contrast, by fulfilling specific expectations like doing homework, they reduce their opportunity to commit delinquent acts (see Hirschi, 1969, 191-192).

The role of work in Hirschi's research was somehow pushed to the background, probably because his populations were primarily students. His focus on work dealt primarily with professional success or acquired status (see Hirschi, 1969, 182).

One of the most central themes of Hirschi and other control theorists is the role of companionship in causing juvenile delinquency. Boys who have delinquent <u>peers</u> have probably been involved in delinquent acts themselves, especially if their attachments to conventional society are weak (see Hirschi, 1969, 161).

Hindelang (1973, 471-487) conducted a partial replication of Hirschi's earlier study and was able to present findings which were in general agreement to those of Hirschi's. The findings, however, that peer attachments and parental attachments were positively related and that peer attachments and self reported delinquency were negatively related, was not supported.

3.2.2 Friday's Control Theory

While Hirschi's theory stressed the individual's bond as the decisive criteria (1969, 16), Friday stressed the importance of role relationship (1980a, 5).

Building on Hirschi's concepts of attachment, commitment, involvement and belief, Friday raised the question regarding the process by which these elements evolve. Acknowledging the disproportionate involvement in crime by young urban males, he recognized the interdependence of the various social levels (structures, institutions, and individuals). Thus, as a macro-sociologically oriented criminologist, Friday was primarily interested in the influence of the structural level as its effects the behavior of the individual by limiting the quality and type of role relationships within social institutions.

In explaining conforming behavior, the vital part of this theory lies in the relation between the development of significant role relationships as a process of social integration and the resulting manifestation of deviant behavior.

Individuals develop an interactional pattern of role relationships which are either integrative, and thus develop attachments, commitments, etc., or they tend to be insular and isolating. For these relationships to be effective in integrating youth, they must be intimate. According to Friday and Hage,

> "... as the intimacy (in relationships) declines ..., the youth is less integrated into society and more likely to be involved in various kinds of crime" (1976, 350).

In later publications, Friday along with Halsey developed four factors with respect to significant role relationships: frequency, scope, choice and overlap (see Figure 29).

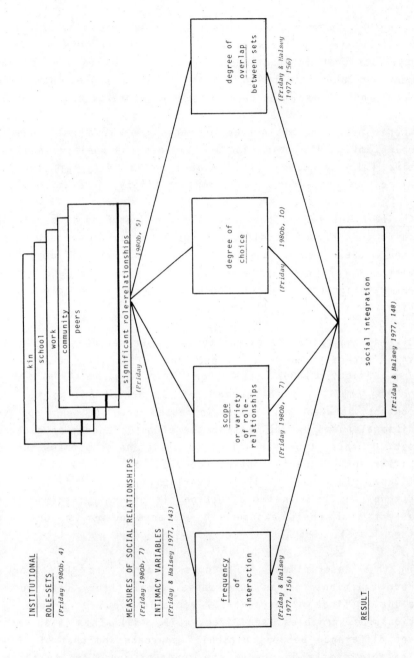

Figure 29: SIGNIFICANT ROLE-RELATIONSHIPS
- A Control Theory - *(Friday & Halsey 1977; Friday 1980b)*

Frequency indicates the number of interactions occuring in a relationship (see Friday, 1980a, 8). Within this concept is the idea that interactions must be numerous for the development of an intimate relationship; and, these interactions should not be isolated to a certain area of the relationship.

Scope speaks to the number or variety of role relationships, which intensifies the exposure to both the positive and negative role sanctions (see Friday, 1980a, 7). High frequency alone does not automatically imply intimacy in relationships.

Choice means having the possibility of entering into relationships that represent different normative systems. In the background there is the assumption that the number of adjustments within a relationship determines its dependency; and, dependent relationships tend to produce conformity and role expectations (see Friday, 1980a, 10).

Overlap indicates the extent to which one set of role relationships interacts with a second set of role relationships (see Friday, 1980a, 11). For example, the first set may be the family and the second set the school or the job. This contact between role sets increases the influence of traditional norms by duplicating the effect of norms in each role set. Of these four variables, the last one is perhaps the main pillar of Friday's entire concept of social integration (1980a, 12; 1980b, 120). Overlapping relationships exert strong pressures in the direction of conformity; they have the effect that one's exposure to diverse norms is constrained (see Simmel, 1955).

In this description, it becomes evident that the theory of role relationships as pure sociological theory does not include attitude or personality variables, but uses role relationships variables (see Dizon, 1979, 159). This is an important difference between Hirschi's approach and that of Friday. The former asks how close the bonds of youth are to the norm structures of society; the latter inquires how many role relationships exist within the different institutional areas the youth possesses and, what is most important, how intimate these relationships are (see Friday and Hage, 1976, 159). Hirschi's work is more micro-sociological in orientation; Friday's is more macro-sociological.

Friday's theory of significant role relationships also distinguishes (similarly as in Hirschi's theory) several areas of relationships or "institutional role sets" (1980a, 4; 1980b, 122-123): kin (family), school, peers, work, and community. The first three areas show corresponding characteristics to those already described by Hirschi.

As an area of life the community represents the social environment outside the family, school and job, also exerting a significant influence upon the socialization process of youth. Especially relevant are certain people in the neighborhood, membership in clubs, churches and other organizations.

A unique problem is posed by the relationship to peers. Normally peers are an integral part of Friday's other four role sets. The importance of the peer relationship is hightened when the relationships to the other role sets are substantially undeveloped. Peers, thus, act in isolation from behavioral definitions provided by other role relations. Given the societal definitions of success and status (â la Merton), role relationships help individuals define themselves. The lack of intimate role relationships within family, school, community and work increases the saliency of the behavioral definitions provided by peers (see Friday and Hage, 1976).

In generalizing role relationship theory to a more socialpsychological level, it can be postulated: people learn cognitions, affections and behaviors in these significant relationships. They also learn role responses to given situational definitions. The process of internalizing social norms (socialization), may be designated as a process of learning which is facilitated by and through intimate role relationships.

Thus far, the theory of role relationships has only been used in a few existing projects, primarily in intercultural comparison research. For example, it was tested by Dizon (1979) in the Philippines in connection with Sutherland's theory of differential association and with Cloward and Ohlin's theory of differential opportunities. Another study done in Belgium by Junger-Tas (1977) testing parts of Hirschi's theory, produced results which tend to support Hirschi's findings concerning the effects of high stakes to conformity creating a susceptibility to "prodelinquent influences" (1969, 161). Junger-Tas states: "... weaker integration in conventional society leads to selecting other marginal friends who in turn reinforce deviant values and diminish barriers to delinquency" (1977, 86).

3.2.3 Further Remarks on Control Theory

In their development of control theory, Hirschi and Friday limited themselves primarily to the antagonists of conforming/non-conforming behavior in trying to explain juvenile delinquency. The implication is that when conformity is achieved, delinquency ceases to be a problem. It is suggested that theories of control should go beyond the criteria of norm-conforming behavior for explaining delinquency. A theory that attempts to explain criminal behavior must also be able to explain non-criminal behavior. The term criminal is a legal term which labels specific behaviors under specific conditions. The most important part of the terms "criminal behavior" or "delinquent behavior" is the word behavior. A theory of behavior should concern itself first with the total phenomenon of behavior rather than being diverted by moral or legal conditions, or be bound by professional disciplines.

Up to now, most control theorists have been primarily concerned with delinquent behavior, and mostly from a sociological perspective. Some considerations which have not been covered have been: the relevance of both physical and cognitive differences; the influence of place and time; the behaviors of adults and of non-delinquent youth; the distinction between role and relationships, and finally, the relevance of an individual's perception of concrete and immediate factors versus the influence of social structures and their processes.

The accomplishments of control theory thus far provide important contributions to the further understanding of external social influences that effect behavior. I suggest, this is not enough. Hirschi himself stated that "criminological research has for too long based its theories on ecological data" (1969, 15). Thus, the extension in the following section has been proposed to evolve yet further.

3.3 Spaceround Integration

> "We are moral beings to the extent that we are social beings."
> Emile Durkheim

Spaceround Integration: A control theory extension

This proposal is an attempt at recognizing behavior in a more phenomenological way (see Dussich and Jacobsen, 1982). It takes into account the macroprocesses and microprocesses of social structures and how they influence behavior through spacerounds.

The term Spaceround (see Figure 30) represents an attempt to conceptually bring together the multifaceted quality of a social psychic happening with given people, with particular

Figure 30: SPACEROUNDS - A Control Theory - *(Dussich & Jacobsen 1982)*

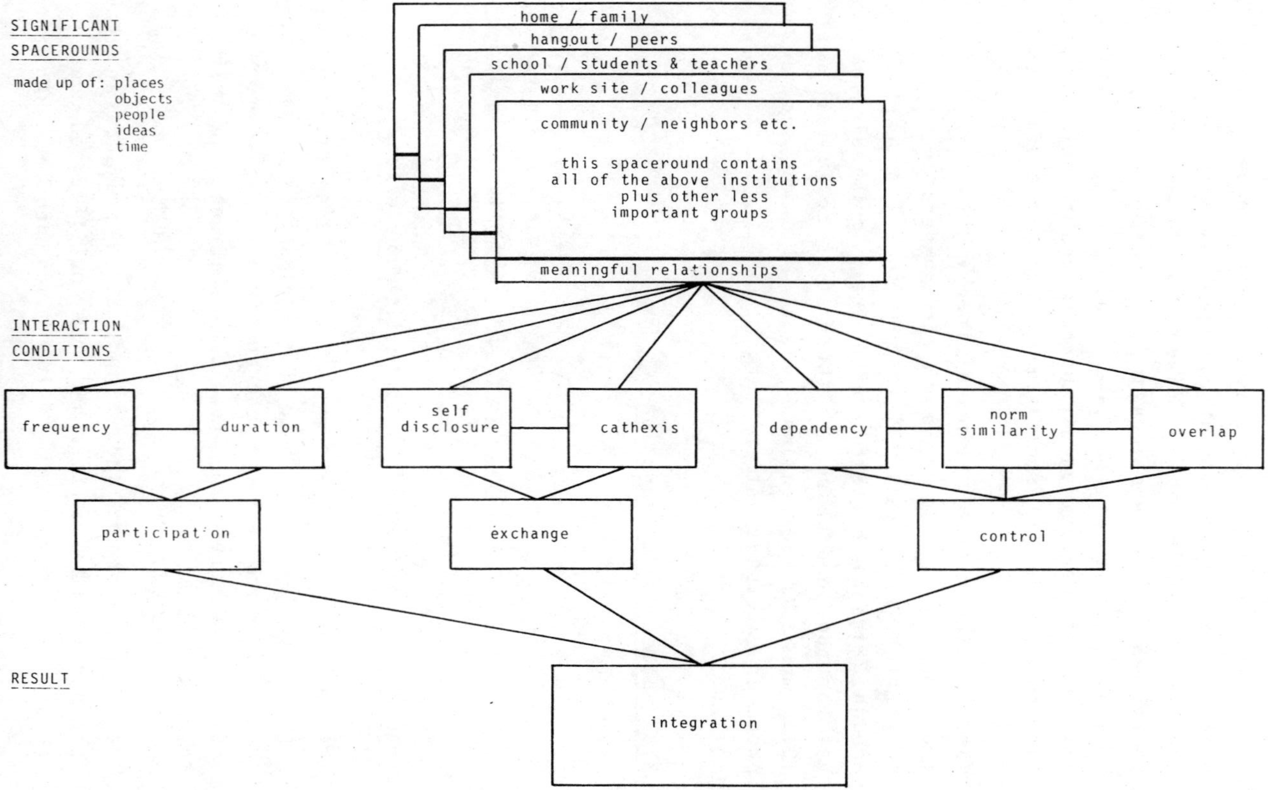

SIGNIFICANT
SPACEROUNDS

made up of: places
objects
people
ideas
time

- home / family
- hangout / peers
- school / students & teachers
- work site / colleagues
- community / neighbors etc.
- this spaceround contains all of the above institutions plus other less important groups
- meaningful relationships

INTERACTION
CONDITIONS

frequency — duration — self disclosure — cathexis — dependency — norm similarity — overlap

participation — exchange — control

RESULT

integration

objects, at a special place, with unique ideas, and only at an express time. This concept of spacerounds was derived from a somewhat similar concept "Placerounds" originally developed by John Lofland (1969) in his book 'Deviance and Identity'. All spacerounds have five main dimensions: people, objects, places, ideas, and time.

The concept people includes the actor and others who participate in a given spaceround. It is my contention that in most spacerounds people represent the most dynamic force. It is through people that relationships are formed and it is through relationships that norms are transmitted.

In the context of this theoretical model, objects also play an important role (hardware, a similar concept also identified by Lofland (1969), refers to physical objects used in interactions which impute a particular identity to the persons associated with it). I contend that objects can and do function as interaction partners and that a range of interactive potential exists also for objects.

Because activities occur in specific locations, these locations become associated with these kinds of activities. These locations are referred to as place. Thus, each spaceround can be identified according to its specific location-place.

The concept of ideas herein refers to all symbolic information that is processed by the persons in a given spaceround. This would include thoughts, language, norms, beliefs, knowledge and imagination. Because each spaceround is unique it is associated with a specific array of ideas.

The term time provides this model with a dynamic change agent that takes into account the continuous modifications which occur among the other four components.

An important character of these dimensions, and hence of spacerounds generally, is that the above mentioned five dimensions interact with a degree of regularity in an identifiable pattern and thus make each spaceround unique.

Significant Spacerounds refers to patterned social phenomena which have special importance to individuals and which may be effected by such macrostructural artifacts as different political systems, different cultures, different governments etc. and such microstructural artifacts as groups, individuals, feelings, ideas etc. These spacerounds may be traditional (family, schools, church) or nontraditional (orphanages, Kibbuzim, prisons, etc.) situations. Examples of some of the more common significant spacerounds are: home/family, hangout/peers, school/students-teachers, work/colleagues, and communities/neighbors. By adding the adjective "significant" spacerounds are limited to those situational settings which are important to individuals and which are similar to the more traditional term social institutions. Each significant spaceround has its own unique set of norms. These norms indicate how the spaceround components should interact describing what behavior is appropriate and what is inappropriate.

The home/family spaceround is generally considered to be the most influential significant spaceround. It is here that the first meaningful relationships usually develop. The home is the place where family activities occur; the family refers to those people who are the interaction partners in this space. The definition of family members include parents, siblings, aunts, uncles, grandparents and any other person (whether related by blood or not) who is a continuing participant of this spaceround.

The hangout/peers spaceround refers to persons and places that are unique for most youth; however, modified facsimiles of this spaceround are also prevelent among adults. A hangout is a place where peering activity occurs and where peers meet on a fairly regular basis. It is a place where they can exercise their own special norms with relative freedom. This place at special times is occupied primarily by people who interact with one another and who are roughly all of the same age, interest, class and culture. While it is true peers interact in other significant spacerounds (especially school and community) this is where they feel the most comfortable.

The school/students and teachers spaceround has somewhat similar features to hangout/peers except that it is a very different place, it is controlled by teachers and school administrators, and it has very different behavioral expectations. It is postulated that this spaceround's significance increases with age up to about eighteen years, and then even more so if one continues on to higher education.

The work/colleagues spaceround is unlike any other, and usually represents the first significant adult spaceround one experiences. The work site is occupied by fellow workers of varying statuses and skills; and, in some situations customers also play an important role in this space. It is postulated that when this particular spaceround becomes dominant, and its norms become different from those of the larger society and the meaningfulness of its relationships are strong, deviant practices can become common place and give rise to white-collar crime. For most, the period of retirement forces an abrupt estrangement from this spaceround often resulting in serious adjustment problems.

The community/neighbors spaceround refers to the area of a town where a person works, lives and/or plays - that is, spends most of his or her time. The people with whom one interacts in this special space are generally referred to as members of a community or neighbors. Thus far, it is the largest significant spaceround discussed and has the most people, objects and ideas. It includes all of the other significant spacerounds plus other people with whom one has frequent contacts (postmen, police, salespersons, neighbors, etc.). Of course, in large cities where the place of employment may be a considerable distance from where one lives and plays, work plays a relatively minor role within the community spaceround.

While this list of five Significant Spacerounds is herein limited to the traditional places of interaction, it is recognized that many other significant spacerounds may exist for people in special circumstances. Some of the uniquely important aspects of Significant Spacerounds are their universality; the relevance of their influence at various points in a person's life; the extent to which this influence shifts from one spaceround to another; and the extent to which interactions in these spacerounds determine how one controls oneself and how one is controlled by the spaceround itself.

The most critical force in these Significant Spacerounds are other people. Thus, within these spacerounds there exist Meaningful Relationships.

<u>Meaningful Relationships</u> represent the direct intimacy bonds between a person and other persons. These relationships are the interactive nexus of each spaceround. It is through these relationships that norms are transmitted and sanctioned. The degree of meaningfulness dictates the extent of conformity and integration. I contend that objects also function as interaction partners and that a range of interactive potential also exists for them. However, for purposes of this discussion, the focus will be primarily on person-to-person interactions which I propose are conditioned or effected primarily by seven basic <u>Interaction Conditions</u>: frequency, duration, self-disclosure, cathexis, dependency, norm similarity, and overlap.

<u>Frequency</u> refers to the number of contacts a person has with another person (see Hirschi, 1969, 160; Friday and Halsey, 1977, 143).

Duration refers to the length of time a given relationship has lasted (see Hirschi, 1969, 160; Dizon, 1981, 9).

Self-disclosure refers to the degree of intimate information which interacting persons permit to pass between each other. It is that character of mutual openness one allows with other persons which results in the sharing of intimate information (see Jourard and Lasakow, 1959; Dizon, 1981).

Cathexis refers to the affective energizing force between a person and another person or an object. It is the investment or value of emotional or mental energy expended between interacting partners (see Dussich, 1982).

Dependency refers to the degree of control another person has over the outcome of an interaction (see Friday, 1980a). This may also be referred to as the power element in a relationship. It is characterized by the control of access to particular resources, materialistic or nonmaterialistic.

Norm similarity refers to the degree to which there is norm consensus between interacting persons (see Nye, 1958). Norms are herein defined as behavioral expectations for which informal sanctions occur. Their influence on most people is usually stronger than formal sanctions.

Overlap refers to the degree of interactions between different spacerounds. To the extent that overlap is high (where many people from different spacerounds interact) the extend of meaningfullness in the corresponding relationships increases (see Friday, 1980a).

It is suggested, these conditions usually occur in the sequence presented above; and thus, can be grouped into three conjugated categories. Frequency and duration are conditions of participation; this is, they provide the opportunity for people to become acquainted with one another and are necessary for the onset of relationships. Self-disclosure, and cathexis are conditions of <u>exchange</u> and involve the give and take elements of relationships. Dependency, norm similarity, and overlap are conditions that fall under the rubric of <u>control</u> and exert a managing influence over relationships. Each of these conditions ultimately plays a critical role in the extent to which meaningful relationships exist. It is through meaningful relationships that a person becomes integrated or not into a given spaceround.

In traditional sociological terms, <u>integration</u> refers to a social process which brings together differing social components (see Fairchild, 1968, 159). When speaking of <u>individual integration</u> in a given spaceround, reference is being made to the process whereby persons learn to deal with the elements of that spaceround and, in so doing, become synchronized* to its components. When persons are well integrated into a particular spaceround, they "fit in" or adapt.

The opposite phenomenon of individual integration is <u>individual isolation</u>. Isolation implies estrangement from interaction within a given spaceround that one is a member of. It is characterized by interactive seperation from most of the usual spaceround activities. The most extreme form of isolation would imply: <u>minimal contacts</u>, <u>low duration</u>, <u>no self-disclosure</u> nor <u>cathexis</u>, a <u>difference in norms</u>, a <u>lack of dependency</u> and <u>no overlap</u> with the persons in that spaceround. <u>Individual dysintegration</u> represents the status of a person whose presence causes problems, one who cannot or will not adapt and one who does not "fit in". This person would have a moderate number of contacts with variable duration, limited self-disclosure and cathexis, a difference in norms, variable dependency and overlap.

---

* Synchronization herein refers to a functional compatibility that exists among components which interact roughly at the same time.

On the other hand, <u>spaceround integration</u> is a condition of the spaceround itself. It implies the synchronization and coordination among the five mutable spaceround components of people, objects, places, ideas, and time. The result of high spaceround integration is a minimum of conflict and a maximum of harmony. The logical opposite of this term is <u>spaceround dysintegration</u>, which describes a condition whereby the interaction components are not "working together" towards common ends and where there is high conflict. The final consideration applies to spacerounds which are seperate from the larger societal activities this is referred to as <u>spaceround isolation</u>. The spaceround itself is not participating in the community, nor does it directly contribute to the community's goals.

It is important to note that the relative significance of spacerounds has not been extensively researched. Hirschi (1969, 31) noted that especially with regard to the relative importance of institutions "... control theory has remained decidedly eclectic ...". Yet another consideration which needs attention is the influence that age has on the relative importance of significant spacerounds. It is reasonable to assume that the first important spaceround is the home/family. This spaceround may become less important when a child enters school. Subsequently as the hangout/peers spaceround begins to evolve into a more autonomous entity it competes in importance with both home and school. When a person leaves school and accepts a job the work/colleagues spaceround takes on increasing importance. At retirement most formerly important spacerounds are no longer available, and by default, the community/neighbors and officials spaceround becomes the most important spaceround for the elderly.

Thus, the main hypothesis of this theoretical model is that:

> If, within a given spaceround, the interaction conditions of frequency, duration, self-disclosure, cathexis, de-

pendency, norm similarity and overlap are high, meaningful relationships will also be high, and individual integration will be maximized.

3.4 The Social Coping Model

> "Unless the individual takes an active part in the process of stress prevention and coping, institutional or governmental policy changes will be of little use."
>
> Cary L. Cooper

A Theoretical Model

This model attempts to present two theoretical roots (the sociological Spaceround Integration Model and the psychological concept of coping theory) which are married into a unified socialpsychological concept and referred to as the theory of social coping. This model attempts to explain how individuals, through their interactions with problems, learn to adapt to norms and ultimately become integrated into their particular social space.

The Social Coping Model is a socialpsychological approach which attempts to explain the dynamics of how people deal with problems in their changing environments. It tries to explain why some people succeed and others fail. It takes into account the macroprocesses of social structures and how they influence individual behavior through Significant Spacerounds; and, it takes into account the microprocesses of cognition and how they influence individual behavior through the Coping Process. Herein coping will mean the successful application of a person's total repertoire in overcoming problems.

The concept which sets the stage and describes the socialpsychological environs of coping at the individual level is the Coping Milieu (see Figure 31). The Coping Milieu is the interactive setting within which an individual's coping process occurs. On a broader social level, these interacting settings are what was previously referred to as spacerounds.

To these spacerounds a person brings resources. Resources (see Figure 32) are defined as available attributes. These are divided into five components: time, physical, psychical, social, and repertoires. Time refers to the constant process of change. Based on a person's resources and particular problems, time exists for each person in varying quantities. Time is the dynamic consumable change-agent which effects the interactions of the other resources, the character of problems, and the way the coping process functions. Time is that limiting commodity available for coping. Physical resources may be divided into personal and nonpersonal. The personal may include: age, sex, race, health, height, weight, etc. Non-personal resources may include attributes which are external to the person such as tools, books, animals, property, clothing, etc. Psychical resources are those personal qualities, principally involving cognitive and motor activities such as: intelligence, personality, education, skills, etc. Social resources are those attributes which refer to a person's relationship to other people such as: sibling position, socio-economic class, social roles, friendship, etc. Repertoire resources refer to those learned behavioral patterns, dependent on interactional experiences with the other four resources, which may be recalled when needed. The repertoire is always in constant interaction with the other resources: it represents both the available response patterns and the transactional mediator between resources (see Figure 32).

Given a spaceround and resources, a person then comes to a problem. A problem is herein defined as a multidimensional external force directed at a person that blocks or interrupts

- 110 -

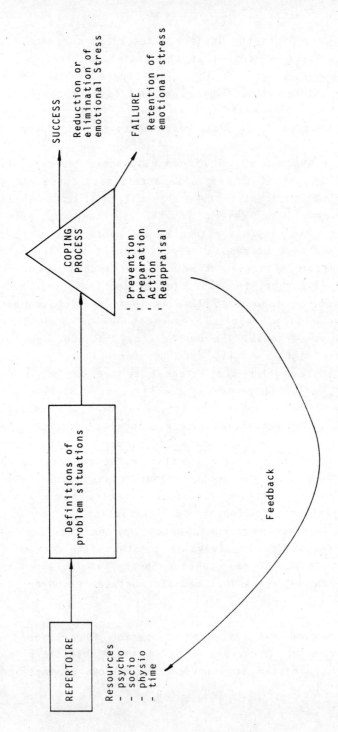

Figure 31: THE COPING MILIEU

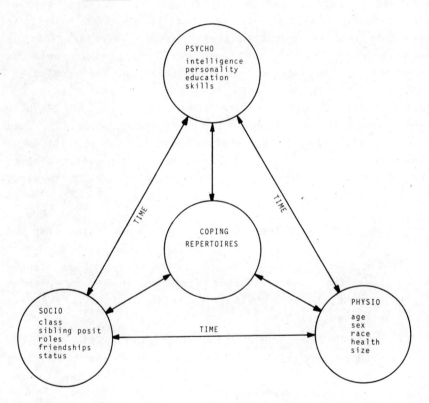

Figure 32: INDIVIDUAL RESOURCES

the status and/or the pursuit of needs or goals which then creates physical tensions (strains). These tensions may be perceived as discomfort, uneasiness, stress, or worry. Each problem is made up of numerous dimensions or continua, each of which may be represented by quantifiable scales. Each problem under consideration can be viewed at a specific moment in time. This problem moment freezes time and therefore fixes a point on each of the many continua. Thus, each continuum contributes (to some degree) to the totality of the problem.

Some examples of continua are shown on Figure 33 "Problem Moment Continua". An example of how this chart could be used to reduce a problem to measureable continua is as follows: A young man has been told by his boss that he has been coming to work late too many times and if he does not stop his tardiness, he will be fired.

Taking the continua in their order of occurance on the diagram:

1. the "Due Continuum" to cope with this problem identifies the time available from the moment of problem awareness (when his boss spoke to him) until the next work day;

2. the "Time Continuum" takes into consideration that the problem has existed from the moment the boss first realized the young man was coming late up to the moment of the warning;

3. the "Person Continuum" takes note that two people are involved in this problem;

4. the "Severity Continuum" focuses on the number issues and since this problem involves a small number of concrete issues it could be rated as "easy";

5. the "Threat Continuum" takes into consideration that this problem could be fixed slightly toward the "life threat" side of the scale as it relates directly to the life important activities of obtaining food, clothing, shelter, etc.;

Figure 33: PROBLEM MOMENT CONTINUA

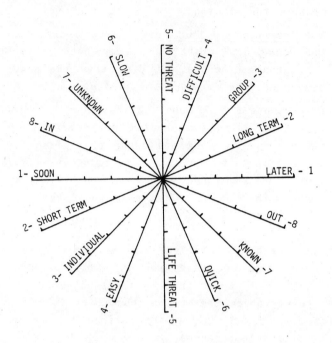

1. DUE CONTINUUM   - Time remaining for problem resolution
2. TIME CONTINUUM   - Length of time problem has existed
3. PERSON CONTINUUM   - Number of persons involved in the problem
4. SEVERITY CONTINUUM   - Complexity of the problem
5. THREAT CONTINUUM   - Extent of threat to a person
6. EVOLUTION CONTINUUM   - Speed with which problem became known
7. FAMILIARITY CONTINUUM - Extent to which problem is familiar to a person
8. CONTEXT CONTINUUM   - Extent to which problem is in or out of context

6. the "Evolution Continuum" would have us consider that the problem became defined as a problem "quickly", i.e. the length of time it took for the young man to realize the warning;

7. the "Familiarity Continuum" makes us consider whether the young man might have ever been confronted with this problem before; if yes, then the point on this scale would be fixed on the "known" side;

8. the "Context Continuum" allows one to consider the extent to which the problem is in or out of context. Coming late to work and being criticized for it is a logical part of what is likely to occur in a job situation. Thus, the problem is very much "in context". The point marked on this continuum would be on the extreme side toward "in".

Using this method all problems can be charted qualitatively and quantitatively. One must keep in mind that more continua could be developed beyond the eight presented here. The relevance of this Problem Moment Continua chart is in its heuristic value and in its ability to portray the uniqueness and transience of problems generally.

In response to the awareness of a problem, a person begins the coping process (see Figure 34). The coping process has four basic phases: prevention, preparation, action, and reappraisal. These processes may be cognitive, emotional, or behavioral, or may occur in combination with each other.

In the prevention phase a person becomes aware of the possibility that a problem may occur. If one has a reasonable anticipation that a problem might occur, specific forms of early-preparation are activated. If there is no anticipation, no early prevention follows.

When it is perceived that a problem will likely occur, the preparation phase can begin. If the response to this awareness

Figure 34: THE FOUR PHASES OF THE PROBLEM RESPONSE PROCESS

AWARENESS OF
PROBLEM POSSIBILITY

PREVENTION

| REASONABLE ANTICIPATION OF A PROBLEM | NO ANTICIPATION OF A PROBLEM |

AWARENESS AND DEFINITION OF AN ACTUAL PROBLEM

"Definition of the situation"

(W.I. Thomas, 1937)

PREPARATION

PREPARATION
- APPRAISAL OF RESOURCES
- REHEARSAL
  "The Work of Worrying" (Janis, 1965)
  The Work of Practicing

ABSENCE OF PREPARATION
- NO APPRAISAL

  No Worrying (Janis, 1965)

  No Practicing

EVENT OCCURS

ACTION

COPING
- LEARNED RESOURCEFULNESS (Meichenbaum, 1973)
- SELF DELIVERED REASSURANCES
- OPTIMISM
- DIMINISHED VULNERABILITY

FAILURE TO COPE
- LEARNED HELPLESSNESS (Seligman, 1973)
- DISAPPOINTMENT IN PROTECTIVE AUTHORITIES
- INCREASED EXPECTATION OF VULNERABILITY (Meichenbaum et al., 1975, 339)

EVENT OVER

REAPPRAISAL

SECONDARY COPING
- REPLAY
- ASSESSMENT

NO SECONDARY COPING
- NO REPLAY
- NO ASSESSMENT

FEEDBACK

and definition of an actual problem is to prepare, then a person begins to appraise his or her resources and starts to rehearse the active coping which is expected. Janis (1965) referred to cognitive (I would suggest emotional also) preparation as "The Work of Worrying". At the behavioral level one might refer to its counterpart as "the work of practicing". When there is no preparation (due to either the inability to perceive or recognize the problem), then no appraisal of resources, no cognitive rehearsal, no worrying, and no practicing occurs.

As soon as the problem event occurs the <u>action phase</u> begins. In this phase a person either brings his or her resources into play to cope with the problem, or does not cope. Coping means successfully applying one's repertoire to deal with the problem at hand. This is an active process which responds to the unique conditions presented by the many problem continua. In this action phase one may use resourcefulness, self delivered reassurances, and a variety of other techniques which serve to diminish vulnerability. Meichenbaum (1973) refers to this general process as "Learned Resourcefulness" which is diametrically opposite to Seligman's (1973) "Learned Helplessness" concept. Learned helplessness is the phenomena where one does not take action in the face of a problem. This failure to cope is the result of expecting to have no control. According to Seligman (1973) this phenomena of helplessness is learned from earlier experiences where a person's actions had no influence on the outcome of his or her behavior. This conviction of non controllability results in learned helplessness. The by-product of this conviction is: one does nothing to deal with problems, becomes disappointed in the inability of authorities to protect and consequently expects increased vulnerability.

After the action phase is over the <u>reappraisal phase</u> occurs. In this phase either secondary coping or no secondary coping takes place. On the one hand if coping occurred there is a kind of replay of what took place: an assessment of the past event occurs. On the other hand, if coping did not take place and the person helplessly accepted the pain and discomfort of the problem, there is no secondary coping, no reply, and no assessment. Regardless of the course taken, the information from this experience becomes part of the repertoire and either modifies the person's coping techniques or reaffirms the futility of doing nothing.

This process of coping with problems and feeding back the reaffirmation of taking action and being able to control the outcome of one's actions, strengthens the coping repertoire for its next encounter. The process of continually trying to strengthen one's repertoire is termed <u>competence striving</u>. Thus, considering a person's social problems and the coping that ensues, one who has a history of successful experiences with increasingly difficult problems, should logically have coping competences capable of handling increasingly difficult problems. It is posited that this process has a snow-ball effect, such that each successful coping experience enriches not only the breadth and depth of repertoires, but also shortens the time needed. This process feeds on itself: it desensitizes the threat and emphasizes the reward. As the time from problem start to problem resolution shortens, the importance of threat is diminished and the importance of reward is increased. This transforms the definitions of threats into challenges (see Meichenbaum et al., 1975) so that one begins to seek out new situations which previously may have been defined as problems but now are defined as challenges.

The process of learning norms, and eventually achieving greater individual integration, follows the basic pattern outlined above. Within given spacerounds, interactions occur which are effected by various social conditions (see Figure 30). The awareness of these conditions are an integral part of one's coping repertoire. Having favorable interaction conditions plays a significant positive role in strengthening one's capacity to cope.

It is suggested that with favorable social conditions and a favorable repertoire a person copes well with his or her problems. The result of these interactions enhances the character of relationships within the spaceround generating norm acceptance and spaceround integration (see Figure 35). Thus, learning to cope within a given spaceround has adaptive significance in terms of being integrated or not.

If the spaceround has legitimate norms like a school or a family, and a person is well integrated, the likelihood of lawful behavior is very high. If the person is not well integrated into a lawful spaceround the likelihood of criminal behavior is high. If the spaceround is illegal, as would be the case for a delinquent gang, members of the Mafia, members of a theft-ring, a terrorist organization, or a white-collar scheme, and the person is well integrated, criminality would very likely also result. If the person is not well integrated into a spaceround that has illegal norms like in a ghetto, the chances of avoiding criminal behavior is high.

Thus, this theory suggests that criminal behavior is a function of both a spaceround's integrative process, and an individual's coping competence.

Figure 35: SPACEROUND COPING MILIEU

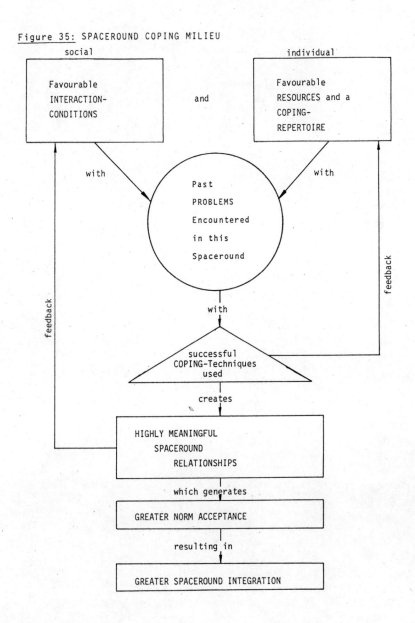

4 General Methodological Information

> "... in the area of interpretative life, variable analysis can be an effective means of unearthing stabilized patterns of interpretation which are not likely to be detected through the direct study of the experience of people. Knowledge of such patterns, or rather of the relations between variables which reflect such patterns, is of great value for understanding group life in its 'here-and-now' character and indeed may have a significant practical value."
>
> Herbert Blumer

4.1 Instruments

4.1.1 Development of the Coping Instrument

In recent years in the social sciences we have seen an increasing trend toward qualitative data collection, away from the pure quantitative highly standardized instruments that project reality on a computer-readable form, and toward instruments which attempt to be dynamic and realistic. However, in spite of the improved quality of their content they are limited to a format that is written in words and thus distant from reality. Considering the measurements of behavior in conflict situations, we wanted to eliminate the danger of standardization using traditional quantitative methods to collect qualitative data. An example was in the pioneer study of Blath, Dillig, and Frey (1980) which dealt with daily conflicts of young prisoners; they tried to collect empirical data of specific strategies of conflict solving in different situations. Using five short descriptions of interpersonal problems at work which were given to the clients in written form, they were required to answer 28 different Likert-scale response categories (see Blath et al., 1980, 83).

An example of such a problem situation follows:

> For three weeks you have been on a new job. Your work colleagues don't know that you were in prison. Today, for the third consecutive time, you've come to work half an hour too late. Twice you overslept and this time you had something else to do. Your colleagues are angry about this situation. One says, "Can't you ever be on time?" (see Blath et al., 1980, 83) (translated).

Using this type of written questionnaire one might assume that all clients receive the information in the same form and that they understand this information in the same way. However, the last point is doubious, for we know from information research, that information in written form is selectively received and selectively understood.

One soon realizes that any further elaboration of the problem situations would become so extensive that the written information would not be understood. Moreover, the clients would soon become tired, their attention would diminish and the attempted standardization of the situation would become endangered in a vain attempt toward instrument optimization.

This leads to a second problem that many written questionnaires of this type have, and that is that the individual differences of the clients account for much of the variance rather than the variation being a function of the independent variable. Examples would include: the attention span of clients being different, reading skill differences, different emotional states of the clients, etc. Individual skills in such problem situations are often hidden: a client is first required to perceive a situation audio-visually thru the written word and then cognitively work on the problem. The population that we used and that Blath et al. (1980) used, showed that prison releasees communicate best verbally and visually rather than through the written word. Researchers should expect that an adaptation from the client's familiar (and more concrete) communication level is preferred over the abstract written level. When external validity means to describe reality as it exists for the client, then the researcher in this case threatens a basic methodological rule of empirical research. It would seem to be even more absurd to require the client than to solve problems in this unfamiliar mode.

Thus, we were sure that if we used written problem situations, we couldn't achieve a valid measurement; and to observe real-life coping (due to ethical, economic and analytic limitations) was not feasible; thus we tried to develop a new method of information gathering that would come as close to the real-life experiences of our clients as possible.

In the same way as in the above mentioned research with the behavior of young prisoners on the job, this project was provided with conflict situations that took into account not only the behavioral intentions, but also the dynamics of the interaction itself. We therefore avoided the possibility of invalidating the answers by providing them with artificial options to describe their behavioral intentions but instead let the clients solve the problems unbiased and subjectively.

In an unsuccessful pretest of problem situations previously generated, we tried to get parolees to resolve a list of prepared problems. We were soon told by the parolees that the situations were artificial. They meant the problems were not from their perspective but from our perspective. Thus, in order to develop a more valid instrument it was necessary to conduct an elaborate analysis of parolee problems so as to accurately identify their own everyday problem situations. In this analysis we had the parolees tell us about their problems. From this list of problems five categories of life areas were developed. This enabled us to determine which life areas were the most often mentioned as being problematic and to what extent. The result was: family, officials, community, work and peers, respectively.

Thus, as a result of the pretesting, we were able to limit ourselves to one skit from the four most relevant spacerounds: family, community, officials, workplace, and tried to find one particular conflict situation typical for each respective spaceround. The situations of family and workplace had the highest degree of conflict present, while the situations from the spaceround community were very elaborated but only had medium degrees of conflict. From the peers spaceround there was only a minimal amount of conflict present.

In an attempt to find a solution to our dilemma of trying to simulate real-life problem situations we came up with the idea of video film presentations. The content of four of the original texts were used exactly as they were given in the interview, except that they were shortened (see Figures 36 to 40). We felt the client could be visually placed in a situation that was as close to reality as we could create. This might convincingly relate all the necessary information the client would need to find a solution to the conflict presented. These video films were made using the so called "subjective camera" technique. This means that the viewer experiences the situation on the screen as though he were part of the unfolding drama. In this way it might be easier for the client to take on the problem solving role. The films did not include the solution, but stopped just short of the moment when one would expect a solution to follow.

Standardization of an instrument is primarily concerned with the stimulus segment: that part of the instrument which causes a respondant to elicit a response. In this instance, the stimulus segment of our instrument was the "problem situation" skits. One of the main reasons for using video skits was to be able to present the exact same situation to each parolee being studied. In addition to presenting the same stimulus we tried to aim these skits at a concrete level of comprehension rather than at an abstract level. This was done to take into account the greater difficulties in abstract tests often encountered by offenders than among non offenders.

Another attempt to increase the instruments' relevance to the parolee was to make it as realistic as possible. In fact, we wanted to simulate real-life situations as much as possible. Moving as far away from an <u>in vitro</u> testing situation and as close to an <u>in vivo</u> situation we eliminated as many aspects of artificiality as possible. The major advantage of situational instruments is that they require far fewer assumptions concerning the generalizability of the results (see Goldfried and Kent, 1972). Efforts were also taken to aim the skits at the same socio-cultural level as that of the average parolees. This was achieved by matching the visual elements (clothes, furniture, etc.) and the auditory elements (speech levels, jargon, clarity, speed, etc.) of each skit with a subjective judgement of the typical parolee's sociocultural background.

Another important consideration in structuring the instrument was whether or not we should provide each respondent with a situational goal. This meant that since each skit presented a problem, and our question to the parolee was "How would you solve this problem?", knowing what direction to go in or knowing what one wanted was critical in his devising a strategy for solving the problem. On the one hand, we did not want to provide the parolee with so much structure that he would only have limited response possibilities, nor did we want to leave the response situation so open ended as to get too wide an area of variance. Additionally, we were concerned that if we gave too much information as to what the person's goal might be it would be robbing him of expressing his own goal setting skills (which are part of his coping repertoire). Thus, the compromise was to provide an implied goal in the dialogue text at the conclusion of each skit. A further consideration dealing with responses that were mostly attempts at saying that which was socially desirable and encouraging that which was in fact a genuine problem solving strategy. That is to say, to what extent would the parolee tell us what he thought we wanted to hear, and how far would what he told us be from what he would do in real-life. In a sense, we wanted to be sensitive to the lie factor (or the difference between wishful thinking and actual behavior).

During the instrument testing phase, an interesting dilemma developed with regard to response variance. With an open ended question after each skit: "How would you solve this problem?", we felt certain that a wide variety of answers would follow. This was not the case; in fact, we discovered that due to the strong conflict we presented in each of the skits, an "either or" (fight or flight) response occured so that we were getting an extremely small degree of response variation. This was resolved with a softening of the conflicts. That is to say, each problem situation was reworked so as to reduce the emotional content of the skit and to provide the respondent with more response options. This worked well and the parolees' responses were subsequently more varied and took longer for them to consider.

Differences in the way the skits were interpreted initially seemed to pose an important problem for us. In our attempt to standardize the instrument, we erroneously expected the perceptions to be similar. However, upon realizing that a person's unique perceptions and subsequent definition of the problem represents an important aspect of that person's coping ability, we decided to get each respondent to clarify his perception of each skit through the interviewer/respondent interaction and ultimately to use this information as part of the measurement of coping.

The final methodological concern was that of insuring that the client was identifying with his role in the video skit. To increase this process we not only took problem areas that were most frequently named and picked the most typical problem situation from a pre-study of problem areas, but we used a device known as "the subjective camera". This means that in each skit, the actors played to the camera as though it were another person (the parolee himself). It was as though the actors were talking with the respondents directly. Each parolee was placed directly in front of a large, color television screen in a quiet darkened room with only the interviewer present; further, the parolee was reminded by both the interviewer and the video skit announcer, that he should place himself in the role of the person being spoken to in the skit. These special considerations seemed to work quite well; in some instances, some of the parolees would actually start responding to the situation with comments before the voice playing the parolee would end.

4.1.2 Development of the Coping Dimensions Scale

In the construction of new instruments one must contend with internal and external validity and find an optimal balance between these two methodological requirements. With regard to external validity, the data is expected to represent reality, as honestly as possible. With regard to internal validity the requirement is that only that data which is necessary for answering a hypothesis be collected.

The key question is then, are we really measuring real-life coping. In order to answer this question and to measure the coping responses a list of 15 possible coping dimensions (criteria) were developed. These were put before a panal of experts made up of psychologists, sociologists and criminologists. Each dimension was explained, discussed and presented as continua. Each expert took the list of dimensions and wrote out definitions for the extremes of each of the dimensions. These definitions were collected and combined into one list with two composite definitions for each dimension (one per extreme). Subsequently this list of fifteen dimensions was reduced to thirteen due to some overlap and ambiguity (see Figure 41). It should be mentioned that before the experts were asked to make their judgements they participated in a two day workshop where the theory of coping and its operationalization was presented and discussed. The purpose of these dimensions served as a measurement tool for the coping responses of those persons studied. Each dimension was organized as a Likert scale with the extremes of each explained. Thus, each person's response to a skit were evaluated according to this dimension scale and received a score between 13 and 91; the higher score representing low coping ability and the lower score representing high coping ability. Using this list of coping dimensions as a composite score did not preclude our using individual dimensions as single variables; it is our opinion that using them as single variables reduces the chance for systematic variance and gives the analysis more flexibility.

In order to insure greater validity, consistency and reliability of this phase of the instrument's development we had three separate raters independently score the parolees response scores. The results of these three raters were then averaged and used as one score for the final data input. Figure 42 shows the mean values for each of the three raters for all thirteen dimensions.

4.1.3 Development of Control Theory Questionnaire

This instrument was based on the theory of spaceround integration. This theoretical model suggested a wide range of social structures and relationships which were operationalized in the instrument. The questionnaire also contained items

- 129 -

Figure 42: RATER MEAN VALUES FOR ALL 13 COPING DIMENSIONS

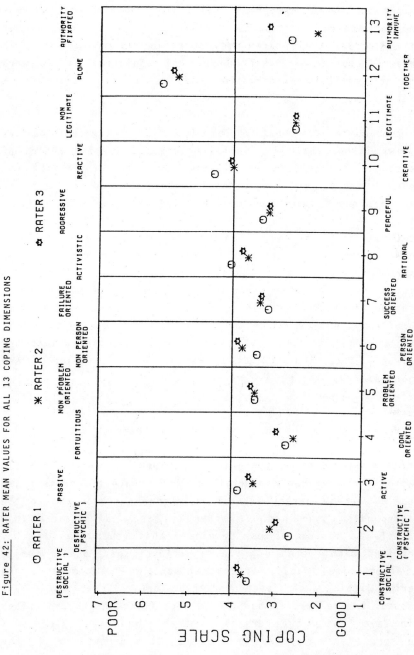

designed to obtain demographic data. This demographic information was needed to establish a pool of data for variables as well as cross verify previously obtained information on each research subject. A small number of additional items were aimed at verifying information that related to coping attitudes.

The procedure was used to develop this instrument was as follows: first, each key variable suggested by the theory of spaceround integration was listed; then the hypothesis for these variables and their relationships were developed; for each hypothesis dummy tables were developed so as to clarify the nature of data to be collected in order to answer the hypothesis in question; from these dummy tables a list of questionnaire items was developed. This first draft of the instrument was pretested using 8 parolees from another district. The information from the pretest was item analyzed with special attention being given to the parolee's understanding of the item, the variation of response patterns, item validity and item reliability. Based on these considerations and analyses, the final 88 item instrument was developed (see Figure 43).

4.1.4 Development of the Integration Instrument

The main dependant variable in the theory of Spaceround Integration is individual integration. This concept addresses the process whereby persons strive to become synchronized to the spaceround's components. In order to assess or measure this variable an instrument was developed that would ask five key questions within each of five significant spacerounds: family of orientation, family of procreation, work, community, and peers. Within each spaceround five basic areas where addressed: one related to how the subject felt, "at the relationship level" with the persons in that particular spaceround; the second area related to the subject's perceptions of how well he fit into that particular spaceround; the third area addressed the subject's perceptions of how the persons in that spaceround reacted to him; the fourth area dealt with the subject's perception of his involvement or participation with the people in that particular spaceround; and, the fifth area dealt with the subject's perceptions of whether or not his presence created problems.

This instrument (see Figure 44) was not used directly with the research subjects, but rather was completed by a person who listened to the taped interview of each subject and based on specific interview criteria, made his judgements.

4.1.5   The Problem Moment Continua System (PMCS)

Before one can analyze the impact of a problem, one should qualify and quantify the problem itself. Thus, the PMCS was developed as a heuristic device not only to measure problems but to graphically portray their uniqueness and transience.

For purposes of this report a problem is defined as a multi-dimensional external force directed at a person that blocks or interrupts the status and/or the pursuit of needs or goals which then creates physical tensions. These tensions may be perceived by the effected persons as discomforting, uneasy, stressful, worrysome, and occupying one's thoughts and feelings. Each problem is made up of numerous dimensions or continua, each of which may be represented by quantifiable scales. Each problem under consideration may be viewed at a specific moment in time. This problem moment freezes time and therefore fixes a point on all of the many continua and provides an opportunity to analyze a given problem both quantitatively and qualitatively. Further, the PMCS allows us to measure to what extent each continuum contributes to the totality of the problem under consideration (see Figure 33).

Figure 33 presents nine examples of continua. Each continuum represents a particular aspect of a problem which can be plotted on a scale of -5 to +5. In analyzing the data, these continua can be correlated with responses. Each continuum can be used separately, or in combination or as a composite. Separately one could correlate single variables with each continuum. In combination, some of the continua are related, e.g. those dealing with time (1, 2, and 6); thus, time as a problem could be combined into one variable and correlated with other variables. As a composite, even though it is difficult to combine some of the continua which are dissimilar, it can be forced into a kind of "crisis scale" and thus used to compare one problem with another.

Due to the subjectivity of these judgements it is important to develop a reliability procedure by using at least three judges for plotting decisions on the continua and then averaging the three judgements into one score.

4.1.6 Classification Method for Social Class

Some of the data collected in this study was used to classify the subjects according to their social class. This classification was accomplished with the assistance of an instrument developed by Kleining and Moore (1968).

Information was gathered on the following items:

1. Schools attended by father,
2. Final grade father attended while at school,
3. Father's date of graduation,
4. Father's field of study,
5. Father's profession,
6. School attended by mother,
7. Final grade mother attended while at school,
8. Mother's date of graduation,

9. Mother's field of study,
10. Mother's profession.

The data from the questionnaire was classified according to social class. It was collected by research with a standardized interview:

Information was gathered on:

- Schools attended by the father,
- Final grade father attended while at school,
- Father's date of graduation,
- Father's profession (educated in),
- Father's profession (practiced),
- Schools attended by the mother,
- Final grade mother attended while at school,
- Mother's date of graduation,
- Mother's profession (educated in),
- Mother's profession (practiced).

This social class selection method was based on 70 professions which were used as status-indicators. The classification was based on the following nine social classes:

- Upper class,
- Upper middle class,
- Intermediate middle class,
- Lower middle class (non-industrial),
- Lower middle class (industrial),
- Upper lower class (non-industrial),
- Upper lower class (industrial),
- Lower lower class,
- Destitute.

The class selection was made by using information provided by the subjects as to their parents professions. If the classification selection based on these data became problematic, supplemental data, such as the number of years school attended, school completed, and income, were taken into account. If father or mother were currently unemployed or sick for a long time or retired from work, the classification was based on the profession last practiced.

4.2 Obtaining Access to Subjects

According to the Data Protection Law of the Federal Republic of Germany (Das Deutsche Bundesrecht. 391. Lieferung - April 1977), special rules and regulations existed concerning the use of data. The Data Protection Law exists for the protection of personal data from misuse in terms of storage, transfer, change and expungement of data.

The Law protects the personal data of

   a. governmental agencies of other public offices,
   b. natural or judical persons, companies of other unions of persons of private law for private purposes, and
   c. of natural or judical persons, companies of other unions of persons of private law for extraneous purposes, from storage, change, expungement or transfer.

This law does not cover data from the press or TV stations. The transfer of data to administrative agencies outside the public use is only admissible if the data are necessary for the fulfillment of agency duties. In terms of research this means if there is a higher priority of interest in that subject than to protect the personal data. In all cases for personal data to be used, an application must be made and a general agreement obtained from the Minister of Justice of that state.

One of the major problems of this study was getting access to parolee data. According to the Data Protection Law, transfer of personal data to institutions outside the criminal justice system is prohibited. There is, however, one major exception of this law. Data on subjects can be released providing the research is of top priority. The data, then, may only be released when an agreement is made between a subject and a researcher.

For this study, an application was made to the Minister of Justice of Lower Saxony. At first, permission could not be obtained. The Minister of Justice referred us to the President of the Higher Regional Court of Celle, the parole officers of this region, and to the Presidents of the seven Regional Courts. After contacting all these people, access to the clients records was finally obtained.

There was, however, one difficulty. We had to obtain an agreement from each of the parole officers and from each of the clients affected. This was a very time consuming process and very difficult to accomplish. As the onset many of the parole officers were convinced that we were working for the Ministry of Justice in some watch-dog role and that we were evaluating their work. Once we received parole officer permission, they in turn had to go to each one of their clients to ask permission. This entire process took approximately 6 months.

5 The Coping/Supervision Study*

> "Stress refers, then, to a very broad class of problems differentiated from other problem areas because it deals with any demands which tax the system, whatever it is, a physiological system, a social system, or a psychological system, and the response of that system."
>
> R.S. Lazarus

This primarily methodological coping study focused principally on the postulate:

> The extent to which a person can cope in a given space-round is proportional to the successful experiences he or she has had with similar problems and the abundance of resources available.

Since it was beyond the realm of this project to measure past successful experiences, one of the main concerns with this research was with explaining differences in coping behavior based on both personal characteristics and different space-round circumstances.

In an effort to better understand the dynamics of coping this exploratory research was based on the following postulates:

---

* This chapter is an updated reanalyzed version of an earlier paper published in Germany under the title: "Social Coping bei jungen Delinquenten unter Bewährung". (In: H.-J. Kerner, H. Kury, K. Sessar (Eds.): Forschungen zur Kriminalitätsentstehung und Kriminalitätskontrolle. Köln: Carl Heymanns Verlag, 1983).

1. Since coping occurs in a multi-variate context, some of its qualities will be related to the individual and some will be related to the situation.

2. Using a sample of different individuals and four different situations to cope with, it should be possible to identify coping behavior clusters that are unique to certain situations and to certain types of persons.

3. Those coping clusters that are unique to individuals will be by-products of individual social psychological phenomena and will not significantly change with different situations.

4. Those coping clusters that are unique to situations will change with each situation and will not be significantly effected by individual differences.

5.1 Data Collection

In order to explore the above postulates it was necessary to interview a sample of young German offenders who were or had recently been under supervision (Bewährung)[1]. The subjects of this study were eighty-one young male adults (between the ages of 17 and 32 years; with an age range of 15 years; the mean was 23.1 years; the median was 24.5 years and the mode was 22 years), from the state judicial district of Hannover, and had been adjudicated under the German youth laws.

The instrument for measuring coping was especially designed for this study (see Dussich and Jacobsen, 1982) and resulted from a prestudy dealing with the problems of young males under

---

[1] Bewährung in German practice means to prove oneself. It is comparable to community supervision and is broken down into two forms: Strafaussetzung zur Bewährung (Probation), and Strafrestaussetzung zur Bewährung (Parole).

supervision (see Dussich, Jacobsen, and Iwannek, 1983). This prestudy showed that the spacerounds most often mentioned as requiring coping (having problems) were: family (27.3 %), civil servants (23.4 %), community (18.2 %), work (17.5 %), and peers (13.6 %).

Based on these findings an instrument was designed which took into account the most typical (most often mentioned) problem situation within each of the first four spacerounds identified (family, civil servants, community, and work). For the "family" spaceround the most typical problem situation was identified as conflicts at the dinner table over school and friends. For the "civil servants" spaceround the most typical problem situation identified was frustration at the employment office. For the "community" spaceround the most typical problem situation identified was hassles with neighbors. For the "work" spaceround the most typical problem situation identified was conflicts with the boss.

Using actual samples from these four problem situations, four short skits were written but without the solutions. These skits were then acted out by professional actors and actresses before a video camera using the "subjective camera" technique[2]. This technique helped to personalize the presentation of the problem to the viewer and thereby helped to increase the identification of the viewer with the particular spaceround portrayed and the problem situation presented. Thus, each of the subjects were shown the four video skits one at a time and after each one they were asked how they would solve the problem just seen. Each response was recorded on tape and subsequently reduced to written text for purposes of analysis.

---

2 The "subjective camera" technique is where the person viewing becomes the central character, he is not seen, only heard. The actors and actresses play to the camera and react to the voice that represents the viewer.

Using this type of instrument helped take the subjects as close to real-life situations as possible and still maintain standardization over the test-stimulus.

The role of the interviewers was to be non-committal and serve as facilitators, encouraging subject spontaneity and responsiveness. It was important for the interviewers to help the subjects elicit an abundance of information so that ultimately there would be adequate data for scoring each of the 13 coping dimensions. Each subject's response was open-ended and unstructured; our intent was to obtain as direct and honest a response as possible without influencing the flow of information in any way.

The two interviewers used for this study were given special theory and practice training. Theory, in terms of interview dynamics as well as understanding the principle elements of the Social Coping model. Practice, in terms of learning the techniques of interviewing and practicing them on simulated subjects through role-playing.

Some of the main limitations of this data collection method were that:

- not withstanding the similarity of the simulations to real-life, there were elements of artificiality to the problem solving situations such as: whether the problem situations were similar to the subject's own real-life conditions, portraying the problem situations through the use of video equipment, and the influence of the ever-present interviewer (to mention the most apparent ones);

- a degree of differential interviewer/subject interaction existed in each interview and probably accounts for some small but insignificant amount of variance;

- the technical quality of the video skits was not professional and may have somewhat reduced the sense of simulation reality as well as perhaps creating a slight distraction for the subjects viewing the video skits.

In spite of these limitations, it is judged that the degree of error they may have caused was insignificant.

The main assumptions of this study primarily focus on the measurement situation. Thus, I assume that: the <u>ceteris paribus</u> principle was in effect; the subjects were representative of all youth under supervision in the Hannover area; the video skits were authentic enough to generalize to real-life situations; all subjects acted in their normal way; all subjects received the problem stimulus (skits) in the same basic way and with essentially the same impact; and, the thirteen dimensions are adequate measures of real-life coping.

The Interview Technique

How does one go about getting information from clients as to how they would solve conflict situations? There were several possibilities available from which only a few of the most important ones were considered. One way would have been to ask clients to show their intended behavior through the use of multiple choice questions. This would have had the disadvantage of not being able to place the dynamics of the conflict situation into written form. Furthermore, the client would have been asked to transform his behavior to a communication level not his own. Besides, it would have been easy for him to give answers which he believed were expected (the effects of social desirability).

A second possibility would have been to ask the client to describe a similar or equal situation from his own life which was similar to the simulated conflict situation. The advantage here would have been that we would not have asked about his intended actions but rather about actual behavior which he had displayed in the past. This could have provided us with an understanding of the dynamics of the situation surrounding the solution. Also, this could have occurred on a familiar communication level. He could have displayed his problem solving behavior at the verbal and nonverbal levels by using gestures and facial expressions in addition to the spoken word. Disadvantages of this interview technique are that the effects of social desirability are hard to avoid, the situations revealed by the clients and their actions belong to the past, and the consequences have already been resolved and thus cannot be verified by the interviewer. Additionally, it could have been that the video skits had little similarity to the situations experienced by clients. In these cases the conflict situations might hurt more than help the measurement process.

A third possibility in the collection of conflict situation behavior could have been to let the clients take the role of the subject in the video skit and let them solve the conflicts immediately following the film's action. In this instance the interviewer would not give them solutions, but rather would work as a motivator continously providing stimuli almost as a counterpart to the client. If the client was willing, this method could become similar to a real role playing situation. It could be possible after a short warm-up phase, for the interviewer to let the client act as a subject, thus allowing the interviewer to note client flight reactions as well as social desirability responses and to further encourage him so as to force him to deal with the conflict situation in a more direct and serious way. It is our opinion that this technique could better deal with the dynamics of problem solving as it not only allows static but also dynamic solutions to conflicts. However, this technique lacked reliability.

In preparing for the use of this interview technique we expected few optimal sessions. We expected that the clients would try to escape more from the conflict or adapt which means to show a conflict solution which he thought was expected of him (social desirability). Frequently it was noted, that because of fear or because of difficulty in forming answers, clients would stop talking. Therefore, it became important to reconfront clients with the facts of the skit. When he would try to escape from a particular problem, he had to be brought back into the original field of the skit.

The sessions usually ended when the client had no more answers to give or when he felt the problem was resolved. An example was: the client suggesting that by giving in, or by giving up, or by suggesting a compromise, the problematic relationship came to an end. In these cases the interviewer tried to help the client find some solution. The interviewer's technique was to reflect back to the client what he had just stated, to show a sincere interest in what was being said and to encourage him along the way. This technique was primarily used in order to keep the response patterns directed towards the original skit rather than allowing the subject to modify the original problem situation. It was also important in this technique to keep the response opportunities as open-ended as possible. That is, if a client was not able to generate a solution response or if he was not willing to solve the problem at this point, permit the session to come to an end.

5.2 Data Reduction

After all taped interview responses were reduced to texts, three raters (who were also given extensive training in the Social Coping model as well as in the definitions of the 13 coping dimensions) independently rated each subject's four skit responses using the 13 dimensions. Each dimension was scored on a seven point Likert scale requiring the rater to make a judgement as to how high or low a given subject's response scored on each of the 13 dimensions. The three raters' scores were then averaged and used as one score for the analysis.

The above reduction procedures were used to determine the <u>nature</u> and <u>strength</u> of the coping response. The <u>abundance</u> of the coping response was determined by simply counting the total number of words elicited in response to each of the four video skits. This content analysis procedure gave an objective and valid method for quantifying each response and, was used directly as a continous variable in the final analysis.

5.3 Findings

The three-way factor analysis using <u>all four video skit responses</u> (aggregate analysis) as a single score showed that the dimensions which seem to belong to Factor I (which we called Normative) were:

	loadings
9. Peaceful/Aggressive	.782
1. Constructive/Destructive	.725
11. Legit/Non-legit	.646
6. Person/Non-person	-.420
13. Authority Immune/Fixated	-.606

Those which seem to belong to Factor II (which we called Outcome) were:

	loadings
7. Success/Failure	.803
2. Constructive/Destructive-psychic	.710
4. Goal/Fortuitous	.707

Those which seem to belong to Factor III (which we called Coping) were:

	loadings
10. Creative/Reactive	.858
3. Active/Passive	.810
5. Problem/Non-problem	.778
8. Rational/Activistic	.773
12. Together/Alone	.593

Taking the factor analysis a step further by rotating the factors with the Kaiser normalization procedure the factor loadings were looked at with each separate skit response. As expected, each skit produced a different pattern of dimension scores and consequently a different factor structure (see Figures 45 to 48).

Looking at the factor loadings for the Family skit responses (see Figure 45) "Argument at Supper", one can see that there are three distinct clusters: eight dimensions are heavily loaded in Factor I, five dimensions are heavily loaded in Factor II, and two dimensions fall under Factor III. Dimensions 2 and 13 share double loadings in Factors II and III. All but one of the dimensions in Factor I are quite strong and dimensions 1, 9, and 11 share Factor I with the aggregate analysis. For Factor II, the dimensions 2, 4, 6, 7, 12, and 13 are mixed in strength with only 2, 4 and 7 present in the aggregate analysis pattern. In Factor III, two dimensions produced weak and shared loadings, and shared none of the dimensions with the aggregate analysis. Thus, the coping responses of the Family skit are rather unique when compared with the four skit aggregate analysis. The most critical (loadings above .900) dimensions for this skit were: the Constructive/Destructive-Social, Success/Failure, and Rational/Activistic.

Figure 45: SPACEROUND: THE FAMILY
           SKIT 1: Argument at Supper

COPING DIMENSIONS (N = 81)	FACTORS		
	I	II	III
1 CONSTRUCTIVE/DESTRUCTIVE-SOCIAL	.932*	.002	-.256
2 CONSTRUCTIVE/DESTRUCTIVE-PSYCHIC	.172	.651*	.502
3 ACTIVE/PASSIVE	.835	.271	.205
4 GOAL/FORTUITOUS	.169	.691*	.106
5 PROBLEM/NONPROBLEM	.875	.169	.128
6 PERSON/NONPERSON	.042	.500	.106
7 SUCCESS/FAILURE	.112	.994*	-.055
8 RATIONAL/ACTIVISTIC	.919	.214	-.088
9 PEACEFUL/AGGRESSIVE	.879*	-.090	-.126
10 CREATIVE/REACTIVE	.820	.351	.184
11 LEGIT/NON-LEGIT	.736*	-.121	-.163
12 TOGETHER/ALONE	.459	.304	.122
13 AUTHORITY IMMUNE/FIXATED	-.320	.568	.603

* Also heavily loaded in the aggregate analysis (6).

For the Community "Friendly Neighbor" skit responses (see Figure 46), the dimensions 1, 9, and 11 in Factor I are the same as in the aggregate skit analysis. In Factor II, the three dimensions 2, 4, and 7 are also represented in the aggregate analysis. In Factor III, there are only dimensions 6 and 12 with 12 also appearing in the aggregate analysis. The most critical (loadings above .900) dimensions were: Constructive/Destructive-Social, and Problem/Non-problem.

The third skit also focused on the Community, but dealt with a "Disappointment at the Employment Office" problem situation. The factor analysis for this skit response (see Figure 47) is the most unusual of the four separate analyses. Factor I is relatively empty with only two heavily loaded dimensions being present and both are found in the aggregate analysis. Factor II is somewhat stronger with five heavily loaded dimensions, only one (4) being similar to the aggregate analysis. Factor III, compared to other spacerounds, is rather unusual by having nine dimensions with heavy loadings (two of which are shared double loadings with Factor II). Four of these dimensions are also in the aggregate analysis. The most critical (loadings above .800) dimensions were: Constructive/Destructive-Social, and Creative/Reactive.

The fourth and final skit focused on the spaceround Work using the problem situation "Argument with the Boss" (see Figure 48). This factor analysis of the Work spaceround is the most similar to the aggregate analysis. In Factor I, of the six heavily loaded, five were from the same factor as in the aggregate analysis. Factor II contains four loadings of which dimensions 2, 4, and 7 are also in the aggregate analysis. Factor III has five dimensions, all of which are the same as for the aggregate analysis. Thus, this skit produced coping response patterns that most closely represented the aggregate analysis than any of the other three spaceround skits. The most critical (loadings above .800) dimensions were: Constructive/Destructive-Psychic, Peaceful/Aggressive, and Creative/Reactive.

Figure 46: SPACEROUND: COMMUNITY/AT THE APARTMENT
SKIT 2: The Friendly Neighbor

COPING DIMENSIONS (N = 81)	FACTORS		
	I	II	III
1 CONSTRUCTIVE/DESTRUCTIVE-SOCIAL	.917*	.003	-.258
2 CONSTRUCTIVE/DESTRUCTIVE-PSYCHIC	-.119	.674*	.437
3 ACTIVE/PASSIVE	.858	.212	.075
4 GOAL/FORTUITOUS	.120	.621*	.075
5 PROBLEM/NONPROBLEM	.917	.128	.178
6 PERSON/NONPERSON	-.251	.279	.506
7 SUCCESS/FAILURE	.267	.866*	.133
8 RATIONAL/ACTIVISTIC	.896	.186	.212
9 PEACEFUL/AGGRESSIVE	.861*	-.098	-.317
10 CREATIVE/REACTIVE	.756	.279	.382
11 LEGIT/NON-LEGIT	.770*	-.097	-.202
12 TOGETHER/ALONE	.202	.080	.385
13 AUTHORITY IMMUNE/FIXATED	-.480	.428	.470

* Also heavily loaded in the aggregate analysis (6).

Figure 47: SPACEROUND: COMMUNITY/CIVIL SERVANT
SKIT 3: Disappointment at the Employment Office

COPING DIMENSIONS (N = 81)	FACTORS		
	I	II	III
1 CONSTRUCTIVE/DESTRUCTIVE-SOCIAL	.224	.880	.057
2 CONSTRUCTIVE/DESTRUCTIVE-PSYCHIC	-.411	.330	.620
3 ACTIVE/PASSIVE	.257	.654	.539*
4 GOAL/FORTUITOUS	-.062	.647*	.586
5 PROBLEM/NONPROBLEM	.339	.693	.304
6 PERSON/NONPERSON	-.082	.148	.251
7 SUCCESS/FAILURE	-.043	.415	.644
8 RATIONAL/ACTIVISTIC	.284	.533	.559*
9 PEACEFUL/AGGRESSIVE	.707*	.193	.002
10 CREATIVE/REACTIVE	.090	.296	.857*
11 LEGIT/NON-LEGIT	.691*	.138	-.026
12 TOGETHER/ALONE	.186	.065	.390*
13 AUTHORITY IMMUNE/FIXATED	-.393	-.115	.616

* Also heavily loaded in the aggregate analysis (7).

Figure 48: SPACEROUND: WORKPLACE
SKIT 4: Argument with the Boss

COPING DIMENSIONS (N = 81)	FACTORS		
	I	II	III
1 CONSTRUCTIVE/DESTRUCTIVE-SOCIAL	.775*	.047	.425
2 CONSTRUCTIVE/DESTRUCTIVE-PSYCHIC	-.079	.857*	.239
3 ACTIVE/PASSIVE	.383	.453	.732*
4 GOAL/FORTUITOUS	.032	.780*	.306
5 PROBLEM/NONPROBLEM	.393	.362	.700
6 PERSON/NONPERSON	-.422*	.380	.134
7 SUCCESS/FAILURE	.157	.770*	.320
8 RATIONAL/ACTIVISTIC	.627	.334	.626*
9 PEACEFUL/AGGRESSIVE	.874*	-.100	.192
10 CREATIVE/REACTIVE	.334	.350	.818*
11 LEGIT/NON-LEGIT	.708*	.053	.314
12 TOGETHER/ALONE	.011	.290	.777*
13 AUTHORITY IMMUNE/FIXATED	-.502	.610	.226

* Also heavily loaded in the aggregate analysis (13).

When considering all four separate skit analyses side-by-side (see Figure 49), it becomes apparent that some dimensions react to the different skits while others do not. Those dimensions which remained stable in the one factor over all four skits were called Strong Trait Dimensions. This implied that regardless of the changing situation presented by the different skits, the response dimensions remained within the same factor throughout. These dimensions were: 4, 9, and 11. Two of these Strong Trait Dimensions (9 and 11) fell in Factor I, and one (4) fell into Factor II. Another category of dimensions was called the Moderate Trait Dimensions. These were dimensions that with one major exception remained all within one factor. In Factor I there was one such Moderate Trait Dimensions (1). In Factor II there were also two of these Trait Dimensions (2 and 7). In Factor III there was one such dimension (12). All together there were 10 trait dimensions found.

Dimensions 3, 6, 8, 10, and 13 were categorized into Moderate State Dimensions. One Strong State Dimension appeared (5); this one had strong loadings in all of the three factors. Comparing the four skit aggregate response analyses to Figure 49, it is fairly clear where the main support for the loadings came from. Perhaps the most interesting findings stemming from these factor analyses were the presence of the three Strong Trait Dimensions and one Strong State Dimension.

Strong Trait	Strong State
9. Peaceful/Aggressive	5. Problem/Non-problem
11. Legitimate/Nonlegitimate	
4. Goal/Fortuitous	

It is also noteworthy that in each of the three factors both trait and state dimensions were found, thereby suggesting the importance of both types of dimensions in the coping process.

Figure 49: FACTOR ANALYSIS USING FOUR SEPARATE SKIT RESPONSES (N = 81)

COPING DIMENSIONS	FACTORS												Dimension Key
	I (Normative)				II (Outcome)				III (Others)				
	FA	FN	EO	WP	FA	FN	EO	WP	FA	FN	EO	WP	
1 CONSTRUCTIVE/DESTRUCTIVE-SOCIAL	.932	.917		.775			.880						b
2 CONSTRUCTIVE/DESTRUCTIVE-PSYCHIC					.651	.674		.857	.502←		.620		b
3 ACTIVE/PASSIVE	.835	.858					.654←				.539←	.732	c
4 GOAL/FORTUITOUS					.691	.621	.647	.780					a
5 PROBLEM/NONPROBLEM	.875	.917					.693					.700	d
6 PERSON/NONPERSON			-.422		.500			.380		.506	.251		c
7 SUCCESS/FAILURE					.994	.866		.770			.644		b
8 RATIONAL/ACTIVISTIC	.919	.896		.627←			.533				.559←	.626	c
9 PEACEFUL/AGGRESSIVE	.879	.861	.707	.874									a
10 CREATIVE/REACTIVE	.820	.756									.857	.818	c
11 LEGIT/NON-LEGIT	.736	.770	.691	.708									a
12 TOGETHER/ALONE	.459←				.304←				.385	.390	.779		b
13 AUTHORITY IMMUNE FIXATED		-.480 Δ		-.502←	.568←	.428 Δ		.610	.603←	.470 Δ	.616		c

Key: a STRONG "TRAIT" DIMENSIONS   (3)
      b MODERATE "TRAIT" DIMENSIONS (4)
      c MODERATE "STATE" DIMENSIONS (5)
      d STRONG "STATE" DIMENSIONS   (1)

FA - Family
FN - Friendly Neighbor
EO - Employment Office
WP - Workplace
Δ - Triple loadings
← - Double loadings

An additional analysis was computed to determine the external validity of the coping instrument with an objective measure of coping behavior, namely the word count. The word count was derived from the total number of words a subject used in responding to each skit. Correlating word count with coping scores for each of the spacerounds the following data were produced:

Spacerounds	r	p
Family (FA)	.1619	.076
Friendly Neighbor (FN)	.4724	.001
Employment Office (EO)	.4784	.001
Work Place (WP)	.4443	.001
all four together	.3976	.001

These data indicated that all the coping response situations were positively correlated and, with one exception (FA), highly significant with the word count variable. In order to further explore the relations between word count and coping an analysis was conducted to investigate the differences among the 13 coping dimensions.

The results were as follows: (see Figure 50)

It is rather apparent that most of the dimensions correlated positively and significantly with the word count variable. The two exceptions were dimensions 9 and 11, both strong "trait" dimensions belonging to the Normative Factor. The remaining "trait" dimension (4) was further analyzed to see how its correlation would be influenced by the four different skits.

Figure 50: COPING DIMENSIONS ACROSS ALL 4 SKITS CORRELATED WITH WORD COUNT (N = 80)

	r	p
1	.2886	.005
2	.3939	.001
3	.4563	.001
4^1	.3071	.003
5	.4303	.001
6	.4786	.001
7	.4172	.001
8	.4421	.001
9^2	-.0124	.457
10^*	.5586	.001
11^2	.1252	.134
12	.3535	.001
13	.2746	.007
Trait Dimensions (4+9+11) together	.1773	.058
Total of 13 Dimensions together	.3976	.001

[1] "Trait" Outcome

[2] "Trait" Normative

* Most positively correlated

The results follow:

Spacerounds	r	p
Family (FA)	.1924	.044
Friendly Neighbor (FN)	.1600	.078
Employment Office (EO)	.3428	.001
Work Place (WP)	.3941	.001

It appeared that most of the correlation strength that dimension 4 had, came from the Employment Office and Work Place skits.

5.4 Conclusions

In the composite analysis (see Figure 49), the three factors which clustered the coping dimensions into three groups, Normative, Outcome, and Others, each provided a separate point of reference. Those belonging to the Normative Factor (I), especially the "trait" dimensions 1, 9, and 11, suggested forms of coping responses that were related to behaviors sanctioned by group norms. One might go so far as to say that dimensions in this factor suggested behaviors which were idealized by societal norms. The loading of each of these three dimensions were quite strong, indicating they were the main contributors for the Normative Factor.

Dimensions 2, 4, and 7 consistently found in the Outcome Factor (II), suggested forms of coping responses that were related to efficiency. These three dimensions were both empirically related (according to their loadings) and theoretically similar (especially 4 and 7). The highest loading in the factor analysis (.994) was obtained from the family skit response to dimension 7. This suggests that the family skit provided an ideal problem situation to elicit the success/failure coping response, in comparison to the other skits.

The Others Factor (III) was not as clearly represented by specific dimensions as were the Normative and Outcome Factors. In the composite analysis, dimensions 12 and 13 fell into this third factor. Both these dimensions seemed related to the concept of dealing with other persons.

These findings would suggest that the subjects in this study responded to coping situations in three basic ways: with concern for normative expectations, with a focus toward behavioral outcomes, and with a special orientation to interpersonal coping skills. The Normative Factor explained 22.7 % of the variance (in the aggregate analysis) and contained five dimensions suggesting that normative considerations occupy an important role in the coping phenomena tested in this study. While the theoretical support for the role of norms in the integration process is adequately represented by both the concepts of "norm similarity" and "norm acceptance" found in the Spaceround Integration portion of the Social Coping Model, the role of norms in the coping process needs to be further stressed.

The logical place in the Social Coping Model to emphasize this normative factor would be with regard to viewing norm awareness as generally as a social resource and as a critical component of an individual's coping repertoire. Thus, these data suggest that behaving in normative ways is particulary important in the coping process. Based on these findings, it seems reasonable to say that to behave normatively depends on: the presence of norms, the optimal social climate for becoming aware of norms, the motivation for accepting norms, and the current situational conditions which permit normative behavior to be expressed.

The second factor, the Outcome Factor, even though it explained a much smaller amount of the variance (6.3 %), it also played an important role in the coping process. It implied that the coping responses concerned with Outcomes are discernable. Since this factor was dominated by the Trait Dimensions 2, 4 and 7, the theoretical significance of this factor suggests that it could fall within the realm of individual resources. These data further suggest that the concern for or absence of concern for Outcomes plays an important role in the total coping phenomena. This idea fits in well with the Social Coping Model, in that the extent of specific learned skills (in this case - outcome orientations) may figure in with an individual's resources, which then come into play during the actual coping activity and appears to be related to the two opposite coping concepts of Learned Resourcefulness (see Meichenbaum, 1973) and Learned Helplessness (see Seligman, 1975).

The third factor, the Coping Factor, explained 47.7 % of the variance and thus, played the most important role in the coping phenomena. The dimensions (10, 3, 5, 8, and 12) in the aggregate analysis which fell within this factor suggested that together they were responsible for the largest amount of variance. Theoretically, they represent a wide variety of coping skills which seem to be similar. It should be noted that these three factors together accounted for 76.7 % of the total variance. This means that 23.3 % of the remaining variance is accounted for by other less pronounced factors.

The mix of Trait and State Dimensions in all three factors suggests the importance of both environmental as well as individual influences in the coping phenomena. This conclusion is not only supported by the Social Coping Model and this research, but is also in keeping with other recent trends in coping research (see Arndt-Pagé et al., 1983, 188). The Social Coping Model incorporates this mix both in the use of the resource concept, which emphasizes that the coping repertoire draws from social, psychic, and physical elements; it also suggests that the spaceround (coping milieu) and the nature of the problem also play an important role in the dynamics of real-life coping (see Dussich and Jacobsen, 1982).

Since the 13 coping dimensions were not specifically designed to measure the extent to which trait or state dimensions came into play, it would be beyond the limits of this study to suggest which type of dimension played the more dominant role in real-life coping. What does seem clear is that both types were present in all four problem situations (skits) and that each problem situation called for a distinctly different pattern of coping dimensions.

A final comment with regard to the correlations of the word count variable and the various coping response variables. While these two variable categories are relatively unimportant, per se, they do provide a measure of external validity. The word count is an <u>objective</u> behavioral measure of the subjects' responses to the standard skit. However, the coping scores were derived from the <u>subjective</u> judgements of three raters. It is interesting that the only two dimensions which did not show a significant correlation were the two dimensions Peaceful/Aggressive and Legitimate/Non-legitimate, both of which (according to the composite analysis) also happen to be strong "trait" dimensions in the Normative Factor. If one were to argue that the high number of positive and significant correlations derived from the other dimensions with the total word count was the result of the raters' being subjectively influenced by the quantity of words present in the response texts of each subject, the principle would only be valid if it applied to all 13 dimensions. These two exceptions seem to suggest another rule (also supported by the Social Coping Model's concept of the repertoire and its influence on coping): that, while a subject's coping repertoire may logically produce a large number of words as a by-product of its richness, at least for the above two exceptions (9 and 11), the quantity of words seem to have no apparent influence on the qualitative nature of these two dimensions. Thus, these exceptions seem to prove the validity of the rule.

6 The Success/Failure Study

The major thrust of this sub-study was designed to determine which variables were relevant in distinguishing the differences between success and failure of young parolees. The Social Coping Model was used as the theoretical backdrop for this investigation.

Earlier in this report (sections 3.3 and 3.4) we stated that the theory of Social Coping is a social psychological model that combines elements from a current sociological theory known as Control Theory with psychological theories of coping (see Dussich and Jacobsen, 1982). Traditional Control Theory has been primarily concerned with social aspects of controlling behavior, while coping theory has been primarily concerned with intrapsychic aspects of dealing with stress. The theory of Social Coping represents an attempt at explaining the dynamics of how people deal with problems in their changing environment. It takes into account both the social conditions of interaction and the individual processes of coping. The concept which sets the stage and describes the social psychological environs for coping is called "spaceround". Spaceround is a phenomenologically oriented concept that provides an interactive setting within such macrostructural artifacts as political systems, cultures, governments etc. and such microstructural artifacts as groups, individuals, feelings, ideas, etc., where a person's social coping processes occur.

This study focused on coping techniques and the two outcomes of parole: success and failure. The purpose was to determine whether those individuals with stronger and more abundant coping skills did better in real-life situations than those with weaker and fewer skills. That is, whether the concept of coping, measured by the 13 coping dimensions of Dussich and Jacobsen (1982) (see Figure 41), was able to differentiate between young parolees who had experienced success and those who had experienced failure. Success was defined as the completion of parole. In contrast, failure was defined as not completing the parole period.

It is beyond the scope of this investigation to review studies relating to success and failure of parolees. In spite of this limitation, our hypotheses were derived from the literature of control theory and social coping. The hypotheses for this study are as follows:

Hy_1: Among those who are successful with parole, the <u>most important significant spaceround</u> is either <u>the family or work</u>, with community as less important and peers as least important.

Hy_2: Among those youth who failed with parole, the <u>most important significant spaceround</u> will be peers, <u>with work</u> as less important than with family, and community as least important.

Hy_3: For those parolees who are successful, the relative importance of spacerounds will reflect the pattern: <u>adolescence</u> - school, family, peers, community; <u>youth</u> - school, family, peers, community; <u>adults</u> - school/work, family, peers, community.

Hy_4: For those who failed, the relative <u>importance of significant</u> spacerounds will reflect <u>the pattern:</u> <u>adolescence</u> - peers, school, family, community; <u>youth</u> - peers, community, school, family; <u>adults</u> - community, peers, work, family.

Hy_5: The strength of positive <u>interactional conditions</u> will be higher for successful parolees than for those who failed.

Hy_6: Among the successful parolees, the extent of <u>meaningful relationships</u> will be higher than among those who failed.

Hy_7: Among those who are successful, the extent of <u>integration</u> in conventional significant spacerounds will be greater than among those who failed.

Hy_8: Those who are successful will have stronger <u>resources</u> than those who failed.

Hy_9: Among those who are successful, fewer indicators of <u>helplessness</u> will be found compared to those who failed.

Hy_{10}: Among those who are successful, more indicators of <u>resourcefulness</u> will be found compared to those who failed.

Hy_{11}: Among those who are successful, the <u>coping skills</u> will be stronger than among those who failed.

Hy_{12}: Among those who are successful, the strength of <u>"Trait" dimensions of coping</u> will be stronger than among those who failed.

6.1 Data Collection

In order to test the above twelve research hypotheses a sample of thirty-five youthful offenders who had recently been under parole were measured.

The 35 subjects of this study were (between the ages of 17 and 30 with an age range of 15 years; the mean was 23.1 years; the median was 23.5 years and the mode was 22 years) males from the judicial state district of Hannover, Germany. They were all under parole during the years 1981 and 1982 and had been adjudicated under the German Youth Law.

The <u>successful</u> subjects of this sub-study consisted of twenty-one young males ranging in age from 23 to 30: the mean was 25, the median was 26.5 and the mode was 24. The successful subjects were interviewed at the Criminological Research Institute, in Hannover.

In contrast, there were fourteen young males classified as <u>failures</u> ranging in age from 17 to 23; the mean was 20.4, the median 20, and the mode 21. The difference in ages, between the successes and the failures (about 4 years) was an artifact of the cross sectional method used. Those who had already achieved success, had already completed their full parole periods and were no longer under supervision; their parole lasted an average of thirty-six months. Those who failed on parole cut their parole period short and were again in prison; their parole lasted an average of twelve months. With regards to the social-demographic variables, the data indicated that the majority of successful and failure clients were single, had both parents living together and where serving sentences for theft.

The failure subjects came from the Hameln/Tündern Youth Prison of Lower Saxony, Germany. The subjects were selected by first looking at the official prison files according to the following criteria:

- they were all sentenced as youth under the German Youth Laws,
- they had all been supervised under parole according to sections 88, 89 of the youth law,
- they had all recidivated during their parole period and thus were back in prison as parole violators,
- they were all German citizens, and,
- they were all from Lower Saxony.

All but three persons asked in prison consented to becoming research subjects in this project. The reason for their cooperativeness can be attributed to at least the following three general factors: First, inmates in this institution are generally familiar with researchers. Since most of the inmates had already had some experience with questionnaires and interviews and were not threatened by the prospect of working with yet another research project. Second, since the better part of those in this prison hope to receive parole, (which is in large part dependent upon their behavior while in prison), it was likely that most of the subjects we interviewed saw their participation with us as an asset. In this regard a number of times subjects made reference to this point. Third, to increase the chance of their consenting to be interviewed it was necessary to establish a maximum of trust and credibility between the interviewer and the prospective subject. Thus, each prospect was spoken to and informed that we represented an independent research institute with no official ties to the prison, to the courts, to the police or to the parole officials. Furthermore, the information collected was protected by law, and the information would not be given to others under any circumstances and that their responses would not effect the length of their sentence.

In the hopes of further motivating the inmates to participate, we tried to get them to feel as though they had a unique chance to be a part of an important activity, something with humanitarian significance. The inmates spoken to were told about how the project results could be used to improve the situation for other offenders in the same situations as themselves. For some, this seemed to be an important reason in their motivation to participate. Some even asked if they could receive a copy of the final results.

In only three instances did subjects not participate: In one case the subject was contacted through a prison official who informed him of our project, and even though the inmate said he wanted to participate, he missed three consecutive appointments to be interviewed. In the second case, the subject explained objections to this type of research at great length. Even our lengthy clarifications did not convince him. He preferred that the time which was reserved for free time activities, be used in the appropriate way and not (according to the inmate) "wasted on unimportant research!". In the third case the subject based his refusal on his bad experiences with parole supervisors. He said they gave information to the police which resulted in his being sent back to prison. In spite of our assurances about data protection and that we were an independent institute, he was not convinced: "That's what they all say, the parole supervisors also told me the same thing; that's the reason I won't agree to be interviewed; if they tricked me why should I help them out!"

Some of the main limitations of this data collection method were that:

- the similarity of the simulation to real-life not withstanding, there were non-the-less elements of artificiality to the problem solving situations, especially with regard to whether the problem situations were similar to the subject's own real-life situations; the use of video equipment and the presence of the interviewer, to mention the most apparent ones;

- a degree of differential interviewer/subject interaction existed in each interview and probably does account for some small amount of variance;
- the atmosphere of the two interview sites were somewhat different; as mentioned above the successful subjects were interviewed in the research institute, while those who recidivated were interviewed in prison;
- the technical quality of the video skits was not professional and may have somewhat reduced the sense of reality as well as perhaps created a slight distraction for the subjects viewing these skits.

In spite of these limitations, it is judged that the degree of error they may have caused was extremely small.

The instruments for collecting the coping data for this study were the same discussed earlier in this report for the previous study (see section 5.1). However, the other information, socio-demographic and Spaceround Integration, were collected with a specially designed questionnaire. This questionnaire had eighty-eight items (see section 4.1.3) and was used in an interview setting prior to the coping skits (explained in chapter 5).

For the most part, the items were a mixture of straight forward informational questions and Likert scale type questions. For the Likert scale type questions, a special card was shown to the subject clearly indicating the response options available. This technique was found to be better than expecting the subjects to remember the abstractions of the various sizes and directions of the item response patterns.

Each interview lasted on the average of fifty-five minutes: the questionnaire generally took thirty minutes and the coping skits and responses took about twenty-five minutes. Each entire interview was taped so as to eliminate the need for the interviewer to record the responses, but more important to allow the interview to proceed with eye to eye contact in a relaxed conversational mode. In each instance, the subject was asked if he minded that the session was being taped; all subjects gave their consent.

6.2 Data Reduction

All interview responses were then reduced to texts, three raters (who were also given extensive training in social coping theory as well as in the definitions of the 13 coping dimensions) independently rated each subject's four responses using the 13 dimensions. Each dimension was scored on a seven point Likert scale requiring the rater to make a judgement as to how high or low a given subject's response scored on each of the 13 dimensions. The three raters' scores were then averaged and used as one score for the purpose of analysis.

The above reduction procedure was used to measure the <u>strength</u> of the coping response; the <u>abundance</u> of the coping response was measured by simply counting the total number of words elicited in response to each of the four video skits. This content analysis procedure gave an objective method for quantifying each response; and, was used directly as a continous variable in the final analysis.

The location of the interviews differed between the two groups: the successful subjects were interviewed in the research institute, while the failures were interviewed in prison. The exact same two interviewers were used for both groups. Analysis of variance between the two interviewers indicated no significant differences.

6.3 Findings

The findings of this sub-study were organized into sub-sections according to the hypotheses addressed. The format for each sub-section is as follows:

- hypothetical statement,
- rational for the hypotheses,
- data presentation,
- discussion of the findings,
- conclusions.

Hy. 1 and 2

In hypothesis one, it was proposed that among those youth who are <u>successful</u> with parole, the <u>most important significant spacerounds</u> would be both the Family and Work, with Community as less important and Peers as least important. After examining the data, however, a different pattern emerged (see Figure 51): Community was the most important, then Family, then Peers, and then Work being the least important spaceround.

For hypothesis two, it was postulated that among those youth who <u>failed</u> with parole, the <u>most important significant spaceround</u> would be Peers, with Work as less important than with Family, and Community as least important. According to these data (see Figure 51), the unsuccessful subjects claimed that Community was the most important spaceround to them, then Work, Family, and Peers being the least important.

The reasons for developing these two hypotheses were to first determine the characteristic profile for the two groups of parolees, second, to compare each of the four spacerounds between the successes and failures, and third, to suggest what the prioritization would be for two subject groups based on the Spaceround Integration Model.

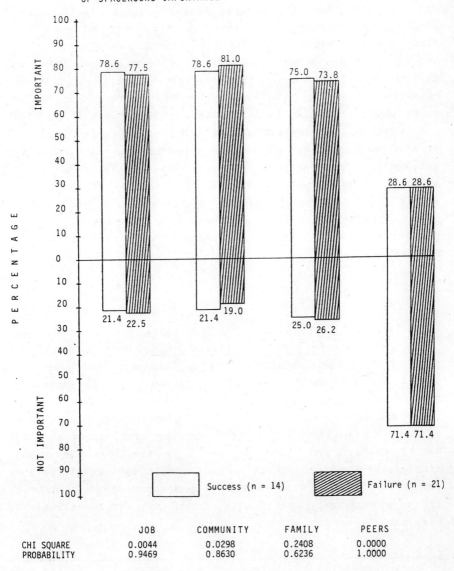

Figure 51: THE PERCENTAGE OF SUCCESS / FAILURE WITH REGARD TO EXTENT OF SPACEROUND IMPORTANCE

It is interesting to note that no significant differences between successful and failure subjects showed up in any of the spacerounds. A surprising finding, however, was the identical importance both groups gave to Peers. The role that Peers played in previous control theory research, has not yet clarified this somewhat elusive variable. For the most part, previous research has dealt with self reported delinquency and non delinquency; thus, it is inappropriate at this stage of our research to stretch the comparisons to success and failure among youthful German parolees. In any case, both these officially identified deviant groups stated that currently, Peers were a low importance spaceround compared to Work, Community, and Family. The two profiles were basically found to be the same. These findings placed Work and Community at about equal levels of importance, Family a bit lower and Peers as the least important spaceround of these four. Therefore, based on the above findings, the null hypothesis was accepted for both hypotheses.

Hy. 3

This hypothesis proposed that for those parolees who were successful, the relative importance of spacerounds would reflect the following pattern: as adolescents[*] (14 years and under) it would be stated that School was the most important, then Family, Peers, and Community would be the least important; subjects classified as youths (between 14 and 21 years of age) would claim that School was the most important, then Peers, Family, and Community would be the least important; finally, the subjects classified as adults (all those above 21 years of age) would state that the spaceround Work would be the most important, then Family, Community, and Peers would be the least important.

---

* Data pertaining to adolescents were obtained by asking each subject questions that related to his life prior to his fourteenth year.

The category "Adult" indicated a high (46 %) score for Family and low scores for Work (15 %) and Peers (15 %).

In summary, these data in Figure 52 suggest a rather interesting Family/Peer comparison for the two categories Adolescent/Adult. This comparison is depicted in the following table:

	Family	Peers
Adolescent	1	11
Adult	6	2

$$X^2 = 9.38 \quad p = .002$$

While the patterns expected were not obtained, these findings did show an interesting effect of age on spaceround prioritization. It essentially showed that as adolescents, successful parolees selected the Family as being low in importance with Peers as very important; however, as adults these same successful parolees judged their Family as more important than Peers. None-the-less, based on the overall findings the null hypothesis was accepted.

Hy. 4

In hypothesis 4 it was stated that for those who are failures, the relative importance of significant spacerounds would reflect the following patterns: as adolescents, they would claim that Peers were the most important, then School, and then Family as the least important; the youth would claim that Work was most important, then School, and then Family as the least important spaceround; adults would select Community as the most important spaceround, then Peers, then Work, and finally, Family as the least important.

The reason for this hypothesis was to investigate the effect of age on the changing prioritization of spaceround importance among the failure parolees.

Figure 52: THE RELATIVE SPACEROUND IMPORTANCE FOR SUCCESSFUL SUBJECTS

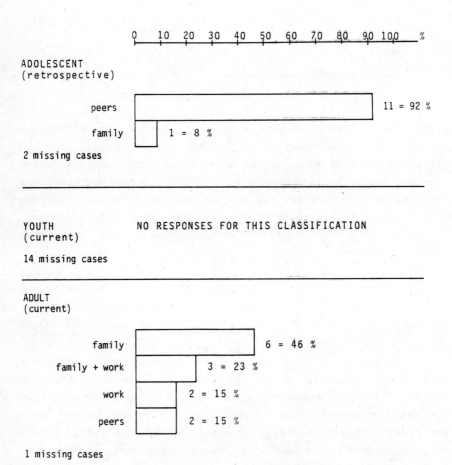

As Figure 53 shows, the response rates for this analysis were too low to draw conclusions from. The only point worth noting was the absence of Peers being mentioned for the "Youth" and "Adult" groups. Due to the lack of significant findings the null hypothesis was accepted.

Hy. 5

This hypothesis stated that the <u>strength of interaction conditions</u> would be higher for successful parolees than for those who fail.

The reason for this hypothesis was to investigate whether there were differences on each interaction condition in the six main spacerounds between the parolees who failed and those who succeeded. The interaction conditions of Frequency, Self Disclosure, Dependency, Norm Similarity, and Overlap were examined for the spacerounds Family of Orientation, Family of Procreation, Work, Community, Civil Servants, and Peers.

For <u>Family of Orientation</u>, no significant differences between the successes and the failures were found with the interaction conditions of Self Disclosure, General Dependency, Cognitive Dependency[*], Norm Similarity, and Overlap. There was, however, an interesting finding with regards to the Financial Dependency[**] question "Do you regularly get money from your parents?". Figure 54 shows that this question was answered in the negative, significantly more by successful subjects than by the failures ($p = .013$). This finding could be construed to mean

---

[*] Cognitive Dependency was a variable developed from the Dependency Condition to focus on the cognitive character of interactions.

[**] Financial Dependency was also developed from the Dependency Condition to focus on the financial aspect of interactions.

Figure 53: THE RELATIVE SPACEROUND IMPORTANCE FOR
FAILURE SUBJECTS

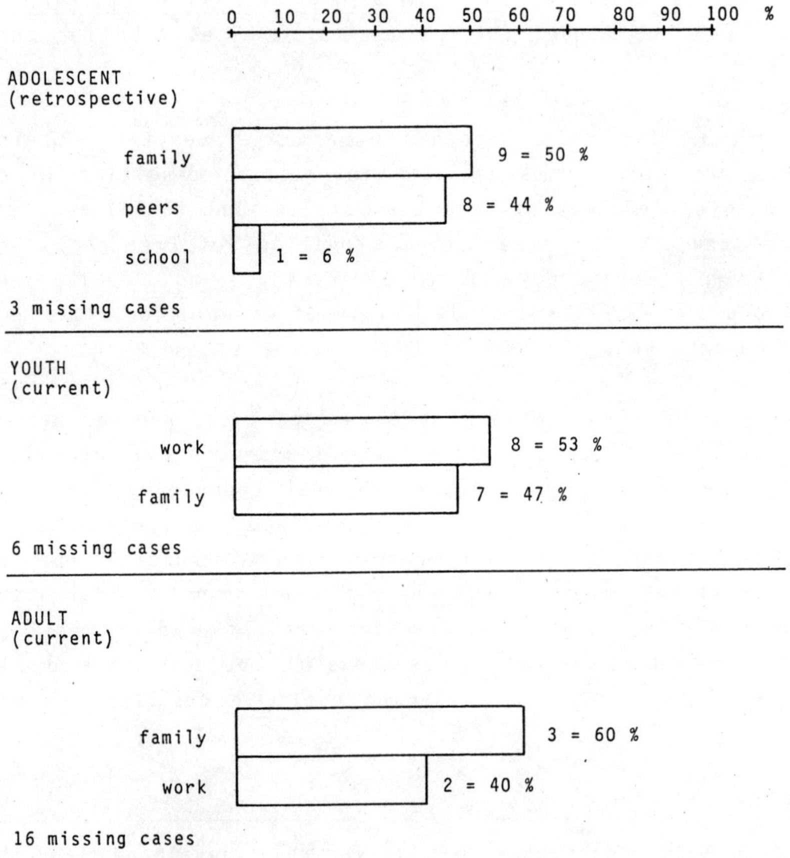

```
                0   10  20  30  40  50  60  70  80  90  100  %
```

ADOLESCENT
(retrospective)

- family — 9 = 50 %
- peers — 8 = 44 %
- school — 1 = 6 %

3 missing cases

YOUTH
(current)

- work — 8 = 53 %
- family — 7 = 47 %

6 missing cases

ADULT
(current)

- family — 3 = 60 %
- work — 2 = 40 %

16 missing cases

Figure 54: SUCCESS AND FAILURE FINANCIAL DEPENDENCY IN THE FAMILY OF ORIENTATION

Do you regularly get money from your parents?

	1 yes	2 sometimes	3 no	missing cases
Success (S)	0	0	100%(11)	(3)
Failure (F)	13.3%(2)	33.3%(5)	53.3%(8)	(8)

t = 2.69   df = 24   p = .013
$\bar{x}_S$ = 3.00 $\bar{x}_F$ = 2.40

Figure 55: SUCCESS AND FAILURE FREQUENCY OF CONTACT IN THE FAMILY OF ORIENTATION

How often are you now together with these persons from your family?

	1 never	2 monthly or less often	3 weekly or once every 14 days	4 2-3 times per week	5 4-6 times per week	6 daily	missing cases
Success (S)	0	36.4%(4)	18.2%(2)	0	0	45.5%(5)	(3)
Failure (F)	11.8%(2)	41.2%(7)	47.1%(8)	0	0	0	(4)

t = 3.20   df = 26   p = .004
$\bar{x}_S$ = 4.00 $\bar{x}_F$ = 2.35

"Do you need money from your parents?". Thus, for a person who is striving for success and giving himself reasurances of his ability to cope, the answer would appear to be logical. A relatively strong significant relationship was also found between success and failures with the condition Frequency ($p = .004$). Figure 55 indicates that about half of the successful clients were in daily contact with members of their family compared to the majority of failures who claimed to be in contact with their family "weekly or once every 14 days" and "monthly or less often".

For the spaceround <u>Family of Procreation</u>, two out of the eight interaction conditions proved to be noteworthy: Frequency of interaction was much higher for the successful subjects than for the failure subjects ($p < .000$). Figure 56 shows that the majority of successful parolees were in contact with their Family of Procreation daily compared to the failures who claimed to be in contact weekly or once every 14 days. These differences, however, could be attributed to the fact that the failure subjects were institutionalized during their interview and perhaps related this item to their current situation in spite of instructions to the contrary. Finally, these data show that the successful subjects claimed to be significantly less Emotionally Dependent[*] when compared to the failure subjects ($p = .025$). Figure 57 shows the distribution of these responses between the successful and failure subjects.

For the spaceround <u>Work</u>, one of the interaction conditions found to be significant was Norm Similarity ($p = .052$). Figure 58 shows that all the successes indicated they were "never" influenced by their fellow workers. Two conditions were close to acceptable levels of significance (above the .05 level); these were Cognitive and Emotional Dependency items

---

[*] Emotional Dependency was a variable developed from the Dependency Condition to focus on the emotional character of interactions.

Figure 56: SUCCESS AND FAILURE FREQUENCY OF CONTACT IN THE FAMILY OF PROCREATION
Recently, how often have you been together with your wife/girl friend/betrothed?

	1 never	2 monthly or less often	3 weekly or once every 14 days	4 2-3 times per week	5 4-6 times per week	6 daily	missing cases
Success (S)	0	0	0	18.2%(2)	0	81.8%(9)	(3)
Failure (F)	7.1%(1)	35.7%(5)	50.0%(7)	7.1%(1)	0	0	(7)

$t = 9.76$ $df = 23$ $p < .000$
$\bar{x}_S = 5.64$ $\bar{x}_F = 2.57$

Figure 57: SUCCESS AND FAILURE EMOTIONAL DEPENDENCY IN THE FAMILY OF PROCREATION

Do you always try to say what your wife/girl friend/betrothed wants to hear from you?

	1 yes	2 mostly	3 sometimes	4 seldom	5 never	missing cases
Successful (S)	0	0	18.2%(2)	36.4%(4)	45.5%(5)	(3)
Failure (F)	7.7%(1)	7.7%(1)	46.2%(6)	23.1%(3)	15.4%(2)	(8)

t = 2.41 df = 22 p = .025
$\bar{x}_S$ = 4.24 $\bar{x}_F$ = 3.31

Figure 58: SUCCESS AND FAILURE NORM SIMILARITY AT WORK

Do you have the same opinion about life as your colleagues?

	1 yes	2 no	missing cases
Successful (S)	40.0%(2)	60.0%(3)	(0)
Failure (F)	0	100.0%(8)	(13)

x^2 = 3.7818
p = .0518

(p = .064 and p = .082) which showed that successful subjects were less dependent. These findings are depicted in Figure 59 and in Figure 60.

For the spaceround Community, no significant relationships were found for Frequency, Self Disclosure, Overlap, or Norm Similarity. Significance was found, however, for Cognitive Dependency (p = .011) and Emotional Dependency (.044). Figure 61 and Figure 62 indicate that the successful subjects expressed less dependence than the failure subjects.

For the spaceround Peers, no significant associations (below the .05 level) were found for Overlap, General or Controlling Dependency[*], or Self Disclosure. Nevertheless, Figures 63 and 64 illustrate two conditions found to be close to significance[**]. These included Frequency, where most of the successful subjects claimed to have had more contact with their Peers than the failure subjects (p = .079); and Norm Similarity, where the successful subjects had significantly less with their Peers than the failure subjects (p = .072). Thus, these data suggest that the successful subjects were in contact with their Peers more than the failure subjects but did not seem to share the same opinions about life with their Peers; whereas the failure subjects had low Frequency of interaction with their Peers, but did share high Norm Similarity.

---

[*] Controlling Dependency was also a concept generated out of the Dependency interaction condition and stressed a strong controlling influence by starting the question with the words "Before you do something ...".

[**] In a previous item the question was posited, "Are there cliques or groups that are important to you?" From this item 78.6 % (11) of the successful and 57.1 % (12) of the failure parolees indicated no; thus, subsequent questions about Peers only involved the small percentage of subjects remaining, 21.4 % (5) and 42.9 % (9), respectively. Participation in the Peers spaceround was very sparse.

Figure 59: SUCCESS AND FAILURE COGNITIVE DEPENDENCY AT WORK

Do your fellow workers have an influence on what you think or the way you live?

	1 yes	2 mostly	3 sometimes	4 seldom	5 never	missing cases
Successful (S)	0	0	0	0	100.0%(6)	(8)
Failure (F)	0	0	12.5%(1)	37.5%(3)	50.0%(4)	(13)

$t = 2.04$ $df = 12$ $p = .064$
$\bar{x}_S = 5.00$ $\bar{x}_F = 4.38$

Figure 60: SUCCESS AND FAILURE EMOTIONAL DEPENDENCY AT WORK

Do you try to say, what your fellow workers want to hear from you?

	1 yes	2 mostly	3 sometimes	4 seldom	5 never	missing cases
Successful (S)	0	0	0	0	100.0%(6)	(8)
Failure (F)	0	16.7%(1)	16.7%(1)	16.7%(1)	50.0%(3)	(15)

$t = 1.94$ $df = 10$ $p = .082$
$\bar{x}_S = 5.00$ $\bar{x}_F = 4.00$

Figure 61: SUCCESS AND FAILURE COGNITIVE DEPENDENCY IN THE COMMUNITY

Are you influenced by these people in what you think and how you live?

	1 yes	2 mostly	3 sometimes	4 seldom	5 never	missing cases
Successful (S)	0	0	12.5%(1)	0	87.5%(7)	(6)
Failure (F)	36.4%(4)	0	27.3%(3)	9.1%(1)	27.3%(3)	(10)

t = 2.87   df = 17   p = .011
$\bar{x}_S$ = 4.75 $\bar{x}_F$ = 2.91

Figure 62: SUCCESS AND FAILURE EMOTIONAL DEPENDENCY IN THE COMMUNITY

Do you always try to say what you think your neighbors, colleagues, etc. expect to hear from you?

	1 yes	2 mostly	3 sometimes	4 seldom	5 never	missing cases
Successful (S)	0	0	0	25.0%(2)	75.0%(6)	(6)
Failure (F)	27.3%(3)	9.1%(1)	0	27.3%(3)	36.4%(4)	(10)

t = 2.17   df = 17   p = .044
$\bar{x}_S$ = 4.75 $\bar{x}_F$ = 3.36

Figure 63: SUCCESS AND FAILURE FREQUENCY OF CONTACT WITH PEERS

How often have you been together with these people recently?

	1 never	2 monthly or less often	3 weekly or once every 14 days	4 2-3 times per week	5 4-6 times per week	6 daily	missing cases
Success (S)	0	0	0	33.1%(1)	33.1%(1)	33.1%(1)	(11)
Failure (F)	25.0%(2)	12.5%(1)	25.0%(2)	12.5%(1)	25.0%(2)	0	(13)

$t = 1.98 \quad df = 9 \quad p = .079$
$\bar{x}_S = 5.00 \quad \bar{x}_F = 1.67$

Figure 64: SUCCESS AND FAILURE NORM SIMLARITY WITH PEERS

Do you believe that you have the same opinion as those in your group about the way one should live?

	1 yes	2 yes, surely	3 no	missing cases
Successful (S)	0	0	100.0%(3)	(11)
Failure (F)	44.4%(4)	22.2%(2)	33.3%(3)	(12)

$t = 2.01 \quad df = 10 \quad p = .072$
$\bar{x}_S = 3.00 \quad \bar{x}_F = 1.89$

Finally, for the spaceround Civil Servants*, a significant relationship was found only for the condition Frequency. The successful subjects indicated that they were in contact with Civil Servants more Frequently than the failure subjects. This strong significant difference (p < .000) is shown in Figure 65. It is worth mentioning that both the successful and failure parolees did not meet Civil Servants on a daily basis, nor 4-6 times per week, nor 2-3 times per week. However, the majority of successful subjects were in contact with Civil Servants about monthly or less often when compared to the majority of the failures who claimed that they were never in contact with Civil Servants. There were no significant differences found in this spaceround for the conditions General and Emotional Dependency, Norm Similarity or Self Disclosure.

Due to the number of independent variables (32) for this hypothesis it was not appropriate to make a blanket acceptance or rejection of the null; however, when the data were grouped according to each separate interaction condition a number of interesting patterns emerged. For the condition of Frequency, out of six spacerounds, four (FOO, FOP, Peers, and CS) showed significant (p < .05) differences between successful and failure subjects, and for the remaining two spacerounds (WP, Com.) significance was not achieved, probably due to low response rates; however, the same trend emerged, i.e. the successful subjects had more frequent contact with persons in all spacerounds. A composite Frequency score across all spacerounds was created and analyzed using the ANOVA. This showed the interaction condition Frequency significantly differentiated between success and failure (F = 20.8286; p < .0001; eta^2 = .3869). Furthermore, the direction of the mean suggested

---

* In the context of this study, Civil Servants primarily meant parole supervisors, employment office officials, and housing officials.

Figure 65: SUCCESS AND FAILURE FREQUENCY OF CONTACT WITH CIVIL SERVANTS

How often are you now in contact with civil servants?

	1 never	2 monthly or less	3 weekly or once per 14 days	4 2-3 times per week	5 4-6 times per week	6 daily	missing cases
Successful (S)	14.3%(2)	64.3%(9)	21.4%(3)	0	0	0	(0)
Failure (F)	76.0%(16)	19.0%(4)	4.8%(1)	0	0	0	(0)

$t = 3.91$ $df = 33$ $p < .000$
$\bar{x}_S = 2.0714$ $\bar{x}_F = 1.2857$

Figure 66: SUCCESS AND FAILURE EXTENT OF MEANINGFUL RELATIONSHIPS WITH CIVIL SERVANTS

Are there civil servants (like parole officers, social workers) who are of importance to you?

	Important Persons Mentioned	No Important Persons Mentioned	Totals
Successful (S)	21.4 % (3)	78.6 % (11)	100.0 % (14)
Failure (F)	19.0 % (4)	81.0 % (17)	100.0 % (21)

$x^2 = .0298$
$p = .8630$

that successful parolees had much higher levels of interactions in these spacerounds than those who failed. Thus, the research hypothesis is supported for this interaction condition.

For the condition Self Disclosure, no significance was obtained across all six spacerounds; however, in those instances where trends did exist (as with Community and Work Place), it could be suggested that successful parolees express slightly more Self Disclosure than those who failed. The null hypothesis is accepted for this interaction condition.

The Dependency condition was divided into five variables: General, Financial, Cognitive, Emotional, and Controlling. No significant differences were noted for the General Dependency items; however, within the spacerounds Family of Orientation and Civil Servants, the successful parolees responded in the direction of less dependency, while with Peers the successful parolees indicated more dependency.

The Cognitive Dependency items produced significance ($p = 0.11$) in the Community and almost reached an acceptable level of significance in the Work Place spacerounds ($p = .064$), with no significance in the Family of Orientation. The unusual results were that for the first two findings (C and WP), the successful subjects displayed less dependence rather than more dependence.

With the condition Financial Dependency, significance between the successfuls and the failures occurred in the Family of Orientation spaceround but not in the Family of Procreation spaceround; however, in both spacerounds the direction of findings suggests that successful subjects viewed themselves as less dependent than their failure counterparts.

For the variable Emotional Dependency significance was again found for the Family of Orientation spaceround as well as within the Community spaceround. Significance was not found in the Work Place and Civil Servant spacerounds. In all four of these spacerounds the responses indicated that the successful parolees again claimed to be less dependent.

The final variable, Controlling Dependency, produced no significant differences; however, the responses suggested a slight increase of Dependency for successful subjects in the spacerounds Family of Procreation and Peers.

Considering the direction of the five aspects of dependency which did not go in the expected direction, the null hypothesis is accepted.

For the interaction condition Norm Similarity four (FOO, FOP, Com., and CS) spacerounds produced no significant differences. The spaceround Work Place did produce a significant difference (p = .052) in the expected direction, i.e. successful parolees showed a higher Norm Similarity. Within the Peers spaceround the difference was close to significance (p = .072) and was opposite to that hypothesized, i.e. the successful subjects indicated they did not have similar norms as their peers. In light of the predominant absence of significant differences, the null hypothesis was accepted.

The final condition, Overlap, produced no significant differences between the two groups of parolees in the four spacerounds tested (FOO, FOP, Com., and Peers). Thus the null hypothesis was accepted.

Focusing on all the interaction condition findings that were significant, as well as the suggested trends from non significant findings, it would appear that successful parolees have more frequent contacts within the spacerounds tested (except WP) and expressed less dependency (except with Peers) in most spacerounds tested. Related to this less dependency phenomena of the successful parolees, was the finding that they claim not to share the same norms as their peers.

Hy. 6

Among the successful parolees, the <u>extent of meaningful relationships</u> within each spaceround will be higher than among those who failed.

This hypothesis was developed to determine whether the variable meaningful relationship would be responded to differently among the successful parolees and those who failed. This hypothesis was based on the theoretical premise that meaningful relationships play a very important role as a <u>social resource</u> in the lives of young parolees to the extent that their presence or absense would be decisive in helping them become successful.

The data for this hypothesis, as shown in Figures 66 to 71, indicate no significant differences existed between successful parolees and those who failed. However, the direction of these data suggest that the successful parolees had a slightly higher extent of meaningful relationships in the spacerounds of Family of Orientation, Family of Procreation, Civil Servants, and Community, but lower extent of meaningful relationships in the spacerounds Peers and Work.

Additionally, in considering the data shown in Figure 72, the successful parolees stated their most meaningful relationships were with mother (35.7 %), brother (21.4 %), then father (14.4 %), while the failures named brother (33.3 %), father (23.8 %), then mother (14.3 %).

Hy. 7

This hypothesis states that among those who are successful, the <u>extent of integration</u> in conventional significant spacerounds will be greater than among those who failed.

Figure 67: SUCCESS AND FAILURE EXTENT OF MEANINGFUL RELATIONSHIPS WITH THE COMMUNITY

Are there persons in the community that you consider very important?

	Important Persons Mentioned	No Important Persons Mentioned	Total
Successful (S)	57.2 % (8)	42.8 % (6)	100.0 % (14)
Failure (F)	52.4 % (11)	47.6 % (10)	100.0 % (21)

x^2 = .0768
p = .7817

Figure 68: SUCCESS AND FAILURE EXTENT OF MEANINGFUL RELATIONSHIPS WITH PEERS

Identify the persons or groups in your age, who are now the most important to you?

	Important Persons Mentioned	No Important Persons Mentioned	Total
Successful (S)	21.4 % (3)	78.6 % (11)	100.0 % (14)
Failure (F)	38.1 % (8)	61.9 % (13)	100.0 % (21)

x^2 = 1.0827
p = .2981

Figure 69: SUCCESS AND FAILURE EXTENT OF MEANINGFUL RELATIONSHIPS AT WORK

Are there persons at your place of work, who are currently important for you?

	Important Persons Mentioned	No Important Persons Mentioned	Total
Successful (S)	42.9 % (6)	57.1 % (8)	100.0 % (14)
Failure (F)	47.6 % (10)	52.4 % (11)	100.0 % (21)

x^2 = .0768
p = .7817

Figure 70: SUCCESS AND FAILURE IMPORTANCE OF FAMILY OF ORIENTATION

Are your parents, brothers and sisters still important for you today?

	yes	sometimes	no
Successful (S)	71.4 % (10)	7.1 % (1)	21.4 % (3)
Failure (F)	66.7 % (14)	14.3 % (3)	19.0 % (4)

x^2 = .4266
p = .8079

Figure 71: SUCCESS AND FAILURE EXTENT OF MEANINGFUL RELATIONSHIPS WITH THE FAMILY OF PROCREATION

When yes, identify those persons who are the most important from your own family:

	Important Persons Mentioned	No Important Persons Mentioned	Total
Successful (S)	35.7 % (5)	64.2 % (9)	100.0 % (14)
Failure (F)	28.6 % (6)	71.4 % (15)	100.0 % (21)

x^2 = .1989
p = .6556

Figure 72: SUCCESS AND FAILURE EXTENT OF MEANINGFUL RELATIONSHIPS WITH THE FAMILY OF ORIENTATION

Please name the most important persons in your family, thus all persons to whom you are related before your 14th year of life? (1st ranked persons)

	Father	Mother	Brother	Sister	Grand-mother	Aunt	Other Persons	No Answer
Successful (S)	14.4%(2)	35.7%(5)	21.4%(3)	(0)	7.1%(1)	(0)	(0)	21.4%(3)
Failure (F)	23.8%(5)	14.3%(3)	33.3%(7)	9.5%(2)	4.8%(1)	4.8%(1)	4.8%(1)	4.8%(1)

x^2 = 5.2121
p = .5169

The reason for this hypothesis was to see if the variable integration differentiated between those who were successful and those who failed. From the theoretical perspective, those who are the better integrated are influenced more by the control conditions of a given spaceround and their behavior should be more conforming.

With regard to the extent of individual integration within each spaceround between successful subjects and failure subjects, no significant differences were found. However, when the integration values from all conventional spacerounds (minus Peers) where combined into a single aggregate variable, the successes had a significantly (t = 2.01; p = .053) higher degree of individual integration. This finding occured in spite of the limited legally defined terms of success and failure. If the successful and failure subjects were to be redefined in more behavioristic terms looking at the individual's social growth, taking into account the improvement of personal relationships, enhancement of the employment situation and less involvement in overall deviant behavior, it would be logical to further hypothesize that integration would play an even more important role in distinguishing between successful and failure subjects. Thus, based on these findings, the null hypothesis was rejected and the research hypothesis was supported.

Hy. 8

This hypothesis states that those who are successful will have stronger resources than those who are failures.

The rationale for this hypothesis was to test the extent and type of resources that would differentiate between successful parolees and those who failed. The Social Coping Model suggests that persons who have more resources have a better chance to cope with their problems. Thus, if those with more resources were also those who succeeded, the concept of resources could be an important theoretical and practical tool in explaining the dynamics of success and failure. To answer this hypothesis, social resources, demographic resources, and the parolee's coping skills were examined.

Social Resources

One important social resource that clearly distinguished between those who succeeded and those who failed was contact Frequency with an important member of their Family of Orientation. Those who succeeded on parole were in contact two or three times a week compared to the failures who were in contact monthly ($t = 3.20$; $df = 26$; $p = .004$). Furthermore, the data indicates that among the successful subjects, the extent of contact for those persons identified as currently being most significant persons is as follows:

	%	n
Mother	63.6	7
Brother	18.2	2
Sister	9.1	1
Father	9.1	1
Σ	100.0	11
missing	-	3

For the failure subjects, however, the extent of contact with persons identified as the most important is quite different:

	%	n
Father	35.3	6
Mother	29.4	5
Sister	11.8	2
Grandmother	11.8	2
Brother	5.9	1
other persons	5.9	1
Σ	100.0	17
missing	-	4

The successful parolees claimed that they had more contact with their mother, whereas the failure subjects stated that they had more contact with their father. In considering the qualitative and quantitative aspects of these findings, there are slight indications in support of the hypothesis; yet, because no acceptable levels of significance were achieved, the null hypothesis was accepted.

Another social resource Frequency of contact clearly distinguished between success and failure subjects within Family of Procreation ($t = 9.76$; $df = 23$; $p < .0001$). The successful client's contact was almost daily whereas for the failure clients their contact was weekly.

A third social resource for successful subjects was Norm Similarity within the Work spaceround (chi square $= 3.7818$; $p = .058$), and the subjects who failed on parole had greater Norm Similarity to their peers than did the successful subjects.

In examining the spaceround Peers, the successful subjects (100 %) further claimed that their friends had not been convicted of crimes, compared to 11.1 % of the subjects who failed ($t = 4.47$; $df = 10$; $p < .001$).

The successful subjects were also significantly in more contact with their Civil Servants (parole officer, housing officer, social worker) than the failures ($t = 3.91$; $df = 33$; $p < .0001$). Most (64.3 %) of the successful subjects were in contact monthly or less often with Civil Servants compared to most (76.2 %) of the failures who claimed they never had contact with Civil Servants.

The subjects who failed on parole, participated significantly more in the Community spacerounds than the successful subjects ($t = 2.25$; $df = 26$; $p = .033$). The two dominant places where the failure subjects socialized at were sport clubs and the local bars. Of the successful subjects 87.5 % stated they were never influenced by the Community, compared to 27.3 % of the subjects who failed parole.

Demographic Resources

In examining the demographic resources (age, education, vocation training), the successful clients were significantly older than the failures (t = .803; p < .0001), the successful parolee was better educated (t = 2.09; p = .044) (see Figure 73), and they had more vocational training (t = 4.32; p < .0001) (see Figure 74).

Coping Resources

Finally, the parolee's coping skills were also examined. It was found that the overall coping score for successful clients was significantly higher than for unsuccessful clients (t = 2.17; p = .038).

Taking into account all categories of resources, these data suggested that successful parolees were distinguished by having weekly interaction with their mothers and daily contact with their wives. Their opinions were very similar to their work colleagues and very different from their peers. They also did not have friends who had been convicted of crimes. They were in contact with civil servants (usually their parole officers) at least monthly. They had minimal participation in their community and thus were not influenced by it very much. These successful parolees were older (about 24 years old), had one year more formal education, as well as one year more vocational training. Finally, they had better coping skills to deal with the kind of common problems which confronted most parolees. Thus, in light of the above significantly stronger resources, the null hypothesis was rejected and the research hypothesis was accepted.

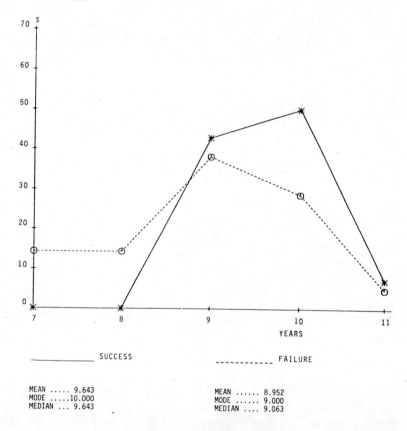

Figure 73: ELEMENTARY SCHOOL EDUCATION

——————— SUCCESS   - - - - - - - FAILURE

MEAN 9.643
MODE 10.000
MEDIAN ... 9.643

MEAN 8.952
MODE 9.000
MEDIAN 9.063

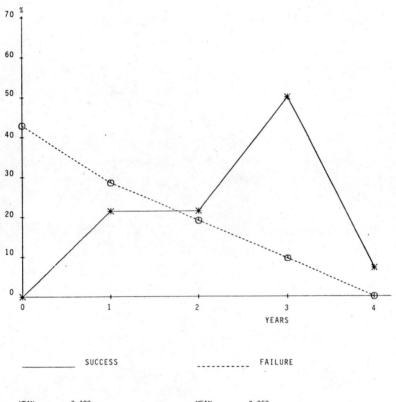

Figure 74: VOCATIONAL SCHOOL EDUCATION

————— SUCCESS   ------------ FAILURE

```
MEAN ...... 2.429        MEAN ...... 0.952
MODE ...... 3.000        MODE ...... 0.000
MEDIAN .... 2.643        MEDIAN .... 0.750
```

Hy. 9

For this hypothesis it was stated that among those who are successful, fewer indicators of helplessness will be found compared to those who are unsuccessful.

This hypothesis was developed to test whether or not the specific variable helplessness could be a distinguishing characteristic between those youth who succeed on parole and those who fail.

With regard to the coping dimensions Active/Passive, the main indicator for helplessness and resourcefulness, a somewhat significant relationship was found with the Employment Office skit (F = 3.3996; p = .0742; eta^2 = .0945) in the expected direction. However, when asked direct questions about different aspects of coping and helplessness (questions 83, 84, and 85) no significance was found between the two groups.

These findings suggested that the direct behavioral measure of helplessness was a more valid indicator of helplessness, since actual behavior was observed, measured and analyzed in response to four different problem situations. It appeared that asking the subjects questions about their being helpless elicited a socially desireable answer rather than one which could serve as an accurate indicator of this characteristic. This comparison also suggested the significant value of using the skit approach to get at coping type information.

It is interesting to note that the skit which elicited a significant difference between the two groups of parolees was the skit that focused primarily on the individual himself (Employment Office). There was almost no influence from others in this decision situation: the subject had to decide within his own mind rather than in response to the influences of parents, neighbors, boss or work colleagues. It may be that in order to find those variables which identify parolees who have the ability to succeed, measures must be devised to eliminate outside social influences.

Thus, these data suggested that the successful parolees were less helpless than those who failed. Consequently, the null hypothesis is rejected and the research hypothesis was supported.

Hy. 10

It was stated in this hypothesis that among those who are successful, more indicators of resourcefulness will be found compared to those who are unsuccessful.

The reason for developing this hypothesis was to try to find out whether successful parolees could be differentiated from the failures based on their ability to use their various resources. Each of the three dimensions measured a somewhat different aspect of resourcefulness: 1-Constructive/Destructive-Social was concerned with the ability of a parolee to use his social resources to fulfill normative expectations; 3-Active/Passive was focused on a person's ability to activate existing resources; and 10-Creative/Reactive was aimed at measuring behavior that dealt with a subject's ability to be creative and develop new resources.

The data show that over all four skits the following results occured:

Dimensions	F	p	Success $\bar{x}$	Failure $\bar{x}$
1-Constructive/ Destructive-Social	3.2730	.0795	3.5714	4.0952
3-Active/Passive	3.4422	.0725	3.2857	3.8095
10-Creative/Reactive	4.4196	.0432	3.7143	4.4286
Composite score: all three dimensions	4.3005	.0460	3.1429	3.5714

These data suggests that the successful parolees had significantly higher scores (more resourcefulness) on each of these dimensions. Thus, the null hypothesis was rejected and the research hypothesis was supported.

Hy. 11

It was hypothesized that among those who are successful, the coping skills will be stronger than among those who are unsuccessful.

The reason for this hypothesis was to test the core variable of this research effort: does coping skill play a major role in differentiating between youthful parolees who succeed and those who fail.

The data, broken down into all 13 dimensions over all four skits plus the overall composite score, are presented below:

	F	p
1 Constructive/Destructive-Social	3.2730	.0795*
2 Constructive/Destructive-Psychic	.3564	.5546
3 Active/Passive	3.4422	.0725*
4 Goal/Fortuitious Oriented	.0660	.7988
5 Problem/Non Problem Oriented	7.1995	.0113**
6 Person/Non Person	1.9132	.1759
7 Success/Failure	.5657	.4573
8 Rational/Activistic	4.8233	.0352**
9 Peaceful/Aggressive	3.3673	.0755*
10 Creative/Reactive	4.4196	.0432**
11 Legitimate/Non Legitimate	.8923	.3517
12 Together/Alone	2.9333	.0961*
13 Authority Immune/Fixated	.0835	.7744
Overall Composite	4.6895	.0377**

*$p < .10$ **$p < .05$

These data show that eight of the 13 dimensions had significance of $p < .10$, and three had significance level of $p < .05$. The important variable for this hypothesis was the overall composite score which showed that successful parolees were significantly (p = .0377) different than the failure parolees well within the acceptable limits of statistical probability.

It is important to note that the instrument used for measuring coping behavior in this project was used for the first time. It had a number of dimensions (6, 12, and 13) that did not hold up very well under the factor analysis done in the previous Coping/Supervision sub-study. Further, it should be mentioned that analyses up to now had been done based on the assumption of linearity. It was feasible that a curvilinear function may have been operating in those other dimensions which did not prove to be significant. None-the-less, in this researcher's opinion these data were sufficient to reject the null hypothesis.

Hy. 12

For this hypothesis it was stated that the strength of "Trait" dimensions among those who were successful were stronger than among those who failed.

The main reason for having developed this hypothesis was to ascertain whether the dimensions identified in the earlier Coping/Supervision Sub-Study by factor analysis as "Trait" dimensions would distinguish between successful and failure subjects.

The factor analysis in the previous study identified seven "Trait" Coping Dimensions (1, 2, 3, 7, 9, 11, and 12); these were used to distinguish between the success and the failure parolees. Separately and as a composite score, "Trait" as a variable showed no significant difference; however, three dimensions, 1-Constructive/Destructive-Social (F = 3.2730; p = .079), 9-Peaceful/Aggressive (F = 3.3673; p = .076), and 12-Together/Alone (F = 2.93; p = .096) showed slightly significant differences.

With only three weak exceptions, these data suggested that the "Trait" dimensions were not particularly valuable in differentiating between successful parolees and those who failed. If higher and more significant F values for these dimensions had been obtained, it would have been appropriate to suggest that trait dimensions of individual coping skills partially accounted for the differences between those parolees who succeeded and those who failed. However, keeping in mind the possibility of curvilinear functions, the three dimensions that were somewhat significant ($p < .10$), the low number of subjects tested and the fact that in six of the seven "Trait" dimensions the successful subjects had stronger coping scores, it is still reasonable to hypothesize that trait dimensions play an important role in the success/failure process. None-the-less, the obtained F values and significance levels were not within acceptable limits; thus, the null hypothesis was accepted.

6.4 Conclusions

At this point it is important to remind the reader that this study was not designed to test or replicate control theory postulates (old or new). Thus, one of the main assumptions of this sub-study is that the theorems of Spaceround Integration and Social Coping are valid.

The first group of hypotheses (1-7) focused on concepts from the Spaceround Integration model in trying to distinguish between parolees who failed and those who succeeded. The second group of hypotheses (8-12) used variables from the broader model of Social Coping to find differences between failure and successful subjects. Out of the first group of seven hypotheses two research hypotheses were accepted and five null hypotheses were accepted. From the five Social Coping hypotheses all of the five research hypotheses were accepted.

These results suggested that with regard to the officially defined success and failure subjects used in this study, the more sociological concepts of the Spaceround Integration Model were not as effective in differentiating between the two groups as were the more psychological concepts of the Social Coping Model. Two explanations seem reasonable at this point: either the Spaceround Integration postulates were too broad and not oriented at the individual level enough to be sensitive to the differences, or the general area of social phenomena addressed by the Spaceround Integration Model in fact made little difference when comparing success and failure. That is to say, either a) the theory was inappropriate, or b) social conditions didn't play a major role in distinguishing between success and failure, or c) both. Hirschi, writing about differences in "delinquent activity between high and low-stake boys" as a result of greater or lesser exposure to criminal influences, suggested that these influences (or what one could call subtle social influences), "are beyond the reach of control theory" (1969, 161). On the other hand it appears that the social coping postulates served as better indicators for distinguishing between the successful and failure subjects. The same points mentioned above, would seem appropriate as explanations for the Social Coping hypotheses, that is, a) the instrument was adequately sensitive, in which case it would follow that b) the phenomena under investigation were principally psychological in nature, thus c) both were in effect.

In spite of the acceptance of five null hypotheses for the Spaceround Integration hypotheses, some of the data obtained are worth discussing. In the first two hypotheses the relative importance of spacerounds was investigated. It was found that no significant differences existed; however, the profile which resulted from this analysis showed that both groups of youthful parolees judged their Peers as being relatively <u>less</u> important compared to Work, Community and Family. This finding seemed to support (at least in principle) the statement by

Hirschi that "since delinquents are less strongly attached to conventional adults than non delinquents, they are less likely to be attached to each other" (1969, 140-141). The statement of Friday and Hage (1976) that "as the saliency of the peer groups increases, so too does the probability of delinquency" does not seem to be applicable to the findings of this study. In fact it was found that the successful subjects (reflecting on their adolescence) rated their Peers as significantly more important than the parole failures did. A possible explanation for these findings would be one proposed by Yablonsky where he suggested that the youth who is able to assume constructive social roles is the one who is well socialized. On the other hand the one who "emerges from a social milieu that trains him inadequately for assuming constructive social roles" is the one who has had defective socialization, lacks social feelings and is not capable of having "human feelings of compassion or responsibility for another" (1963, 196). This lack of "trust, warmth, affection or support" with peers was also confirmed by Junger-Tas (1977, 84).

The successful subjects identified Peers as being more important than Family, significantly more than the failures. Speaking of non-delinquents, if Yablonsky's (1963, 196) principal also applied to successful subjects, it might help explain why the successful subjects (prior to their 14th year) identified Peers as more important than Family when compared to the failures. It might be that these successful subjects learned how to develop new relationships outside the Family which then became useful in becoming successful later in life, i.e. during their parole period. Other findings from this study supporting this notion would be that the successful subjects had stronger personal resources, more frequency of contact with members of all spacerounds and less emotional dependency with their Family of Procreation, at Work and in the Community.

The next and perhaps most important Spaceround Integration hypothesis was number five. This hypothesis was broken down into five sub-hypotheses, one for each interaction condition tested. The null hypothesis was accepted for all sub-hypotheses except for the Frequency hypothesis. In retrospect it was inappropriate to hypothesize across all spacerounds equally as each produced different findings for the same interaction condition. This realization is especially congruent with the spaceround Peers.

Hypothesis six dealt with meaningful relationships and although the null hypothesis was accepted the data turned up the interesting qualitative finding that prioritization of the most meaningful relationships for successful subjects were, in order of importance, mother, brother, sister, and father, compared to the failure subjects who claimed, in order of importance, father, mother, sister and grandmother. While Hirschi (1969, 100-107) suggested no differences existed between delinquents and non delinquents in terms of mother's or father's influence, it is difficult to generalize his findings to our parolees' success/failure findings.

Another important finding, with respect to the Spaceround Integration Model and the distinction between successful and failure subjects, was the data derived from testing hypothesis seven. These data suggested that the extent of a parolee's integration is an important determinant of whether he will be a success or failure. If we operationally define success on parole as an indicator of law-abiding behavior and failure as an indicator of law-breaking behavior, then previous control theory research which equates integration to conformity (see Hirschi 1969; Friday and Halsey 1977; Junger-Tas 1977) would support these findings.

Considering the Social Coping hypotheses, in each instance significant differences were found between the parolees who succeeded and those who failed. The first of these was hypothesis eight which focused on resources. In fact the information from the remaining hypotheses are all embodied into this one hypothesis. Using these results two profiles were suggested for the typical parolee who succeeded and for the typical parolee who failed:

General profiles for the two research groups based on the significant differences:

Successes	Failures
- contact with <u>mothers</u> (over fathers) 2-3 times per week	- contact with <u>fathers</u> (over mothers) weekly to monthly or less
- similar life opinions from their work colleagues	- different life opinions from their work colleagues
- different opinions from their peers	- similar opinions as their peers
- no friends with criminal records	- some friends with criminal records
- at least monthly contact with the employment and parole office	- almost no contact with any civil service office
- low participation in the communitiy (sports clubs, neighbors, or pubs)	- high participation in the community (sports clubs, neighbors, or pubs)
- most were 24 years old	- most were 21 years old
- had more schooling (10 years)	- had less schooling (9 years)
- had more vocational training (2 years)	- had less vocational training (1 year)
- better coping skills	- weaker coping skills
- stronger resourcefulness	- less resourcefulness
- few indicators of helplessness	- more indicators of helplessness
- greater extent of individual integration	- greater extent of individual isolation

These differences suggest not only different individual characteristics, but also different interaction patterns. The successfuls are better integrated especially with regard to having more frequent and positive contacts within conventional spacerounds like their Family of Orientation, Family of Procreation, Work Place, Peers without criminal records, Civil Servants, and Schools. Also, they are more resourceful, less helpless and generally have stronger coping skills.

The failures, on the other hand, are more isolated from traditional spacerounds and have their main contacts with Peers (some of which have criminal records) in Community hangouts (sport clubs and pubs, which are also Peer spacerounds). They are also less resourceful, more helpless and generally have weaker and fewer coping skills.

In retrospect, the hypotheses which were derived from the more psychological concepts of coping seemed to yield somewhat more fruitful results in terms of accepting or rejecting the null hypotheses. This observation is not made to suggest the discriminative dominance of one discipline over the other. It is merely mentioned as a categorical observation which is probably more an indictment of our research instruments or methods than anything else.

Considering the response scores from all 13 coping dimensions for each skit plus the composite scores across all four skits, Figures 75 thru 79 provide F values, p values and the means.

In spite of the frustratingly low sample size and low response rates, overall, this study fulfilled its primary goal of exploring the social control and social coping differences between successful parolees and parolees who failed within the framework of the Social Coping Model.

Figure 75: SUCCESS AND FAILURE DIFFERENCES ON 13 COPING
DIMENSIONS FOR SKIT 1: Argument at supper

Dimensions	F	p	$\bar{x}$ S		F
1	2.1450	.1525	4.7143	<	5.333
2	.0064	.9370	2.9286	~	2.9348
3	.9599	.3343	4.2143	<	4.6190
4	1.4023	.2448	3.3571	>	3.0000
5	.4020	.5304	4.0000	<	4.2857
6	.0658	.7992	3.3571	>	3.2857
7	.0000	1.0000	3.4286	=	3.4286
8	1.6957	.2019	4.3571	<	4.9048
9	1.0152	.3210	3.9286	>	4.3810
10	2.3783	.1326	4.5714	>	5.1905
11	.3615	.5518	3.0714	<	3.2857
12	.1317	.7190	6.3571	>	6.1905
13	.0581	.8111	2.3571	>	2.4286
Composite	.2474	.6222	3.9286	<	4.0476

$\bar{x}$ Key: 1 = high
         7 = low

Figure 76: SUCCESS AND FAILURE DIFFERENCES ON 13 COPING
DIMENSIONS FOR SKIT 2: The friendly neighbor lady

Dimensions	F	p	$\bar{x}$ S		$\bar{x}$ F
1	2.2794	.1406	3.6429	<	4.4762
2	.0071	.9334	2.7857	>	2.7619
3	1.4286	.2405	3.5714	<	4.0952
4	.0759	.7847	2.5000	<	2.5714
5	4.4882	.0417	3.0714	<	4.0952
6	1.7944	.1895	3.5000	>	3.0952
7	.2197	.6423	3.0000	>	2.9286
8	3.0415	.0905	3.5714	<	4.5238
9	3.5893	.0669	3.2143	<	4.1905
10	.6776	.4163	4.2857	<	4.7143
11	.4632	.5009	2.7143	<	3.0000
12	.0764	.7839	6.1429	<	6.2857
13	.6492	.4262	2.2857	>	2.0000
Composite	.7820	.3829	3.4286	<	3.6667

$\bar{x}$ Key: 1 = high
7 = low

Figure 77: SUCCESS AND FAILURE DIFFERENCES ON 13 COPING DIMENSIONS
FOR SKIT 3: Disappointment at the employment office

Dimensions	F	p	$\bar{x}$ S		F
1	.1153	.7364	2.7143	>	2.6190
2	.6140	.4389	2.4286	<	2.6190
3	3.3996	.0742	2.5000	<	3.0476
4	1.0806	.3061	2.2143	<	2.4762
5	1.8629	.1815	2.5000	<	2.9524
6*	12.0262	.0016	3.8571	<	5.0476
7	.1784	.6755	2.7143	<	2.8095
8	.9995	.3247	2.6429	<	2.9048
9	.0097	.9221	2.2143	<	2.2381
10	7.2828	.0109	2.5714	<	3.3333
11	.5351	.4696	2.0000	<	2.1429
12	1.6094	.2134	3.6429	<	4.2381
13	1.3986	.2454	2.2143	<	2.4762
Composite	5.4000	.0264	2.5714	<	3.0000

$\bar{x}$ Key: 1 = high
7 = low

* Unusually strong significance
and high F value.

Figure 78: SUCCESS AND FAILURE DIFFERENCES ON 13 COPING DIMENSIONS
FOR SKIT 4: Argument with the boss

Dimensions	F	p	$\bar{x}$ S		$\bar{x}$ F
1	2.5246	.1216	3.3571	<	4.1429
2	.4714	.4971	2.7143	>	2.5714
3	2.6524	.1129	2.8571	<	3.6190
4	.0123	.9122	2.5000	<	2.5238
5	5.8586	.0212	2.7857	<	3.8095
6	.3800	.5419	2.9286	<	3.1429
7	.1454	.7054	3.2143	<	3.3333
8	5.2675	.0282	3.1429	<	4.3810
9	4.3491	.0448	2.9286	<	3.9048
10	4.0745	.0517	3.4286	<	4.4762
11	1.3398	.2554	2.4286	<	2.8571
12*	8.2827	.0070	3.2857	<	5.1429
13	0.0000	1.0000	2.2857	=	2.2857
Composite	4.2573	.0470	2.8571	<	3.4762

$\bar{x}$ Key: 1 = high
7 = low

* Unusually strong significance
and high F value.

Figure 79: SUCCESS AND FAILURE DIFFERENCES ON 13 COPING DIMENSIONS OVER ALL FOUR SKITS:

Dimensions	F	p	$\bar{x}$ S		F
1	3.2730	.0795	3.5714	<	4.0952
2	.3564	.5546	2.6429	<	2.7619
3	3.4422	.0725	3.2857	<	3.8095
4	.0660	.7988	2.7143	>	2.6667
5	7.1995	.0113	3.0714	<	3.9048
6	1.9132	.1759	3.3571	<	3.6667
7	.5657	.4573	3.1429	<	3.2857
8	4.8233	.0352	3.5000	<	4.2381
9	3.3673	.0755	3.1429	<	3.6190
10	4.4196	.0432	3.7143	<	4.4286
11	.8923	.3517	2.5000	<	2.7619
12	2.9333	.0961	4.8571	<	5.4286
13	.0835	.7744	2.2857	<	2.3333
Composite	4.6895	.0377	3.1429	<	3.5714

$\bar{x}$ Key: 1 = high
7 = low

7 Implications for Policy, Practice, and Research

> "It is much easier to determine why offenders continue in criminal careers than it is to understand what makes them quit."
>
> Walter C. Reckless

The following comments were drawn from the four studies and presented in this report: the Youthful Parolee File-Card Pre-Study, the Parole Problems Pre-Study, the Coping/Supervision Study, and the Success/Failure Study.

7.1 Policy

Most of the comments in this section assume the validity of the Social Coping Model. The general policy suggestion which stems from this project would be that an overall approach to the community supervision of offenders, especially those under parole, should take into account the importance of the interaction between situational variables, especially those concerning the family and the parole officer, and individual variables, especially those which focus on real-life coping processes.

The Success/Failure Study showed that most of those who failed parole not only participated less in significant spacerounds, but, in those spacerounds where they did participate they had fewer personal contacts than those who succeeded, especially with regard to Family members (both orientation and procreation), Civil Services (parole office, employment office and housing office) and Peers.

These findings suggest that isolation and parole failure are by-products of some common cause (perhaps faulty socialization as suggested by Yablonsky, 1963) or isolation itself as a cause of parole failure (as stressed by Friday and Halsey, 1977) or both. The Spaceround Integration Model stresses the importance of meaningful relationships in the process of becoming well integrated. The Social Coping Model stresses the importance of social resources in successfully dealing with problems. Considering the empirical and theoretical information together suggests that being isolated (the opposite of being integrated into a spaceround) distinguishes between those youth on parole who succeed and those who fail. Thus, a logical recommendation for parole supervisors would be to place major efforts to reduce their clients isolation in all traditional spacerounds. Special attention should be placed on the interaction conditions of Frequency of contact in traditional spacerounds and Norm Similarity in the work spaceround. Use of trained volunteers is recommended to enhance interactions in traditional spacerounds. A further recommendation would be to develop interpersonal skills training programs for use during the offender's pre-release period so as to enhance the post-release establishment and maintenance of meaningful relationships.

The Coping/Supervision Study and the Success/Failure Study, suggest a number of implications with regard to coping. The Success/Failure Study suggests that successful parolees are able to cope significantly better than those who fail. The spaceround that yielded the highest and most significant coping scores for successful parolees was Work Place in response to the "Argument with the Boss" skit. This particular skit was derived from the Parole Problems Pre-study which found that information from previous research, non-parolees and parole supervisors identified the world of work as being the most problematic. Since the young parolees in this study identified work as one of the least problematic areas (see Figure 17), it would seem reasonable to conclude, that for young parolees, recognizing problems at work and knowing how to cope with them plays an important (if not critical) role in successfully completing parole.

One of the five questions in the integration instrument of the Success/Failure Study also focused on the spaceround Work. It asked "At work, when I am together with my colleagues there are never/seldom/sometimes/frequently/always problems". The results showed that the two groups of exparolees responded similarly by saying they seldom had problems. The results of the Parole Problem Study indicated that current parolees also didn't see work as a serious problem area. Considering both these independent findings it would appear that young offenders on parole as well as after parole were relatively unaware of how problematic the work situation was. Among those who also expressed a lack of awareness were successful parolees, who when tested, coped in a significantly better way when actually confronted with a work place problem. Thus, these findings suggest that part of any kind of pre-parole training program should include work problem awareness and resolution skills in its format. Additionally, parole supervisors should receive special training in job crisis intervention techniques. The role of a supervisor in the management of their clients lives should ideally be concerned with those areas that have proven to be critical in the process becoming successful at Work and in the Family; and, in this role, the supervisor's skill levels should be highly developed.

7.2 Research

Since this project was not primarily directed at testing the Spaceround Integration Model or the Social Coping Model (as both models evolved considerably during the course of this project), it would appear reasonable to organize the two models into more formal theoretical statements which could then be empirically tested better. Those areas of the Spaceround Integration Model which appear to warrant special attention are: the extent to which the interaction conditions effect the meaningfulness of relationships, the relative importance of these conditions, and which conditions explain the greatest amount of variance with regard to an individual's integration.

There appears to be a truism in research which, that which is the most difficult to conduct is usually done the least and is needed the most. In control theory the majority of studies have used the cross sectional approach; however, the nature of much of the theoretical explanations suggest causal links over considerable lengths of time. For example, some of the key concerns deal with the socialization process, the changing importance of meaningful relationships over time, the relative importance of peers over time, and the role of interaction conditions over time. These needs beg the question: are longitudinal studies the only logical method for accurately answering these questions. Caplan, in his exhaustive reformulation and testing of Hirschi's control model, makes this same recommendation especially recognizing the "greater capacity to assure the temporal sequence of the independent and dependent variables" in the longitudinal designs (1978, 373).

Another area of delinquency research that continues to elude researchers is the role of peers in delinquency. The Gluecks (1950, 164) noted that delinquency occurs before the selection of companions, while Reckless (1961, 311) claimed that "companionship is one of the most important universal causes of crime and delinquency among males". Throughout the past three decades such control theorists as Hirschi (1969), Hindelang (1973), Thibauld (1974), Tieman (1976), Junger-Tas (1977), Friday and Hage (1976), Caplan (1978) and Dizon (1981) have dealt with this issue with widely different results. In this project it was noted that successful subjects (as adolescents) claimed that Peers/Hangouts had been the most important spaceround for them. Young parolees claimed that peers were the least problematic people they had to deal with; whereas, non-offender youth indicated that peers were somewhat problematic for them. In spite of more frequent contacts, successful parolees had <u>less</u> norm similarity, <u>fewer</u> meaningful relationships and <u>no</u> criminal friends among peers when compared to those who failed parole. As adults both the successes and failures rated Peers as a spaceround with low importance compared to Work, Community and Family. Thus, it appears that the maze of variables that distinguish between those who are more integrated or those who succeed or, indeed, those who do not become delinquent, are fraught with many subtle complexities that seem to change considerably over that relatively short period of time from adolescence to adulthood. Needless to say, this area of human behavior could greatly benefit from an exhaustive, narrowly focused, longitudinal research effort preferably using a cohort as the main unit of analysis with a recent model of control theory as the theoretical backdrop.

From the theoretical level the link between coping and individual integration is the adaptation to spacerounds. While this link is assumed in both theoretical models, it was not directly tested. Adaptation speaks to the generalized adjustment made in a given setting. The process of <u>becoming</u> adapted through numerous coping events and its relationship to social control would be a logical extension of the present work. It is the conviction of this researcher that only through the inclusion of both coping trait and coping state considerations couched within a socialpsychological framework can the full understanding of becoming successful on parole be approached. I am recommending a comprehensive and eclectic model which would take into account a broader perspective than usually found within a single theory. If striving to account for all of the variance of a given phenomenon is one of the key goals of scientific endeavor, then being open to more descriptions of reality should move us closer in that direction.

Summary

Social Coping of Youth under Supervision

The purpose of this research was to gather information about the ability of youthful parolees in the Hannover area to cope with their lives in the period immediately following their release from prison. More specifically, this research was interested in finding out about the techniques used to achieve success in specific problem areas such as in the family, place of work, with neighbors, among friends, and with civil servants. The value of this research would be realized in its findings to the various agencies which either prepare or assist parolees to succeed as well as to those agencies that make decisions as to whether a sentenced offender will receive parole and whether a parolee is to remain under parole or be released. If this research is able to expand our current knowledge of parolees' use of coping skills, the information could become an important asset to all decisions made with regard to the parole process.

Another important dimension of this research's potential value is in focusing on success. According to the 1979 statistics on youthful offenders in Lower Saxony who were placed on parole after serving time in prison, 59 % succeeded (see Rechtspflege, Fachserie 10, Reihe 5: Bewährungshilfe, 1979, 36-37. Statistisches Bundesamt Wiesbaden (Ed.)). Why they succeeded and how they succeeded is a relative mystery. In the Federal Republic of Germany, this area of concern has been almost totally neglected. Much of what has been done thus far, has been concerned with describing the characteristics of failure.

In the last twenty years about 82 % of the probation and parole research has dealt with adults and only 18.0 % with youth (see Figure 1). When comparing the extent of research conducted between parole and probation, one finds that only 27.9 % has dealt with parole and 72.1 % with probation. This means that the most over-researched client is the adult on probation (57.3 %), and the least researched client is the youth on parole (3.3 %). Thus, this research focused on an under-researched client (the youth parolee) and with a relatively under-researched concern (success).

In an effort to focus on success, this researcher decided to investigate the process of overcoming problems and difficulties by youth on parole. This process of dealing with problematic situations is referred to as coping. Coping, however, is too general a concept to use in a small focused research project. A person attempts to cope with every problem, large or small. Hypothetically, one would be confronted with the totality of youth parolee problem solving. Therefore, another aspect of the coping phenomena was needed.

The logical next step was to consider patterns of coping. The principle question then becomes what types of coping behaviors can be discernable as patterns. Are these patterns meaningful? Do they distinguish between those parolees who are successful and those who are not? Are these patterns influenced by the socialization process and/or by current relationships? How do these patterns cluster and become part of individual coping repertoires? Are coping repertoires different for parolees and probationers, and between those who succeed and those who fail on supervision?

Thus, this line of thought has evolved from a concern for how parolees achieve success, to a more focused inquiry on coping repertoires and their relationships to other variables.

Main Research Questions

- Do coping patterns exist that differentiate between youth parolees who fulfill their parole periods successfully and those who are returned to prison because they failed on parole.

- Do the number of meaningful relationships have an effect on coping patterns?

- Does the intensity of relationships have an effect on coping patterns?

- How are coping patterns effected by other variables such as: age, education, socioeconomic status, family situation, work situation, relationship to peers, etc.?

- What is the inter-relationship between coping, social integration, and other social phenomena?

- What is the relationship of coping to individual resources?

Parole Problem Pre-study

The pre-study focused directly on typical parolee problems. It was conducted by using exploratory interviews of parolees, non-parolees of the same age, parole supervisors, analyzing data from a prerelease study of adults in Nürnberg, FRG and studies reported in American and German parole literature (see Figure 1). From each of these data sources a list of problems emerged which were collapsed into five areas: family, civil servants, community, work, and peers.

Based on the frequency with which problems were mentioned, these areas were prioritized according to data source. Since this was only used in the development of the coping instrument, small samples were used. Consequently, inferences beyond simple comparisons were not made.

Comparing each data source with each other produced different rankings of problems. For each of these problem comparisons three statistical tests were used: Chi-squared, Tau, and Contingency Coefficient. Chi-squared is a test of significance usually used for nominal data to indicate whether our observations differ from what would be expected by chance. Tau is referred to as Kendall's rank correlation coefficient. It is used when at least ordinal data is achieved and a measure of association between two sets of attributes are nominal in character. The Contingency Coefficient is a measure of association between two sets of attributes which are nominal in character.

The Theoretical Overview

The <u>theoretical overview</u> of this research is based on a mixture of predominantly experimental psychological research on coping techniques mostly at the cognitive level and sociological theories of social control. The most relevant theoretical points of this research are:

    a. <u>Coping</u> is subject to the principles of <u>learning</u>. These are specific empirically derived principles that explain the general nature of learning or the functional relationships between "certain antecedant conditions and changes in performance of a task" (English and English, 1958). Since this research is in large part dealing with an analysis of what people do (as oppose to only what they think) and is concerned with the conditions under which they perform (i.e. the response to environmental stimuli), this approach partially falls within the realm of neobehaviorism (see Bandura and Walters, 1959; Hastorf, 1965, 268-284; Henker, 1964).

    b. By using a list of <u>coping dimensions</u> (for a further discussion, see sections 4.4.3 and 4.4.4) an attempt was made to identify those specific patterns that are applicable in many situations. They may more accurately be referred to as coping principles which may be either preparatory or response acts; and, they may be cognitive or behavioral in nature.

c. <u>Coping repertoire</u> is a concept developed to represent a person's constellation of coping techniques. It is herein contended that these repertoires can be identified measured and classified; and, that they vary widely among the general population. Also of primary interest is the size of these repertoires, the way coping techniques are prioritized within them, and to what extent these repertoires are influenced by other social phenomena.

d. <u>Meaningful relationships</u> are clearly a sociological concept that came from the roots of modern sociological thought, especially from the traditions of symbolic interactionism, behaviorism, and the concepts of primary groups, the looking-glass self, and the significant other (see Cooley, 1902; Dewey, 1930; Mead, 1934; and Blumer, 1969). The current use of this concept of meaningful relationships comes from the recent work of Friday and Hage (1976). They used the term "intimate role relationships" (borrowed from Marwell and Hage 1970). This concept of significance or intimacy is discussed by them in terms of "saliency", "meaningfulness", "integration" and "number of activities", in an attempt to characterize the nature of role relationships. In this author's opinion, the term <u>meaningful relationships</u> captures the sense of symbolic interaction better.

e. <u>Social integration</u>, as mentioned earlier, is a broad sociological concept (originating with Durkheim in 1951) applicable to youth crime throughout the world and relating to how people are socialized to the dominant norms of society. The principle spacerounds of socializing activity are, family, school, work, community, and peers. This orientation is used because it is postulated that learning coping techniques is part of the socialization process (see Friday, 1981a; Thibaut and Kelly, 1959).

f. What is important (in terms of its influence) to an individual in a spaceround depends on the meaning of its major <u>interactive components</u>: people, objects, place, ideas, and time. The way a person's repertoire of meanings evolve is through the process of interaction with these five basic components. In the arena of interactions (spacerounds), one is continously confronted with options concerning how to cope. The motivation and the forces which influence this selection process is of major interest to this study.

A Survey of Coping

Coping refers to "things that people do to avoid being harmed by life-strains" (Pearlin and Schooler, 1978, 2). The term coping has a number of closely related concepts such as mastery, defense and adaptation (see White, 1974). This protective function is activated in three primary ways: by altering the conditions that cause the problems; by cognitively controlling the definitions of the problem so that the resultant stress is neutralized; and, by placing comfortable limits on the emotional response to problems (see Pearlin and Schooler, 1978, 2).

Research on coping has been steadily increasing in the last two decades, especially since the early work by Lois Murphy (1962), titled 'The Widening World of Childhood'. Murphy studied children's reaction to threat. She identified three basic steps that characterize the coping process: preparation, coping, and secondary coping. Four years later, Richard S. Lazarus (1966), in his book 'Psychological Stress and the Coping Process', identified similar patterns for adult coping. Today coping is at the center of stress research. One of the first major considerations in studying coping is the importance of developing "taxonomies of life-stressors". In so doing, the specific means of controlling "biological, ecological, psychological and social conditions of stress reactions" would be facilitated (Prystav, 1979, 297).

The sociological dimensions of coping have been considered only to a very limited extent (see Blath, Dillig, and Frey, 1980; Pearlin and Schooler, 1978). These kinds of considerations have gone from a behavioral perspective to a social group perspective. Work in the social and behavior areas of coping have been recognized as being seriously underdeveloped (see Prystav, 1979, 297; Pearlin and Schooler, 1978, 2).

Prior to discussing the techniques or characteristics of coping it is imperative to recognize that socio/psychological environments within which coping techniques function are the two basic givens: <u>social resources</u>, and <u>psychological resources</u>. These two terms refer to what is available to a person that can be drawn upon in the development of coping techniques/repertoires.

Perhaps the most logical way to organize the literature on coping is to use the three basic steps that Murphy (1962), Lazarus (1966), and others (see Janis, 1958; Mandler, 1962; Ax, 1964; Schachter, 1966; Arnold, 1970; Glass and Singer, 1972) have generally used to describe the coping process as mentioned above.

In the <u>preparation phase</u> Meichenbaum et al. (1975) stated that "Much of the coping process is anticipatory in nature and is initiated before a confrontation with a threat or stressor". The results of most of these type studies have pointed to the enormous variability in the ability and style that people use in coping with stress. Preparing or rehearsing for stress is what Janis (1965) called "The Work of Worrying". This worrying process then gives way to coping or self derived reassurances. Meichenbaum (1973) referred to this process as "learned resourcefulness".

In the <u>coping phase</u> an almost unlimited number of possible acts exist. Lazarus et al. (1974) differentiated between two coping modes: direct action and intra psychic. These may be liberally translated into behavioral modes and cognitive modes.

In the secondary coping phase, an attempt is made to focus on the feed-back one gets as a result of trying the vast number of possibilities that could be used to deal with stress.

Control Theory

The four dominant sociological traditions developed in the U.S. for delinquency have been Strain Theories, Cultural Deviance Theories, Labeling Theories, and Control Theories. Strain Theories (also called Anomie Theories) claim that a person is forced into delinquency in order to satisfy legitimate desires that are not provided through conformity to society. Perhaps the best example of a strain theory is that of Robert K. Merton espoused in his book 'Social Theory and Social Structure' (1957). Cultural Deviance Theories claim that delinquency is a middle class perspective which views deviance as conformity to another set of norms. One of the classic cultural deviance theories was propounded by Edwin H. Sutherland and is known as Differential Association (1939).

Control Theories claim that delinquents are amoral beings whose bond to society is broken. The most explicit statement of this theoretical tradition was made by Travis Hirschi (1969) with the publication of his book 'Causes of Delinquency'. Of the four above mentioned approaches, Control Theory seems to best capture the social reality of delinquent behavior. For additional discussions of control theories one should see Kornhauser (1973), Caplan (1978), Becker (1980), Friday (1980a), Weitekamp (1980), and Dussich and Jacobsen (1982).

Further remarks on Control Theory

In their development of control theory, Hirschi and Friday limited themselves primarily to the antagonists of conforming/non-conforming behavior in trying to explain juvenile delinquency. The implication is that when conformity is achieved, delinquency ceases to be a problem. It is suggested that theories of control should go beyond the criteria of norm-conforming behavior for explaining delinquency. A theory that attempts to explain criminal behavior must also be able to explain non-criminal behavior. The term criminal is a legal term which labels specific behaviors under specific conditions. The most important part of the terms "criminal behavior" or "delinquent behavior" is the word behavior. A theory of behavior should concern itself first with the total phenomenon of behavior rather than being diverted by moral or legal conditions, or be bound by professional disciplines.

Up to now most control theorists have been primarily concerned with delinquent behavior, and mostly from a sociological perspective. Some considerations which have not been covered have been: the relevance of both physical and cognitive differences; the influence of place and time; the behaviors of adults and of non-delinquent youth; the distinction between role and relationships, and finally, the relevance of an individual's perception of concrete and immediate factors versus the influence of social structures and their processes.

The accomplishments of control theory thus far provide important contributions to the further understanding of external social influences that effect behavior. We suggest, this is not enough. Hirschi himself stated that "criminological research has for too long based its theories on ecological data" (1969, 15). Thus, the extension in the following section has been proposed.

Spaceround Integration: A control theory extension

This proposal is an attempt at recognizing behavior in a more phenomenological way (see Dussich and Jacobsen, 1982). It takes into account the macroprocesses and microprocesses of social structures and how they influence behavior through spacerounds. The term Spaceround (see Figure 30) represents an attempt to conceptually bring together the multifaceted quality of a social psychic happening with given people, at a special place, with unique ideas, with particular objects, and only at an express time. This concept of spacerounds was derived from a somewhat similar concept, "Placerounds", originally developed by John Lofland (1969) in his book 'Deviance and Identity'. All spacerounds have five main dimensions: people, objects, places, ideas, and time.

Significant Spacerounds refers to patterned social phenomena which have special importance to individuals and which may be effected by such macrostructural artifacts as different political systems, different cultures, different governments, etc. and such microstructural artifacts as groups, individuals, feelings, ideas, etc. These spacerounds may be traditional (family, schools, church) or nontraditional (orphanages, Kibbuzim, prisons, etc.) situations. Examples of some of the more common significant spacerounds are: home/family, hangout/peers, school/students-teachers, work/colleagues, and communities/neighbors. By adding the adjective "significant" we are limiting spacerounds to those situational settings which are important to individuals and which are similar to the more traditional term social institutions. Each spaceround has its own unique set of norms. These norms indicate how the spaceround components should interact describing what behavior is appropriate and what is inappropriate.

Meaningful Relationships represent the direct intimacy bonds between a person and other persons. These relationships are the interactive nexus of each spaceround. It is through these relationships that norms are transmitted and sanctioned. The degree of meaningfulness dictates the extent of conformity and integration. We contend that objects also function as interaction partners and that a range of interactive potential also exists for them. However, for purposes of this discussion, we will focus primarily on person-to-person interactions which we propose are conditioned or effected primarily by seven basic Interaction Conditions: frequency, duration, self-disclosure, cathexis, dependency, norm similarity, and overlap.

In traditional sociological terms, integration refers to a social process which brings together differing social elements (see Fairchild, 1968, 159). When speaking of individual integration in a given spaceround, we are referring to the process whereby persons learn to deal with the components of that spaceround and, in so doing, become synchronized[*] to its components. When persons are well integrated into a particular spaceround, they "fit in" or adapt.

Thus, the main hypothesis of this theoretical model is that:

> If, within a given spaceround, the interaction conditions of frequency, duration, self-disclosure, cathexis, dependency, norm similarity and overlap are high, meaningful relationships will also be high, and individual integration will be maximized.

On the other hand, spaceround integration is a condition of the spaceround itself. It implies the synchronization and coordination among the five mutable spaceround components of people, objects, places, ideas, and time. The result of high

---

* Synchronization herein refers to a functional compatibility that exists among components which interact roughly at the same time.

spaceround integration is a minimum of conflict and a maximum of harmony. The logical opposite of this term is <u>spaceround dysintegration</u>, which describes a condition whereby the interaction components are not "working together" towards common ends and where there is high conflict. The final consideration applies to spacerounds which are seperate from the larger societal activities; this we refer to as <u>spaceround isolation</u>. The spaceround itself is not participating in the community, nor does it directly contribute to the community's goals.

The opposite phenomenon of individual integration is <u>individual isolation</u>. Isolation implies estrangement from interaction within a given spaceround that one is a member of. It is characterized by interactive separation from most of the usual spaceround activities. The most extreme form of isolation would imply: <u>minimal contacts</u>, <u>low duration</u>, <u>no self-disclosure</u>, no <u>cathexis</u>, a <u>difference in norms</u>, a <u>lack of dependency</u> and <u>no overlap</u> with persons in that spaceround. <u>Individual dysintegration</u> represents the status of a person whose presence causes problems, one who cannot or will not adapt and one who does not "fit in". This person would have a moderate number of contacts with variable duration, limited self-disclosure and cathexis, a difference in norms, variable dependency and overlap.

The Social Coping Model

This model attempts to present two theoretical roots (a recent sociological development in control theory and an explanation of a psychological concept - coping theory) which are married into a unified social-psychological concept and referred to as the theory of social coping. This theory attempts to explain how individuals, through their interactions with problems, learn to adapt to norms and ultimately become integrated into their particular social space.

The concept which sets the stage and describes the social-psychological environs of coping is the Coping Milieu (see Figure 31). The Coping Milieu is a phenomenologically oriented concept that describes the coping process within an individual's own interactive setting. On a broader social level, these interacting settings are what was previously referred to as Spacerounds.

To these Spacerounds a person brings resources. Resources (see Figure 32) are defined as available attributes. These are divided into five components: time, physical, psychical, social, and repertoires. Time refers to the constant process of change. Based on a person's resources and particular problems time exists for each person in varying quantities. Time is the dynamic consumable change-agent which effects the interactions of the other resources, the character of problems and the way the coping process functions. Time is that limiting commodity available for coping. Physical resources may be divided into personal and nonpersonal. The personal may include: age, sex, race, health, height, weight, etc. Non-personal resources may include attributes which are external to the person such as tools, books, animals, property, clothing, etc. Psychical resources are those personal qualities, principally involving cognitive and motor activities such as: intelligence, personality, education, skills, etc. Social resources are those attributes which refer to a person's relationship to other people such as: sibling position, socio-economic class, social roles, friendship, etc. Repertoire resources refer to those learned behavioral patterns, dependent on interactional experiences with the other four resources, which may be recalled when needed. The repertoire is always in constant interaction with the other resources: it represents both the available response patterns and the transactional mediator between resources (see Figure 32).

Given spacerounds and resources, a person then comes to a problem. A <u>problem</u> is herein defined as a multidimensional external force directed at a person that blocks or interrupts the status and/or the pursuit of needs or goals which then creates physical tensions (strains).

In response to the awareness of a problem, a person begins the coping process (see Figure 34). The <u>coping process</u> has four basic phases: prevention, preparation, action, and reappraisal. These processes may be cognitive, emotional, or behavioral, or may occur in combination with each other.

This process of coping with problems and feeding back the reaffirmation of taking action and being able to control the outcome of one's actions, strengthens the coping repertoire for its next encounter. The process of continually trying to strengthen one's repertoire is termed <u>competence striving</u>. Thus, considering a person's social problems and the coping that ensues, one who has a history of successful experiences with increasingly difficult problems, should logically have coping competences capable of handling increasingly difficult problems. It is posited that this process has a snow-ball effect, such that each successful coping experiences enriches not only the breadth and depth of repertoires, but also shortens the time needed. This process feeds on itself: it desensitizes the threat and emphasizes the reward. As the time from problem start to problem resolution shortens, the importance of threat is diminished and the importance of reward is increased. This transforms the definitions of threats into challenges (see Meichenbaum et al., 1975) so that one begins to seek out new situations which previously may have been defined as problems but now are defined as challenges. It is suggested that with favorable conditions and a favorable repertoire a person is able to cope with his or her problems. The result of these interactions enhances the character of relationships within the spaceround generating norm acceptance and spaceround integration (see Figure 35). Thus, learning to cope within a given spaceround has adaptive significance in terms of being integrated or not.

Thus, this theory suggests that criminal behavior is a function of both a spaceround's integrative process and an individual's coping competence.

Development of the Coping Dimensions

In order to measure the coping responses a list of 15 possible coping dimensions were developed. These were put before a panel of experts made up of psychologists, sociologists and criminologists. Each dimension was explained and discussed. Each expert took the list of dimensions and wrote out definitions for the extremes of each of the dimensions. These definitions were collected and combined into one list with two composite definitions for each dimension. Subsequently this list of fifteen dimensions was reduced to thirteen due to some overlap and ambiguity (see Figure 41). The purpose of these dimensions served as a measurement tool for the coping responses of those persons studied.

Development of the Control Theory Questionnaire

This instrument was based on the theory of Spaceround Integration. This theoretical model suggested a wide range of social structures and relationships which were operationalized in the instrument. The questionnaire also contained items designed to obtain demographic data. This demographic information was needed to establish a pool of data for variables as well as cross verify previously obtained information on each research subject. A small number of additional items were aimed at verifying information that related to coping attitudes.

Development of the Integration Instrument

The main dependant variable in the theory of Spaceround Integration is individual integration. This concept addresses the process whereby persons strive to become synchronized to the spaceround's components. In order to assess or measure this variable an instrument was developed that would ask five key questions within each of five significant spacerounds: family of orientation, family of procreation, work, community, and peers.

Coping/Supervision Study

This primarily methodological coping study focused principally on the postulate:

> The extent to which a person can cope in a given spaceround is proportional to the successful experiences he or she has had with similar problems and the abundance of resources available.

Data Collection

In order to explore the above postulate it was necessary to interview a sample of young German offenders who were or had recently been under supervision (Bewährung). The subjects of this study were eighty-one young male adults (between the ages of 17 and 32 years; with an age range of 15 years; the mean was 23.1 years; the median was 24.5 years and the mode was 22 years), from the state judicial district of Hannover, and had been adjudicated under the German youth laws.

Conclusion

In the composite analysis (see Figure 49), the three factors which clustered the coping dimensions into three groups, Normative, Outcome, and Others, each provided a separate point of reference. Those belonging to the Normative Factor (I), especially the "trait" dimensions 1, 9, and 11, suggested forms of coping responses that were related to behaviors sanctioned by group norms. One might go so far as to say that the three dimensions in this factor suggested behaviors which were idealized by societal norms. The loading of each of these dimensions were quite strong, indicating they were the main contributors for the Normative factor.

Dimensions 2, 4, and 7 consistently found in the Outcome Factor (II), suggested forms of coping responses that were related to efficiency. These three dimensions were both empirically related (according to their loadings) and theoretically similar (especially 4 and 7). The highest loading in the factor analysis (.994) was obtained from the family skit response to dimension 7. This suggests that the family skit provided an ideal problem situation to elicit the success/failure coping response, in comparison to the other skits.

The Others Factor (III) was not as clearly represented by specific dimensions as were Factors I and II. In the composite analysis, dimensions 12 and 13 fell into this third factor. Both these dimensions seemed related to the concept of dealing with other persons.

These findings would suggest that the subjects in this study responded to coping situations in three basic ways: with concern for normative expectations, with a focus toward behavioral outcomes, and with a special orientation to interpersonal coping skills. The Normative Factor explained 22.7 % of the variance (in the aggregate analysis) and contained five dimensions suggesting that normative considerations occupy an important role in the coping phenomena tested in this study. While the theoretical support for the role of norms in the integration process is adequately represented by both the concepts of "norm similarity" and "norm acceptance" found in the Spaceround Integration portion of the Social Coping Model, the role of norms in the coping process needs to be further stressed.

The logical place in the Social Coping Model to emphasize this normative factor would be with regard to viewing norm awareness as generally as a social resource and as a critical component of an individual's coping repertoire. Thus, these data suggest that behaving in normative ways is important in the coping process. Based on these findings, it seems reasonable to say that to behave normatively depends on: the <u>presence of norms</u>, the optimal social climate for becoming <u>aware of norms</u>, the <u>motivation for accepting norms</u>, and the current situational conditions which <u>permit normative behavior</u> to be expressed.

The second factor, the Outcome Factor, even though it explained a much smaller amount of the variance (6.3 %), it also played an important role in the coping process. It implied that the coping responses concerned with Outcomes are discernable. Since this factor was dominated by the Trait Dimensions 2, 4, and 7, the theoretical significance of this factor suggests that it could fall within the realm of individual resources. These data further suggest that the concern for or absence of concern for Outcome plays an important role in the total coping phenomena. This idea fits in well with the Social Coping Model, in that the extent of specific learned skills (in this case - outcome orientations) may figure in with an individual's resources, which then come into play during the actual coping activity and appears to be related to the two opposite coping concepts of Learned Resourcefulness (Meichenbaum, 1973) and Learned Helplessness (Seligman, 1975).

The third factor, the Others Factor, explained 47.7 % of the variance and thus, played the most important role in the coping phenomena. The dimensions (10, 3, 5, 8, and 12) in the aggregate analysis which fell within this factor suggested that together they were responsible for the largest amount of variance. Theoretically, they represent a wide variety of coping skills which seem to be similar. It should be noted that together Factors I, II, and III accounted for 76.7 % of the total variance. This means that 23.3 % of the remaining variance is accounted for by other less pronounced factors.

The mix of Trait and State Dimensions in all three factors suggests the importance of both environmental as well as individual influences in the coping phenomena. This conclusion is not only supported by the Social Coping Model and this research, but is also in keeping with other recent trends in coping research (see Arndt-Pagé et al., 1983, 188). The Social Coping Model incorporates this mix both in the use of the resource concept, which emphasizes that the coping repertoire draws from social, psychic, and physical elements; it also suggests that the spaceround (coping milieu) and the nature of the problem also play an important role in the dynamics of real-life coping (see Dussich and Jacobsen, 1982).

Since the 13 coping dimensions were not specifically designed to measure the extent to which trait or state dimensions came into play, it would be beyond the limits of this study to suggest which type of dimension played the more dominant role in real-life coping. What does seem clear is that both types were present in all four problem situations (skits) and that each problem situation called for a distinctly different pattern of coping dimensions.

A final comment with regard to the correlations of the word count variable and the various coping response variables. While these two variable categories are relatively unimportant, per se, they do provide a measure of external validity. The word count is an <u>objective</u> behavioral measure of the subject's responses to the standard skit. However, the coping scores were derived from the <u>subjective</u> judgements of three raters. It is interesting that the only two dimensions which did not show a significant correlation were the two dimensions Peaceful/Aggressive and Legitimate/Non-legitimate, both of which (according to the composite analysis) also happen to be strong "trait" dimensions in the Normative Factor. If one were to argue that the high number of positive and significant correlations derived from the other dimensions with the total word count was the result of the rater's being subjectively influenced by the quantity of words present in the response texts of each subject, the principle would only be valid if it applied to all 13 dimensions. These two exceptions seem to suggest another rule (also supported by the Social Coping Model's concept of the repertoire and its influence on the coping process): that, while a subject's coping repertoire may logically produce a large number of words as a by-product of its richness, at least for the above two exceptions (9 and 11), the quantity of words seemed to have no apparent influence on the qualitative nature of these two dimensions. Thus, these exceptions seem to prove the validity of the rule.

Success/Failure Study

The major thrust of this sub-study was designed to determine which variables were relevant in distinguishing the differences between success and failure of young parolees. The Social Coping Model was used as the theoretical backdrop for this investigation.

This study focused on coping techniques and the two objective outcomes of parole: success and failure. The purpose was to determine whether those individuals with stronger and more abundant coping skills did better in real-life situations than those with weaker and fewer skills. That is, whether the concept of coping, measured by the 13 coping dimensions of Dussich and Jacobsen (1982) (see Figure 41), was able to differentiate between young parolees who had experienced success and those who had experienced failure. Success was defined as the completion of parole. In contrast, failure was defined as not completing the parole period.

Data Collection

In order to test the twelve research hypotheses a sample of thirty-five youthful offenders who had recently been under parole were measured.

The 35 subjects of this study were (between the ages of 17 and 30 with an age range of 15 years; the mean was 23.1 years; the median was 23.5 years and the mode was 22 years) males from the judicial state district of Hannover, Germany. They were all under parole during the years 1981 and 1982 and had been adjudicated under the German Youth Law.

Conclusions

These results suggested that with regard to the officially defined success and failure subjects used in this study, the more sociological concepts of the Spaceround Integration Model were not as effective in differentiating between the two groups as were the more psychological concepts of the Social Coping Model. Two explanations seem reasonable at this point: either the Spaceround Integration postulates were too broad and not oriented at the individual level enough to be sensitive to the differences, or the general area of social phenomena addressed by the Spaceround Integration Model in fact made little difference when comparing success and failure. That is to say, either (a) the theory was inappropriate, or

(b) social conditions didn't play a major role in distinguishing between success and failure, or (c) both. Hirschi, writing about differences in "delinquent activity between high and low-stake boys" as a result of greater or lesser exposure to criminal influences, suggested that these influences (or what one could call subtle social influences), "are beyond the reach of control theory" (1969, 161). On the other hand it appears that the social coping postulates served as better indicators for distinguishing between the successful and failure subjects. The same points mentioned above, would seem appropriate as explanations for the Social Coping hypotheses, that is (a) the instrument was adequately sensitive, in which case it would follow that (b) the phenomena under investigation were principally psychological in nature, thus (c) both were in effect.

In spite of the acceptance of five null hypotheses for the Spaceround Integration hypotheses, some of the data obtained are worth discussing. In the first two hypotheses the relative importance of spacerounds was investigated. It was found that no significant differences existed; however, the profile which resulted from this analysis showed that both groups of youthful parolees judged their Peers as being relatively <u>less</u> important compared to Work, Community and Family. This finding seemed to support (at least in principle) the statement by Hirschi that "since delinquents are less strongly attached to conventional adults than non-delinquents, they are less likely to be attached to each other" (1969, 140-141). The statement of Friday and Hage (1976) that "As the saliency of the peer groups increases, so too does the probability of delinquency" does not seem to be applicable to the findings of this study. In fact it was found that the successful subjects (reflecting on their adolescence) rated their Peers as significantly more important than the parole failures did. A possible explanation for these findings would be one proposed by Yablonsky where he suggested that the youth who is able to assume constructive social roles is the one who is well socialized. On the other hand the one who "emerges from a social milieu that trains him inadequately for assuming constructive social roles" is the one who has had defective socialization, lacks social feelings and is not capable of having "human feelings of compassion or responsibility for another" (1963, 196). This lack of "trust, warmth, affection or support" with peers was also confirmed by Junger-Tas (1977, 84).

The successful subjects identified Peers as being more important than Family, significantly more than the failures. Speaking of non-delinquents, if Yablonsky's (1963, 196) principle also applied to successful subjects, it might help explain why the successful subjects (prior to their 14th year) identified Peers as more important than Family when compared to the failures. It might be that these successful subjects learned how to develop new relationships outside the Family which then became useful in becoming successful later in life, i.e. during their parole period. Other findings from this study supporting this notion would be that the successful subjects had stronger personal resources, more frequency of contact with members of all spacerounds and less emotional dependency with their Family of Procreation, at Work and in the Community.

The next and perhaps most important Spaceround Integration hypothesis was broken down into five sub-hypotheses, one for each interaction condition tested. The null hypothesis was accepted for all sub-hypotheses except for the Frequency hypothesis. In retrospect it was inappropriate to hypothesize across all spacerounds equally as each produced different findings for the same interaction condition. This realization is especially congruent with the spaceround Peers.

A subsequent hypothesis dealt with meaningful relationships and although the null hypothesis was accepted the data turned up the interesting qualitative finding that prioritization of the most meaningful relationships for successful subjects were, in order of importance, mother, brother, sister, and father, compared to the failure subjects who claimed, in order of importance, father, mother, sister, and grandmother. While Hirschi (1969, 100-107) suggested no differences existed between delinquents and non-delinquents in terms of mother's or father's influence, it is difficult to generalize his findings to our parolees' success/failure findings.

Another important finding, with respect to the Spaceround Integration Model and the distinction between successful and failure subjects, was the data derived from testing the next hypothesis. These data suggested that the extent of a parolee's integration is an important determinant of whether he will be a success or failure. If we operationally define success on parole as an indicator of law-abiding behavior and failure as an indicator of law-breaking behavior, then previous control theory research which equates integration to conformity (see Hirschi 1969; Friday and Halsey 1977; Junger-Tas 1977) would support these findings.

Considering the Social Coping hypotheses, in each instance significant differences were found between the parolees who succeeded and those who failed. The first of these hypotheses focused on resources. In fact the information from the remaining hypotheses are all embodied in this one hypothesis. Using these results two profiles were suggested for the typical parolee who succeeded and for the typical parolee who failed.

These differences suggest not only different individual characteristics, but also different interaction patterns. The successfuls are better integrated especially with regard to having more frequent and positive contacts within conventional spacerounds like their Family of Orientation, Family of Procreation, Work Place, Peers without criminal records, Civil Servants, and Schools. Also they are more resourceful, less helpless and generally have stronger coping skills.

The failures, on the other hand, are more isolated from traditional spacerounds and have their main contacts with Peers (some of which have criminal records) in Community hangouts (sport clubs and pubs, which are also Peer spacerounds). They are also less resourceful, more helpless and generally have weaker and fewer coping skills.

In retrospect, the hypotheses which were derived from the more psychological concepts of coping seemed to yield somewhat more fruitful results in terms of accepting or rejecting the null hypotheses. This observation is not made to suggest the discriminative dominance of one discipline over the other. It is merely mentioned as a categorical observation which is probably more an indictment of our research instruments or methods than anything else.

In spite of the frustratingly low sample size and low response rates, overall, this study fulfilled its primary goal of exploring the social control and social coping differences between parolees who succeeded and parolees who failed within the framework of the Social Coping Model.

Implications

The following comments were drawn from the four studies presented in this report: the Youthful Parolee File-Card Pre-Study, the Parole Problems Pre-Study, the Coping/Supervision Study, and the Success/Failure Study.

Policy

Most of the comments in this section assume the validity of the Social Coping Model. The general policy suggestion which stems from this project would be that an overall approach to the community supervision of offenders, especially those under parole, should take into account the importance of the interaction between situational variables, especially those concerning the family and the parole officer, and individual variables, especially those which focus on real-life coping processes.

The Success/Failure Study showed that most of those who failed parole not only participated less in significant spacerounds but, in those spacerounds where they did participate they had fewer personal contacts than those who succeeded, especially with regard to Family members (both orientation and procreation), Civil Services (parole office, employment office and housing office) and Peers.

These findings suggest that isolation and parole failure are by-products of some common cause (perhaps faulty socialization as suggested by Yablonsky, 1963), or isolation itself as a cause of parole failure (as stressed by Friday and Halsey, 1977), or both. The Spaceround Integration Model stresses the importance of meaningful relationships in the process of becoming well integrated. The Social Coping Model stresses the importance of social resources in successfully dealing with problems. Considering the empirical and theoretical information together suggests that being isolated (the opposite of being integrated into a spaceround) distinguishes between those youth on parole who succeed and those who fail. Thus, a logical recommendation for parole supervisors would be to place major efforts to reduce their clients isolation in all <u>traditional</u> spacerounds. Special attention should be placed on the interaction conditions of Frequency of contact in traditional spacerounds and Norm Similarity in the work spaceround. Use of trained volunteers is recommended to enhance interactions in traditional spacerounds. A further recommendation would be to develop interpersonal skills training programs for use during the offender's pre-release period so as to enhance the post-release establishment and maintenance of meaningful relationships.

The Coping/Supervision Study and the Success/Failure Study, suggest a number of implications with regard to coping. The Success/Failure Study suggests that successful parolees are able to cope significantly better than those who fail. The spaceround that yielded the highest and most significant coping scores for successful parolees was Work Place in response to the "Argument with the Boss" skit. This particular skit was derived from the Parole Problems Pre-study which found that information from previous research, non-parolees and parole supervisors identified the world of work as being the most problematic. Since the young parolees in this study identified work as one of the least problematic areas (see Figure 17), it would seem reasonable to conclude, that for young parolees, recognizing problems at work and knowing how to cope with them plays an important (if not critical) role in successfully completing parole.

One of the five questions in the integration instrument of the Success/Failure Study also focused on the spaceround Work. It asked "At work, when I am together with my colleagues there are never/seldom/sometimes/frequently/always problems". The results showed that the two groups of exparolees responded similarly by saying they seldom had problems. The results of the Parole Problem Pre-study indicated that current parolees also didn't see work as a serious problem area. Considering both these independent findings it would appear that young offenders on parole as well as after parole were relatively unaware of how problematic the work situation was. Among those who also expressed a lack of awareness were successful parolees, who when tested, coped in a significantly better way when actually confronted with a work place problem. Thus, these findings suggest that part of any kind of pre-parole training program should include work problem awareness and resolution skills in its format. Additionally, parole supervisors should receive special training in job crisis intervention techniques. The role of a supervisor in the management of their clients lives should ideally be concerned with those areas that have proven to be critical in the process of becoming successful at Work and in the Family; and, in this role, the supervisor's skill levels should be highly developed.

Research

Since this project was not primarily directed at testing the Spaceround Integration Model or the Social Coping Model (as both models evolved considerably during the course of this project), it would appear reasonable to organize the two models into more formal theoretical statements which could then be empirically tested better. Those areas of the Spaceround Integration Model which appear to warrant special attention are: the extent to which the interaction conditions effect the meaningfulness of relationships, the relative importance of these conditions, and which conditions explain the greatest amount of variance with regard to an individual's integration.

There appears to be a truism in research which says, that which is the most difficult to conduct is usually done the least and is needed the most. In control theory the majority of studies have used the cross sectional approach; however, the nature of much of the theoretical explanations suggest causal links over considerable lengths of time. For example, some of the key concerns deal with the socialization process, the changing importance of meaningful relationships over time, the relative importance of peers over time and the role of interaction conditions over time. These needs beg the question: are longitudinal studies the only logical method for accurately answering these questions. Caplan, in his exhaustive reformulation and testing of Hirschi's control model, makes this same recommendation especially recognizing the "greater capacity to assure the temporal sequence of the independent and dependent variables" in the longitudinal designs (1978, 373).

Another area of delinquency research that continues to elude researchers is the role of peers in delinquency. The Gluecks (1950, 164) noted that delinquency occurs before the selection of companions, while Reckless (1961, 311) claimed that "companionship is one of the most important universal causes of crime and delinquency among males". Throughout the past three decades such control theorists as Hirschi (1969), Hindelang (1973), Thibauld (1974), Tieman (1976), Junger-Tas (1977), Friday and Hage (1976), Caplan (1978), and Dizon (1981) have dealt with this issue with widely different results. In this project it was noted that successful subjects (as adolescents) claimed that Peers/Hangouts had been the most important spaceround for them. Young parolees claimed that peers were the least problematic people they had to deal with; whereas, non-offender youth indicated that peers were somewhat problematic for them. In spite of more frequent contacts, successful parolees had <u>less</u> norm similarity, <u>fewer</u> meaningful relationships and <u>no</u> criminal friends among peers when compared to those who failed parole. As adults both the successes and failures rated Peers as a spaceround with low importance compared to Work, Community, and Family. Thus, it appears that the maze of variables that distinguish between those who are more integrated or those who succeed or, indeed, those who do not become delinquent, are fraught with many subtle complexities that seem to change considerably over that relatively short period of time from adolescence to adulthood. Needless to say, this area of human behavior could greatly benefit from an exhaustive, narrowly focused, longitudinal research effort preferably using a cohort as the main unit of analysis with a recent model of control theory as the theoretical backdrop.

From the theoretical level the link between coping and individual integration is the adaptation to spacerounds. While this link is assumed in both theoretical models, it was not directly tested. Adaptation speaks to the generalized adjustment made in a given setting. The process of <u>becoming</u> adapted through numerous coping events and its relationship to social control would be a logical extension of the present work. It is the conviction of this researcher that only through the inclusion of both coping trait and coping state considerations couched within a social-psychological framework can the full understanding of becoming successful on parole be approached. I am recommending a comprehensive and eclectic model which would take into account a broader perspective than usually found within a single theory. If striving to account for all of the variance of a given phenomenon is one of the key goals of scientific endeavor, then being open to more descriptions of reality should move us closer in that direction.

Junge Erwachsene, die unter Bewährung stehen, und ihr Social Coping

Die Absicht der vorliegenden Untersuchung bestand darin, Informationen über die Fähigkeiten junger Bewährungshilfeprobanden aus dem Großraum Hannover zu erheben und zu analysieren, welche deren Leben unmittelbar nach der Entlassung aus dem Gefängnis betreffen. Das besondere Interesse galt denjenigen Lebensbewältigungstechniken, die in bestimmten Lebensbereichen wie der Familie, dem Arbeitsplatz, mit Nachbarn, unter Freunden und im Umgang mit Behörden einen erfolgreichen Umgang mit Problemen gewährleisten.

Die Bedeutung dieser Arbeit kann in den Erkenntnissen gesehen werden, die sowohl für die verschiedenen Institutionen wichtig sind, die die Probanden auf ihre Bewährungszeit vorbereiten und sie während dieser Zeit begleiten, als auch für diejenigen Entscheidungsträger, die darüber befinden, ob eine Strafe zur Bewährung ausgesetzt wird bzw. ob ein Proband der Bewährungshilfe unterstellt bleibt oder die Bewährung widerrufen wird. Wenn es dieser Untersuchung gelingt, unser heutiges Wissen über das Problemlösungsverhalten von Probanden zu erweitern, könnten diese Informationen von großer Bedeutung für alle Entscheidungen werden, die bezüglich des Bewährungsverlaufs getroffen werden.

Ein weiterer bedeutender Aspekt dieser Untersuchung liegt in der Konzentration auf die Frage nach dem erfolgreichen Verlauf der Bewährungszeit. Den Statistiken aus dem Jahre 1979 über junge Straftäter in Niedersachsen, die nach Verbüßung eines Teils ihrer Strafzeit der Bewährungshilfe unterstellt wurden, ist zu entnehmen, daß 59 % der Probanden die Zeit unter Bewährung erfolgreich beendeten (vgl. Fachserie 10: Rechtspflege; Reihe 5: Bewährungshilfe, Jahrgang 1979, hrsg. vom Statistischen Bundesamt, S. 36-37). Warum sie erfolgreich waren und wie sie die Bewährungszeit ohne Widerruf beendeten, ist noch relativ unerforscht. Dieser Aspekt wurde in der

Bundesrepublik bis jetzt weitgehend unbeachtet gelassen. Fast alle Untersuchungen zu diesem Thema bestanden hauptsächlich in der Herleitung der Ursachen für mißlungene Bewährungsverläufe.

In den letzten zwanzig Jahren beschäftigten sich ca. 82 % der Untersuchungen zur Bewährunghilfe mit Erwachsenen und nur 18 % mit Jugendlichen (vgl. Tab. 1). Vergleicht man die Anzahl der Untersuchungen über Bewährungshilfe unter dem Aspekt der Strafrestaussetzung bzw. Strafaussetzung, so stellt sich heraus, daß sich nur 27,9 % mit der Strafrestaussetzung zur Bewährung, aber 72,1 % mit der Strafaussetzung zur Bewährung befaßten. Das bedeutet, daß der Erwachsene unter Strafrestaussetzung am häufigsten Gegenstand von Untersuchungen war (57,3 %), im Gegensatz dazu befaßten sich nur 3,3 % der Untersuchungen mit Jugendlichen unter Strafrestaussetzung. Aus diesem Grund konzentriert sich diese Untersuchung auf eine vernachlässigte Klientel (den jungen Probanden) mit einem noch weitgehend unerforschten Anliegen (erfolgreiche Beendigung der Bewährungszeit).

In diesem Sinne haben wir uns entschieden zu untersuchen, wie Jugendliche mit Problemen und Schwierigkeiten des Alltages fertig werden. Dieser Prozeß des Verhaltens in Problemsituationen wird als Coping bezeichnet. Der Begriff des Coping ist jedoch zu allgemein, um als Konzept eines eng umgrenzten Forschungsprojektes benutzt zu werden. Eine Person versucht, jedes Problem zu lösen, ob groß oder klein. Wahrscheinlich würde man mit der Gesamtheit des Problemlösungsverhaltens junger Probanden konfrontiert werden. Daher war es notwendig, noch einen weiteren Aspekt des Coping-Phänomens einzuführen.

Der logisch nächste Schritt war, Coping-Modelle in Betracht zu ziehen. Zur grundsätzlichen Frage wurde damit, welche Muster von Coping-Verhalten voneinander unterscheidbar sind: Sind diese Muster sinnvoll? Unterscheiden sie zwischen Probanden, die ihre Bewährung erfolgreich beenden, und denen, die es nicht tun? Werden diese Modelle vom Sozialisationsprozeß beeinflußt und/oder durch bestehende Beziehungen? Wie gruppieren sich diese Muster und werden damit zu einem Teil des individuellen Coping-Repertoires? Bestehen Unterschiede zwischen den Repertoires der Probanden, deren Strafe von Anfang an zur Bewährung ausgesetzt wurde, und denen, deren Strafe bedingt zur Bewährung ausgesetzt wurde? Bestehen Unterschiede zwischen denen, die ihre Bewährung ohne Widerruf beenden, und denen, deren Bewährung widerrufen wurde?

Es entwickelte sich aus der Fragestellung, warum Probanden ihre Bewährung erfolgreich beenden, eine gezielte Untersuchung über Coping-Repertoires und deren Verbindungen mit anderen sozialpsychologischen Variablen.

Die wichtigsten Forschungsfragen

- Existieren Coping-Muster, die zwischen jungen Probanden unterscheiden, die ihre Bewährung erfolgreich beenden, und denen, bei denen ein Widerruf erfolgt?
- Hat die Anzahl bedeutender Beziehungen mit den Mitmenschen einen Einfluß auf die Coping-Muster?
- Hat die Intensität dieser Beziehungen einen Einfluß auf die Coping-Muster?
- Welchen Einfluß haben andere Variablen wie Alter, Erziehung, sozialer Status, die Situation in der Familie und am Arbeitsplatz, Beziehungen zu Peers etc. auf die Coping-Muster?
- Welche Beziehungen gibt es zwischen Coping, Sozialer Integration und anderen sozialen Phänomenen?
- Welche Beziehungen bestehen zwischen Coping und den individuellen Ressourcen?

Eine Voruntersuchung über Probleme während der Bewährungszeit

Die Voruntersuchung konzentrierte sich hauptsächlich auf typische Alltagsprobleme der Probanden. Durchgeführt wurde diese

Untersuchung mit Hilfe explorativer Interviews mit <u>Bewährungshilfeprobanden</u>, mit jungen Erwachsenen etwa gleichen Alters, die <u>nicht</u> unter Bewährung standen, mit <u>Bewährungshelfern</u> sowie mittels Sekundäranalysen einer wissenschaftlichen Untersuchung über kurz vor der Entlassung stehende <u>Erwachsene</u> zum einen und zum anderen den Forschungsergebnissen, die der amerikanischen und deutschen Literatur über Bewährungshilfe entnommen wurden (vgl. Tab. 1). Jede dieser Quellen brachte eine ganze Reihe von Alltagsproblemen hervor, die wir in fünf Bereiche aufteilten: Familie, Behörden, Gemeinschaft, Arbeitsplatz und Peers.

Basierend auf der Häufigkeit, mit der die Probleme genannt wurden, wurden diese Bereiche den Quellen entsprechend zugeordnet. Da dies nur zur Entwicklung eines Coping-Instruments diente, begnügten wir uns mit kleinen Stichproben. Dementsprechend wurden auch keine Schlußfolgerungen gezogen, die über einfache Vergleiche hinausgingen.

Vergleicht man alle Datenquellen miteinander, erhält man verschiedene Problemhierarchien. Für jeden Vergleich wurden drei statistische Tests benutzt: chi-quadrat, tau und phi. Chi-quadrat ist ein Maß, daß für nominal skalierte Daten benutzt wird, um aufzuzeigen, ob Beobachtungen sich von erwarteten Verteilungen unterscheiden. Tau ist ein Korrelationskoeffizient für ordinal skalierte Daten (nach Kendall). Der Kontingenz-Koeffizient phi ist ein Ähnlichkeitsmaß für nominal skalierte Daten.

Ein theoretischer Überblick

Das theoretische Konzept dieses Projektes baut auf einer Verbindung der vorwiegend experimental-psychologischen Untersuchungen über Coping-Techniken (zumeist auf der kognitiven Ebene) und der soziologischen Untersuchungen zur sozialen Kontrolle auf. Die wichtigsten theoretischen Gesichtspunkte der vorliegenden Untersuchung sind:

a) <u>Coping</u> ist den <u>Lernprinzipien</u> unterworfen. Das sind bestimmte, empirisch hergeleitete Prinzipien, die den allgemeinen Charakter des Lernens erklären, oder die funktionellen Beziehungen zwischen "bestimmten vorrangigen Bedingungen und Veränderungen einer Aufgabe" (English u. English, 1958). Da sich das Projekt größtenteils mit der Beantwortung der Frage beschäftigt, was Menschen tun (im Gegensatz zu dem, was sie denken), und mit den Bedingungen, unter denen sie handeln (als Reaktion auf Stimuli aus ihrer Umwelt), fällt dieser Ansatz zum Teil in den Bereich des Neo-Behaviorismus (Bandura u. Walters, 1959; Hastorf, 1965, S. 268-284; Henker, 1964).

b) Es wurde der Versuch gemacht, durch Anwendung einer Reihe von <u>Coping-Dimensionen</u> (vgl. im weiteren die Diskussion in Kap. 4.4.3 und 4.4.4) spezielle Muster zu identifizieren, die in vielen Situationen wiederkehren. Noch zutreffender wären sie als Coping-Prinzipien zu bezeichnen, die entweder als vorbereitende oder reaktive Handlungen auslegbar sind; und sie können kognitiven oder behavioralen Charakter besitzen.

c) Das <u>Coping-Repertoire</u> ist ein Konzept, das entwickelt wurde, um die Konstellation der Coping-Techniken einer Person darzustellen. Dies bedeutet, daß diese Repertoires identifiziert, gemessen und klassifiziert werden können und daß sie unter der Bevölkerung variieren. Von primärer Bedeutung ist auch die Art, in der die Coping-Techniken eingestuft werden, und der Umfang, in dem diese Repertoires von anderen sozialen Phänomenen beeinflußt werden.

d) <u>Bedeutende Beziehungen</u> sind eindeutig ein soziologisches Konzept, das aus den Wurzeln des modernen soziologischen Denkens entstanden ist, speziell aus den Traditionen des symbolischen Interaktionismus', Behaviorismus' und aus den Konzepten von Primär-Gruppen, der Selbsteinschätzung und des Signifikanter Anderen (Cooley, 1902; Dewey, 1930; Mead, 1934; Blumer, 1969). Das hier gebrauchte Konzept der bedeutenden Beziehungen geht zurück auf die kürzlich erschienene Arbeit von Friday u. Hage (1976). Sie benutzten den Begriff "intimate role relationships" (entnommen aus Marwell u. Hage, 1970). Dieses Konzept der Signifikanz oder Vertrautheit wurde von ihnen mit den Bezeichnungen "Wichtigkeit", "Bedeutsamkeit", "Integration" und "Quantität der Aktivitäten" erfaßt; es galt als Versuch, die Natur der Rollenbeziehungen zu charakterisieren. Nach Auffassung des Autors erfaßt der Terminus "bedeutende Beziehungen" den Sinn der symbolischen Interaktion besser.

e) Die Soziale Integration ist, wie bereits erwähnt, ein umfangreiches soziologisches Konzept (ausgehend von Durkheim, 1951), das für Jugendkriminalität in der ganzen Welt anwendbar ist; es bezieht sich darauf, wie Menschen in die herrschenden Normen der Gesellschaft eingegliedert werden. Die hauptsächlichen Lebensbereiche für die Sozialisation sind Familie, Schule, Arbeitsplatz, Gemeinschaft und Peers. Wir wählten diese Orientierung, weil als gegeben vorausgesetzt werden kann, daß das Erlernen von Coping-Techniken ein Teil des Sozialisationsprozesses ist (Friday, 1981a; Thibaut u. Kelly, 1959).

f) Was (im Hinblick auf seinen Einfluß) für ein Individuum in einem Lebensbereich wichtig ist, hängt von der Bedeutung der wichtigsten interaktiven Komponenten Menschen, Objekte, Ort, Ideen und Zeit ab. Das Repertoire einer Person entwickelt sich durch den Prozeß der Interaktion zwischen diesen fünf Basiskomponenten. In der Arena der Interaktionen (Spacerounds) wird man ständig mit Alternativen konfrontiert, die sich um die Frage drehen, wie man mit einem speziellen Problem fertig wird. Die Motivationen und die Zwänge, die diesen Entscheidungsprozeß beeinflussen, sind von großem Interesse für die vorliegende Untersuchung.

Ein Überblick über Coping

Coping bezieht sich auf Dinge, die Menschen tun, um zu verhindern, daß sie durch Spannungen und Belastungen verletzt werden (Pearlin u. Schooler, 1978, S. 2: "things that people do to avoid being harmed by life-strains"). Dem Begriff Coping entsprechen eine Vielzahl eng miteinander verbundener Konzepte wie Beherrschung (mastery), Abwehr (defense) und Anpassung (adaptation) (White, 1974). Die schützende Funktion wird auf drei zentralen Wegen aktiviert: über die Veränderung der Gründe, die das Problem hervorrufen, über die kognitive Kontrolle der Definition des Problems, so daß der daraus resultierende Druck neutralisiert wird, und über das Setzen von erträglichen Grenzen emotionaler Reaktionen auf Probleme (Pearlin u. Schooler, 1978, S. 2).

Die Coping-Forschung hat in den letzten 20 Jahren ständig an Bedeutung gewonnen, erst recht seit der frühen Arbeit von Lois Murphy ("The Widening World of Childhood", 1962). Sie fand heraus, daß es hauptsächlich drei Schritte sind, die den Coping-Prozeß charakterisieren: die Vorbereitungsphase, die Aktionsphase (Coping) und die Aufbereitungsphase (Secondary Coping). Vier Jahre später identifizierte Richard S. Lazarus in seinem Buch "Psychological Stress and the Coping Process" (1966) ähnliche Muster für das Coping von Erwachsenen. Heute steht Coping im Mittelpunkt der Streßforschung. Eine der ersten wichtigen Überlegungen bei der Untersuchung des Coping-Verhaltens ist die Bedeutung der Entwicklung einer Taxonomie von Stressoren. Bei dieser Vorgehensweise könnte der Weg zur Kontrolle der biologischen, ökologischen, psychologischen und sozialen Bedingungen von Streß erleichtert werden (Prystav, 1979, S. 297).

Soziologische Coping-Dimensionen wurden nur in einem sehr begrenztem Ausmaß berücksichtigt (Blath, Dillig u. Frey, 1980; Pearlin u. Schooler, 1978). Dabei wurden behavioristische bis soziale Gruppen-Perspektiven eingeführt. Die Arbeit mit den sozialen und den Verhaltensanteilen des Coping wurde als ernsthaft unterentwickelt erkannt (Prystav, 1979, S. 297; Pearlin u. Schooler, 1978, S. 2).

Vor der Erörterung der Techniken oder Charakteristika des Coping ist es zwingend notwendig anzuerkennen, daß die sozialpsychologische Lebensbedingungen unter denen die Coping-Techniken Anwendung finden, hauptsächlich die folgenden beiden sind: die _sozialen Ressourcen_ und die _psychologischen Ressourcen_. Diese zwei Begriffe befassen sich damit, was einer Person zur Verfügung steht, um Coping-Techniken bzw. ein Coping-Repertoire zu entwickeln.

Vermutlich läßt sich die Literatur über Coping adäquat mittels der drei Coping-Phasen gliedern, die Murphy (1962), Lazarus (1966) und andere (Janis, 1958; Mandler, 1962; Ax, 1964; Schachter, 1966; Arnold, 1970; Glass u. Singer, 1972) im allgemeinen benutzten, um den Coping-Prozeß - wie oben erwähnt - zu beschreiben.

Für die _Vorbereitungsphase_ stellten Meichenbaum u.a. (1975) fest, daß der Coping-Prozeß größtenteils antizipatorischer Natur ist und vor einer Konfrontation mit Bedrohung oder Streß in Gang gesetzt wird. Die Ergebnisse der Mehrzahl dieser Art von Untersuchungen wiesen auf eine enorme Variation der Fähigkeiten und des Stils hin, mit denen Menschen mit Streß fertig werden. Sich auf Streßsituationen vorzubereiten oder dafür zu proben, nennt Janis "Work of Worrying" (1965). Dieser Prozeß des "Sich-Sorgens" macht den Weg frei für die Problembewältigung oder die Selbstbestätigung. Meichenbaum (1973) bezeichnete diesen Prozeß als "Learned Resourcefulness".

In der Coping-Phase selbst (der Phase aktiven Handelns) existiert eine unbegrenzte Zahl von Handlungsmöglichkeiten. Lazarus u.a. (1974) unterschieden zwischen zwei Coping-Methoden: direktes Handeln und intrapsychische (Re-)Aktion. Dies kann frei übersetzt werden in Verhalten einerseits und kognitiver Auseinandersetzung andererseits.

In der Phase der Aufarbeitung (Secondary Coping) wird der Versuch gemacht, das Feedback zu verarbeiten, das man als Ergebnis der Coping-Phase erhält, indem man eine Vielzahl der Möglichkeiten durchprobierte, die im Umgang mit Streß genutzt werden können.

Kontrolltheorie

Die vier wichtigsten soziologischen Traditionen, die in den USA zur Delinquenz entwickelt wurden, waren die Druck-Theorien, die Theorien der kulturellen Devianz, der Labeling-Ansatz und die Kontrolltheorie. Die Druck-Theorien (auch Anomie-Theorie) besagen, daß eine Person zur Delinquenz getrieben wird, um legitime Bedürfnisse zu befriedigen, die mittels Konformität nicht erlangt werden. Das möglicherweise beste Beispiel für die Druck-Theorie ist das, wofür Robert K. Merton in seinem Buch "Social Theory and Social Structure" (1957) eintritt. Die Theorien der kulturellen Devianz besagen, daß Delinquenz eine Mittelklasse-Perspektive besitzt, die Abweichung als Konformität innerhalb eines anderen Normensystems bezeichnet. Eine der klassischen kulturellen Devianztheorien wurde von Edwin H. Sutherland vorgelegt und ist als "Differential Association" (1939) bekannt.

Die Kontrolltheorien besagen, daß Delinquente unmoralische Menschen sind, deren Bindungen an die Gesellschaft zerstört sind. Die expliziteste Aussage dieser theoretischen Tradition machte Travis Hirschi (1969) mit der Veröffentlichung seines Buches "Causes of Delinquency". Von den oben erwähnten vier Betrachtungsweisen scheint die Kontrolltheorie die soziale Realität delinquenten Verhaltens am ehesten zu erfassen. Ausführliche Diskussionen zur Kontrolltheorie finden sich bei Kornhauser (1973), Caplan (1978), Becker (1980), Friday (1980a), Weitekamp (1980) und Dussich u. Jacobsen (1982).

Weitere Anmerkungen zur Kontrolltheorie

In ihren Entwicklungen der Kontrolltheorie beschränkten sich sowohl Hirschi als auch Friday bei dem Erklärungsversuch der Jugendkriminalität zunächst auf die Antagonismen des konformen/non-konformen Verhaltens. Die eigentliche Bedeutung besteht darin, daß Delinquenz aufhört, ein Problem zu sein, sobald Konformität erreicht ist. Kontrolltheorien sollten jedoch über das Kriterium des non-konformen Verhaltens hinausgehen. Eine Theorie, die versucht, kriminelles Verhalten zu erklären, muß auch in der Lage sein, nicht-kriminelles Verhalten zu erklären. Der Begriff "kriminell" ist ein juristischer Terminus, der ein spezifisches Verhalten unter spezifischen Bedingungen bezeichnet. Der wichtigste Teil der Begriffe "kriminelles Verhalten" oder "delinquentes Verhalten" ist das Wort Verhalten. Eine Verhaltenstheorie sollte sich vorrangig mit dem gesamten Phänomen des Verhaltens befassen, statt sich durch moralische oder juristische Bedingungen ablenken zu lassen oder durch professionelle Disziplinen gebunden zu sein.

Bis jetzt befaßten sich Kontrolltheoretiker hauptsächlich mit delinquentem Verhalten, und dies zumeist aus soziologischer Perspektive. Dabei fanden einige Annahmen bislang noch keine Berücksichtigung: die Bedeutung sowohl physischer als auch kognitiver Unterschiede; der Einfluß von Ort und Zeit; das Verhalten Erwachsener und nicht-delinquenter Jugendlicher; die Unterscheidung zwischen Rolle und Beziehung; und schließlich die Bedeutung der individuellen Wahrnehmung konkreter und unmittelbarer Faktoren im Kontrast zum Einfluß sozialer Strukturen und ihrer Prozesse.

Was die Kontrolltheorie bislang erreicht hat, ist ein wichtiger Beitrag zum besseren Verständnis externaler sozialer Einflüsse auf das Verhalten. Wir vermuten, daß dies nicht genug ist. Hirschi selbst konstatierte, daß die kriminologische Forschung ihre Theorien zu lange auf der Basis ökologischer Daten aufstellte (1969, S. 15). Deshalb wird eine Erweiterung in den folgenden Bereichen versucht.

Spaceround Integration: Eine Erweiterung der Kontrolltheorie

Dieser Vorschlag ist ein Versuch, Verhalten in einer mehr phänomenologischen Weise zu kennzeichnen (vgl. Dussich u. Jacobsen, 1982). Er berücksichtigt die Makro- und Mikroprozesse soziologischer Strukturen und deren Einflüsse auf das Verhalten. Der Terminus Spaceround (vgl. Abb. 30) repräsentiert den Versuch, einen Begriff zu finden für die vielschichtige Qualität sozialpsychologischer Ereignisse für bestimmte Menschen an einem bestimmten Ort mit einzigartigen Ideen mit individuellen Objekten zu einem bestimmten Zeitpunkt. Der Begriff der Spacerounds wurde von einem ähnlichen Konzept abgeleitet, und zwar von dem der "Placerounds", ursprünglich entwickelt von John Lofland in seinem Buch "Deviance and Identity" (1969). Alle Spacerounds haben fünf hauptsächliche Dimensionen: Menschen, Objekte, Orte, Ideen und die Zeit.

Signifikante Spacerounds beziehen sich auf idealtypische soziale Phänomene, die eine besondere Bedeutung für das Individuum haben, und die durch solche makrostrukturellen Artefakte beeinflußt werden wie unterschiedliche politische Systeme, unterschiedliche Kulturen, unterschiedliche Regierungen etc. sowie durch solche mikrostrukturellen Artefakte wie Gruppen, Individuen, Gefühle, Ideen etc. Diese Spacerounds können traditionelle (Familie, Schule, Kirche) oder nicht-traditionelle (Heim, Kibbuz, Gefängnis etc.) Situationen sein. Beispiele für allgemeinere signifikante Spacerounds sind: Elternhaus/Familie, Hang-out/Peers, Schule/Schüler-Lehrer, Arbeitsplatz/Kollegen und Gemeinschaft/Nachbarn. Indem wir das Adjektiv "signifikant" hinzufügen, begrenzen wir die Spacerounds auf diejenigen Situationen, die für Individuen wichtig sind und die dem traditionellen Terminus "soziale Institution" ähneln. Jeder Spaceround hat seine eigenen einzigartigen Normen. Diese Normen zeigen an, wie die Spaceround-Komponenten miteinander interagieren, und definieren jeweils, welches Verhalten angemessen ist und welches unangemessen ist.

Bedeutende Beziehungen repräsentieren die Bindungen zwischen einer Person und anderen. Diese Beziehungen stellen die interaktive Verknüpfung innerhalb jedes Spacerounds dar. Mittels dieser Beziehungen werden die Normen weitergegeben und erhalten Allgemeingültigkeit. Das Ausmaß der Bedeutung dieser Beziehungen bestimmt den Grad der Konformität und Integration. Wir sind der Meinung, daß Objekte genau so funktionieren wie Interaktionspartner und daß von ihnen ebenfalls eine interaktive Leistung ausgeht. In diesem Zusammenhang werden wir uns jedoch vorrangig auf die Beziehung Mensch-zu-Mensch konzentrieren, von denen wir annehmen wollen, daß sie hauptsächlich von sieben Interaktionsbedingungen abhängig sind oder beeinflußt werden: Kontakthäufigkeit, Dauer der Beziehung, Selbstöffnung, Kathexis, Abhängigkeit, Ähnlichkeit von Normen und Überschneidungen.

In den traditionellen soziologischen Begriffen bezieht sich Integration auf einen sozialen Prozeß, der unterschiedliche soziale Elemente verschmelzt (Fairchild, 1968, S. 159). Wenn wir von individueller Integration in einen gegebenen Spaceround sprechen, beziehen wir uns auf einen Prozeß, durch den Personen lernen, mit den Komponenten dieses Spacerounds umzugehen und sich auf diese Weise mit dessen Komponenten zu synchronisieren*. Wenn Personen in einen bestimmten Spaceround

---

* Hierbei bezeichnet Synchronisation die funktionale Kompatabilität, die dann unter den Komponenten besteht, wenn sie etwa zur gleichen Zeit miteinander wirken

gut integriert sind, dann fügen sie sich ein oder passen sich an.

Daraus wird die Grundhypothese dieses theoretischen Modells abgeleitet:

> Wenn in einem gegebenen Spaceround die Interaktionsbedingungen Kontakthäufigkeit, Dauer der Beziehung, Selbstöffnung, Kathexis, Abhängigkeit, Ähnlichkeit von Normen und Überschneidungen in hohem Maße bestehen, so existieren bedeutende Beziehungen, so daß die individuelle Integration ein maximales Ausmaß annimmt.

Auf der anderen Seite ist die Spaceround-Integration eine Bedingung des Spaceround selbst. Das beinhaltet die Synchronisation und Koordination der fünf veränderlichen Spaceround-Komponenten Menschen, Objekte, Orte, Ideen und Zeit. Das Ergebnis dieser hohen Spaceround-Integration ist ein Minimum an Konflikten und ein Maximum an Harmonie. Das logische Gegenstück zu diesem Terminus ist die Spaceround-Dysintegration, die einen Zustand beschreibt, bei dem die Komponenten des Spaceround nicht für ein gemeinsames Ziel arbeiten und daher große Konflikte herrschen. Zuletzt ließen sich Spacerounds vorstellen, die von gesellschaftlichen Aktivitäten isoliert sind; dies bezeichnen wir als Spaceround-Isolation. Weder gehört ein solcher Spaceround selbst zur Gemeinschaft noch trägt er direkt zu den Zielen der Gemeinschaft bei.

Das Gegenteil der individuellen Integration ist die individuelle Isolation. Isolation beinhaltet die Entfremdung von der Interaktion innerhalb eines gegebenen Spaceround, von dem das Individuum ein Teil ist. Dieser Zustand ist durch eine Trennung von den meisten alltäglichen Spaceround-Aktivitäten gekennzeichnet. Die extremste Form der Isolation beinhaltet: sehr wenige Kontakte von kurzer Dauer, keine Selbstöffnung, deutliche Unterschiede zwischen Normen, keine Kathexis, ein Mangel an Abhängigkeit und keine Überschneidungen. Individuelle Dysintegration repräsentiert den Status einer Person, deren Anwesenheit Probleme hervorruft - jemand, der sich nicht anpassen kann oder will, der nicht dazu paßt. Diese Person hätte eine geringe Anzahl an Kontakten von unterschiedlicher Dauer, begrenzte Selbstöffnung und Kathexis, teilweise abweichende Normen, eine geringe Abhängigkeit und wenige Überschneidungen.

Das theoretische Modell des Social Coping

Dieses Modell stellt einen Versuch dar, zwei theoretische Wurzeln (eine neuere soziologische Entwicklung der Kontrolltheorie und die Auslegung eines psychologischen Konzeptes, der Coping-Theorie) in einem einheitlichen sozialpsychologischen Konzept miteinander zu verbinden; es soll als "Modell des Social Coping" bezeichnet werden. Diese Theorie versucht zu erklären, wie Individuen mittels der Auseinandersetzung mit Problemen lernen, sich Normen anzupassen und damit letztlich in ihren spezifischen sozialen Raum integriert werden.

Das Konzept, das die Bühne dafür hergibt und die sozialpsychologische Umwelt für das Coping beschreibt, ist das Coping-Milieu (vgl. Abb. 31). Das Coping-Milieu ist ein phänomenologisch orientiertes Konzept, das den Coping-Prozeß eingebettet in die Interaktions-Gegebenheiten des Individuums darstellt. Auf einer umfassenderen sozialen Ebene repräsentieren diese Gegebenheiten das, was oben als signifikante Spacerounds bezeichnet worden war.

In diese signifikanten Spacerounds bringt eine Person ihre Ressourcen ein. Ressourcen werden definiert als die jemandem zur Verfügung stehenden Eigenschaften (vgl. Abb. 32). Sie sind in fünf Komponenten unterteilt: Zeit, physische, psychische und soziale Eigenschaften sowie das Repertoire.
Die Zeit bezieht sich auf den permanenten Prozeß der Veränderungen. Sie existiert für jede Person in unterschiedlichem

Ausmaß, abhängig davon, welche Ressourcen und spezifischen Probleme eine Person aufweist. Zeit ist das dynamische, verbrauchbare Medium für Veränderungen, die die Beziehungen zwischen den übrigen Ressourcen, den Charakter des Problems und die Art und Weise, in der der Coping-Prozeß funktioniert, beeinflußt. Die Zeit wird damit zu einem knappen Mittel, das nur begrenzt für das Coping zur Verfügung steht.
Physische Ressourcen können in persönliche und nicht-persönliche Ressourcen unterteilt werden. Persönliche Ressourcen umfassen: Alter, Geschlecht, Rasse, Gesundheit, Größe, Gewicht, etc. Nicht-persönliche Ressourcen beinhalten Attribute, die außerhalb einer Person liegen, wie z.B. Werkzeug, Bücher, Tiere, Eigentum, Kleidung, etc.
Psychische Ressourcen sind persönliche Qualitäten, die im allgemeinen kognitive und motorische Aktivitäten einschließen wie: Intelligenz, Persönlichkeit, Erziehung, Fähigkeiten etc.
Soziale Ressourcen sind solche Attribute, die sich auf die Beziehung einer Person zu einer anderen Person beziehen, wie: Stellung unter Geschwistern, sozio-ökonomische Schicht, soziale Rollen, Freundschaften etc.
Die Ressource Repertoire bezieht sich auf erlernte Verhaltensmuster, abhängig von den sich gegenseitig beeinflussenden Erfahrungen mit den anderen vier Ressourcen, die, wenn nötig, abgerufen werden können. Das Repertoire steht in ständiger Interaktion mit den anderen Ressourcen: es repräsentiert sowohl die verfügbaren Reaktionsmuster als auch den transaktionalen Mittler zwischen den Ressourcen (vgl. Abb. 32).

Mit diesen Spacerounds und Ressourcen begegnet eine Person einem Problem. Ein Problem wird hierbei als eine multidimensionale äußere Kraft definiert, die sich auf eine Person richtet und dessen Zustand blockiert oder unterbricht und/oder dessen Streben nach Bedürfnissen oder Zielen stört, so daß eine Spannung entsteht.

In dem Augenblick, in dem eine Person eines Problems gewahr wird, beginnt der Coping-Prozeß (vgl. Abb. 34). Der Coping-Pro-

zeß besteht aus vier Phasen: der Prävention, der Vorbereitung, der Aktion und der Verarbeitung. Diese Prozesse können kognitiv, emotional oder behavioral sein oder aber eine Kombination der drei Auftretensformen.

Der Prozeß der Problemlösung, der Rückmeldung einer Handlung und der Fähigkeit, das Ergebnis einer Handlung zu kontrollieren, stärkt das Coping-Repertoire für die nächste Begegnung mit einem Problem. Der ständige Versuch, das Repertoire zu stärken, wird als _Streben nach Kompetenz_ bezeichnet. Betrachtet man die sozialen Probleme einer Person und das darauf folgende Coping, so sollte jemand, der auf eine Reihe erfolgreicher Erfahrungen mit zunehmend schwierigeren Problemen zurückblicken kann, logischerweise die Kompetenz zum Coping erworben haben und fähig sein, weiterhin auch schwierigere Probleme anzugehen. Es wird postuliert, daß dieser Prozeß einen Schneeball-Effekt in der Form besitzt, daß jede erfolgreiche Coping-Erfahrung nicht nur den Umfang und die Tiefe des Repertoires erweitert, sondern auch die dafür benötigte Zeit verkürzt. Dieser Prozeß beruht auf sich selbst: er macht unempfindlich für Bedrohungen und hebt die Belohnung hervor. Wenn sich die Zeit vom Auftreten des Problems bis zur Lösung verkürzt, verringert sich die Bedeutung der Bedrohung und die Bedeutung der Belohnung nimmt zu. Dadurch wird eine Bedrohung in Herausforderungen umdefiniert (Meichenbaum u.a. 1975), so daß man beginnt, neue Situationen zu suchen, die vorher als Problem definiert wurden, jetzt aber als Herausforderung betrachtet werden. Es liegt nahe, daß eine Person unter günstigen Bedingungen und mit einem günstigen Repertoire fähig ist, mit ihren Problemen fertig zu werden. Das Ergebnis dieses Prozesses betont den Charakter der Beziehungen innerhalb eines Spaceround, wenn er Norm-Akzeptanz und Spaceround-Integration fördert (vgl. Abb. 35). Auf diese Weise gewinnt das Erlernen der Fähigkeit, in einem gegebenen Spaceround Probleme zu lösen, Bedeutung in dem Sinne, daß die individuelle Integration besteht oder nicht.

Dieses theoretische Modell schlägt also vor, kriminelles Verhalten als eine Funktion sowohl des Integrationsprozesses in einen Spaceround als auch der individuellen Coping-Kompetenz zu verstehen.

Die Entwicklung von Coping-Dimensionen

Um das Coping-Verhalten zu messen, wurde eine Liste von 15 möglichen Coping-Dimensionen entwickelt. Diese Liste wurde einem Expertengremium vorgelegt, das aus Psychologen, Soziologen und Kriminologen bestand. Jede Dimension wurde erläutert und diskutiert. Alle Experten übernahmen die Liste der Dimensionen und entwickelten Definitionen für die Extremwerte jeder Dimension, so daß schließlich alle Dimensionen durch ihre beiden Pole gekennzeichnet wurden. Nachträglich wurde die Zahl der Dimensionen wegen einiger Überschneidungen und Mehrdeutigkeiten auf dreizehn reduziert (vgl. Abb. 41). Diese 13 Dimensionen dienten als Meßinstrument für die Antworten der Probanden im Coping-Teil.

Entwicklung des Fragebogens zur Kontrolltheorie

Dieser Fragebogen baute auf die Theorie der Spaceround-Integration auf. Dieses theoretische Modell legt eine Vielzahl sozialer Strukturen und Zusammenhänge nahe, die in den Fragebogen eingearbeitet wurden. Der Fragebogen enthielt auch Items zu einigen demographischen Daten der Probanden, die benötigt wurden, um einen Datensatz zu erstellen, in dem vorher erhaltene Informationen abgesichert werden konnten. Eine kleine Zahl zusätzlicher Items zielte darauf, die Coping-Einstellungen zu validieren.

Entwicklung des Instrumentes zur Integration

Die wichtigste abhängige Variable in der Theorie zur Spaceround-Integration ist die individuelle Integration. Die beschriebene Konzeption richtet sich auf den Prozeß, durch den Personen versuchen, synchron mit den übrigen Komponenten eines Spaceround zu werden. Um diese Variable zu umreißen und zu messen, wurde ein Instrument entwickelt, das fünf Schlüsselfragen zu jeder der fünf signifikanten Spacerounds enthielt: Herkunftsfamilie, Prokreationsfamilie, Arbeitsplatz, Gemeinschaft und Peers.

Die Untersuchung über Coping und Bewährungshilfe

Diese vorrangig methodologische Untersuchung über Coping thematisiert im Prinzip die folgenden Hypothese:

> Das Ausmaß, in dem eine Person in einem gegebenen Spaceround zurechtkommt, ist proportional zu den erfolgreichen Erfahrungen, die sie mit ähnlichen Problemen gemacht hat sowie dem Umfang der verfügbaren Ressourcen.

Datenerhebung

Um die oben genannte Hypothese zu untersuchen, war es notwendig, eine Stichprobe junger Straffälliger zu befragen, die unter Bewährung standen oder vor kurzem noch gestanden hatten. Die Probanden der Untersuchung waren 81 männliche junge Erwachsene im Alter zwischen 17 und 32 Jahren (das Durchschnittsalter betrug 23,1 Jahre; Median: 24,5 Jahre; Modus: 22 Jahre); alle stammten aus dem Landgerichtsbezirk Hannover und waren nach dem Jugendstrafrecht verurteilt worden.

Zusammenfassung

In der Zusammenfassung der Datenanalyse (vgl. Abb. 49) ergaben sich drei Cluster von Coping-Dimensionen, die diese in die Faktoren "Normorientierung im Verhalten", "Streben nach Ergebnissen" und "Die Anderen" gruppierten. Die Dimensionen, die zum Faktor I (Normorientierung im Verhalten) gehörten, speziell die "Trait"-Dimensionen 1, 9 und 11, betreffen verschiedene Formen der Coping-Reaktion, die in Beziehung mit dem durch Gruppennormen sanktionierten Verhalten stehen. Man kann sogar so weit gehen zu sagen, daß die drei Dimensionen dieses Faktors Verhaltensweisen vorgeben, die in den gesellschaftlichen Normen idealisiert werden. Die Ladungswerte jeder dieser drei Dimensionen war sehr stark, zeigten also die Richtung des Faktors I (Normorientierung im Verhalten) an.

Die Dimensionen 2, 4 und 7, die durchweg im Faktor II (Streben nach Ergebnissen) zu finden waren, stellen Formen des Coping-Verhaltens dar, die zur Leistung(sfähigkeit) gehören. Diese drei Dimensionen waren sowohl empirisch (hinsichtlich ihrer Ladungswerte) als auch theoretisch ähnlich (speziell 4 und 7). Die höchste Ladung in der Faktorenanalyse wies Dimension 7 im Lebensbereich Familie auf (.994). Das läßt vermuten, daß die Familie eine ideale Problemsituation bietet, eine erfolgsorientierte/mißerfolgsorientierte Antwort ans Licht zu bringen - eher noch als andere soziale Räume.

Der Faktor III (die Anderen) wurde durch die entsprechenden Dimensionen nicht so deutlich abgebildet wie die Faktoren I und II. Vor allem die Dimensionen 12 und 13 luden auf dem dritten Faktor; beide Dimensionen schienen mit dem Konzept des Umgangs mit anderen Personen in Beziehung zu stehen.

Diese Ergebnisse legen nahe, daß die Probanden der Untersuchung hauptsächlich auf drei Arten mit Alltagsproblemen umgehen: zum einen in Hinblick auf <u>normative Erwartungen</u>, zum zweiten gezielt <u>am Ergebnis orientiert</u> und schließlich ausgerichtet auf <u>zwischenmenschliche Coping-Fähigkeiten</u>. Der Faktor I (Normorientierung im Verhalten) erklärte 22,7 % der Varianz (über alle 4 Skits hinweg) und umfaßte fünf Dimensionen, die besagten, daß normative Erwägungen eine wichtige Rolle spielen in bezug auf das hier untersuchte Coping-Phänomen. Theoretische Unterstützung findet die Rolle der Normen im Integrationsprozeß sowohl durch das Konzept der "Ähnlichkeit der Normen" als auch durch das Prinzip der "Normakzeptanz" im Teil der Spaceround Integration des Social Coping Modells; jedoch ist es nötig, auf die Rolle der Normen im Coping-Prozeß noch näher einzugehen.

Für die Betonung dieses Faktors der Normorientierung würde der geeignete Platz im Social Coping Modell das allgemeine Normenbewußtsein darzustellen, und zwar sowohl als eine soziale Ressource als auch als eine der kritischen Komponenten des individuellen Coping-Repertoire. Auf diese Weise deuten die Daten an, daß normengerechtes Verhalten wichtig für den Coping-Prozeß ist. Stützt man sich auf diese Erkenntnisse, scheint es naheliegend zu sagen, daß normgerechtes Verhalten von folgenden Voraussetzungen abhängt: das Vorhandensein der Normen, ein optimales soziales Klima für die Wahrnehmung der Normen, die Motivation, Normen zu akzeptieren, sowie die gerade herrschenden Bedingungen, die es erlauben, normatives Verhalten auszudrücken.

Obwohl Faktor II (Streben nach Ergebnissen) einen sehr viel geringeren Teil der Varianz aufklärte (6,3 %), spielt er ebenfalls eine sehr wichtige Rolle im Coping-Prozeß. Er besagt, daß Coping-Reaktionen unter dem Aspekt der Orientierung an den Ergebnissen voneinander unterscheidbar sind. Da die "Trait"-Dimensionen 2, 4 und 7 die Richtung dieses Faktors angeben, könnte seine theoretische Bedeutung aus dem Bereich der individuellen Ressourcen abgeleitet werden. Die Ergebnisse lassen ferner darauf schließen, daß das Streben oder aber das mangelnde Streben nach Ergebnissen eine wichtige Rolle für das gesamte Coping-Phänomen spielt. Diese Gedanken entsprechen recht gut dem Modell des Social Coping, in dem das Ausmaß der spezifischen gelernten Fähigkeiten (hier: der Orientierung am Ergebnis) in die individuellen Ressourcen einer Person einfließen; diese werden dann während der eigentlichen Coping-Aktivität ins Spiel gebracht und scheinen mit den beiden gegensätzlichen Coping-Konzepten "Learned Resourcefulness" (Meichenbaum, 1973) und "Learned Helplessness" (Seligman, 1975) in Beziehung zu stehen.

Der dritte Faktor (die Anderen) erklärte 47,7 % der Varianz und spielte somit die wichtigste Rolle im Coping-Phänomen. Die Dimensionen (10, 3, 5, 8 und 12) die diesen Faktor beschreiben legen nahe, daß sie gemeinsam für den größten Teil der Varianz verantwortlich waren. Theoretisch repräsentieren sie eine Vielfalt an Coping-Fähigkeiten, die einander ähnlich zu sein scheinen. Es sollte nicht unerwähnt bleiben, daß die Faktoren I, II und III gemeinsam 76,7 % der gesamten Varianz erklärten, die restlichen 23,3 % der Varianz also von weniger ausgeprägten Faktoren erklärt wurden.

Die Mischung von "Trait"- und "State"-Dimensionen in allen drei Faktoren hebt die Bedeutung sowohl der Umwelteinflüsse als auch der individuellen Einflüsse im Coping-Phänomen hervor. Dieser Schluß wird nicht nur durch das Modell des Social Coping und diese Untersuchung unterstützt, sondern auch durch neuere Trends in der Coping Forschung (Arndt-Pagé, et al., 1983, S. 188). Das Modell des Social Coping verkörpert diese Mischung bei der Anwendung individueller Ressourcen, wobei nachdrücklich darauf hingewiesen wird, daß das Coping-Repertoire sich aus sozialen, psychischen und physischen Elementen zusammensetzt; es drückt aber ebenso aus, daß das Coping-Milieu und die Art des Problems auch eine wichtige Rolle in der Dynamik des real-life-Coping spielen (Dussich u. Jacobsen, 1982).

Da die 13 Coping-Dimensionen nicht speziell dafür entwickelt wurden, die Rolle der "Trait"- oder "State"-Dimensionen zu erfassen, kann es auch nicht Aufgabe dieser Untersuchung sein zu klären, welche dieser beiden Dimensionen die bedeutendere Rolle im real-life-Coping spielt. Was deutlich geworden zu sein scheint, ist, daß beide Arten in allen vier Problem-Situationen vorkommen und daß jede Problemsituation ein ausgeprägtes eigenes Muster der Coping-Dimensionen hervorrufen.

Zuletzt noch ein Hinweis auf die Korrelation zwischen der Variablen "Anzahl von Wörtern" und den unterschiedlichen Coping-Variablen. Während diese beiden Kategorien von Variablen eigentlich relativ unwichtig sind, so bieten sie doch einen Maßstab für die externale Validität an. Die Anzahl der Wörter sind ein objektives Maß für das Verhalten der Probanden. Die Coping-Scores wurden dagegen aus den subjektiven Urteilen der drei Beurteiler abgeleitet. Interessant ist, daß nur zwei Coping-Dimensionen keine signifikante Korrelation zeigten, und zwar die Dimensionen friedlich/aggressiv und legitimiert/nicht legitimiert; und beide waren starke "Trait"-Dimensionen im Faktor I (Normorientierung im Verhalten). Falls man annehmen sollte, daß die große Zahl positiver und signifikanter Korrelationen bei den übrigen Dimensionen ein Ergebnis des Umfanges der Antworten gewesen sei, durch den die Beurteiler beeinflußt worden seien, so müßte dies für alle 13 Dimensionen gültig sein. Die zwei referierten Ausnahmen scheinen eine andere Regel (unterstützt durch das Modell des Social Coping über Coping-Repertoire und dessen Einfluß auf den Coping-Prozeß) zu bestätigen: während das Coping-Repertoire eines Probanden als Nebenprodukt seines Erfahrungsschatzes folgerichtig eine große Zahl von Wörtern bedingt, so stellen wenigstens die oben erwähnten zwei Dimensionen eine Ausnahme dar, denn bei ihnen schien die Quantität keinen sichtbaren Einfluß auf die Qualität zu haben. Somit mögen die beiden Ausnahmen die Validität zu bestätigen.

Die Untersuchung über Erfolg und Mißerfolg

Das Hauptanliegen dieses Teils der Untersuchung bestand darin, die Variablen zu bestimmen, die wichtig sind für die Unterscheidung zwischen Erfolg und Mißerfolg junger Bewährungshilfeprobanden. Dabei stellte das Modell des Social Coping den theoretischen Hintergrund für diese Untersuchung dar.

Diese Untersuchung thematisierte die Coping-Techniken und die zwei objektiven Ergebnisse der Unterstellung unter Bewährungshilfe: Erfolg und Mißerfolg. Zweck der vorliegenden Untersuchung war es, festzustellen, ob Probanden mit stärker ausgeprägten und reichlich vorhandenen Coping-Fähigkeiten besser mit lebensnahen Situationen fertig werden als solche mit schwächer ausgebildeten und wenigen Fähigkeiten. Mit anderen Worten: es sollte geprüft werden, ob das Coping-Konzept mit den 13 Dimensionen, die von Dussich u. Jacobsen (1982) (vgl. Tab. 14) entwickelt wurden, fähig ist, zwischen jenen Probanden zu unterscheiden, die erfolgreiche Erfahrungen machten und denen, die einen Mißerfolg erleben mußten. Erfolg wurde als Beendigung der Bewährung ohne Widerruf definiert, Mißerfolg im Gegensatz dazu, als Beendigung der Bewährung durch Widerruf.

Datenerhebung

Um die zwölf Hypothesen zu beantworten, wurde eine Stichprobe von 35 jungen Straffälligen untersucht, die erst kürzlich die Bewährungszeit beendet hatten.

Die 35 männlichen Probanden dieser Untersuchung waren zwischen 17 und 30 Jahre alt (das Durchschnittsalter betrug 23,1 Jahre; Median: 23,5 Jahre; Modus: 22 Jahre); alle stammten aus dem Landgerichtsbezirk Hannover. Sie standen während der Jahre 1981 und 1982 unter Bewährung und waren nach dem Jugendstrafrecht verurteilt worden.

Zusammenfassung

Diese Ergebnisse machen deutlich, daß - in Hinblick auf die offiziell definierten Aussagen über Erfolg und Mißerfolg - die mehr soziologisch orientierten Konzepte unserer Kontrolltheorie bei der Unterscheidung dieser beiden Gruppen nicht so effektiv waren wie die eher psychologisch orientierten Konzepte des Coping-Modells. Zwei Erklärungen scheinen hierfür naheliegend: entweder waren die Voraussetzungen für die Spaceround-Integration zu breit und nicht ausreichend am Individuum orientiert, um Unterschiede erfassen zu können, oder das allgemeine Umfeld des sozialen Phänomens, das durch das Modell der Spaceround-Integration angezielt wurde, machte tatsächlich nur kleine Unterschiede beim Vergleich von Erfolg und Mißerfolg aus. Das kann also bedeuten, daß (a) entweder die Theorie ungeeignet ist oder (b) die sozialen Bedingungen keine große Rolle bei der Unterscheidung von Erfolg und Mißerfolg spielen, oder (c) beides zutrifft. Hirschi schreibt über die Unterschiede zwischen den delinquenten Aktivitäten von "high- and low-stake boys" als Ergebnis einer größeren oder geringeren Gefahr, kriminellen Einflüssen ausgesetzt zu sein, er vermutet, daß diese Einflüsse (oder was man als subtile soziale Einflüsse bezeichnet) außerhalb der Reichweite der Kontrolltheorie lägen (1969, S. 161). Andererseits scheint es, daß die Voraussetzungen des Social Coping bessere Indikatoren für die Unterscheidung zwischen erfolgreichen und nicht erfolgreichen Probanden darstellen.

Die gleichen, bereits oben erwähnten Maßstäbe scheinen als Erklärung für die Hypothesen zum Social Coping geeignet zu sein, also daß (a) das Instrument ausreichend empfindlich ist, was zur Folge hätte, daß (b) das zu unterscheidende Phänomen prinzipiell psychologischer Natur sei, so daß (c) beides zur Geltung käme.

Trotz der Akzeptanz von fünf Null-Hypothesen für die Hypothesen zur Spaceround-Integration, sind es einige der Daten wert diskutiert zu werden. In den ersten beiden Hypothesen wurde die relative Bedeutung der Spacerounds untersucht. Wir stellten fest, daß keine signifikanten Unterschiede bestanden; das Profil zeigte jedoch, daß beide Gruppen der jungen Probanden ihre Peers als relativ <u>unbedeutend</u> beurteilten im Gegensatz zu den übrigen Spacerounds Arbeitsplatz, Gemeinschaft und Familie. Diese Erkenntnis scheint zumindest grundsätzlich die Aussage Hirschis zu untermauern, der sagte: "Da Delinquenten weniger stark den konventionell denkenden Erwachsenden zugetan sind als nicht-delinquente Jugendliche, ist ihr Kontakt untereinander auch nicht so stark" (1969, S. 140f.). Die Aussage von Friday u. Hage 1976 ("Wenn die Bedeutung der Peers-Gruppe wächst, dann steigt auch die Wahrscheinlichkeit der Delinquenz") scheint nicht mit den Ergebnissen unserer Untersuchung übereinzustimmen. Tatsächlich stellten wir fest, daß erfolgreiche Probanden ihre Peers als signifikant wichtiger einschätzten als die nicht erfolgreichen Probanden. Dieses Resultat ist Teil der Beantwortung von Hypothese 3. Eine mögliche Erklärung für diese Ergebnisse gibt Yablonsky mit der Feststellung, daß ein Jugendlicher, der fähig ist, konstruktive soziale Rollen einzunehmen, sich auch gut in die Gesellschaft einfügen kann. Andererseits ist derjenige, der aus einem sozialen Milieu stammt, das ihn nur ungenügend darauf vorbereitet, konstruktive soziale Rollen einzunehmen, jemand, dessen Sozialisation unvollkommen bleibt, dem es an sozialen Gefühlen mangelt und der nicht fähig ist, menschliche Gefühle wie Mitgefühl und Verantwortung anderen gegenüber zu entwickeln (1963, S. 196). Dieser Mangel an Vertrauen, Wärme, Zuneigung oder Unterstützung bei Peers wurde auch von Junger-Tas bestätigt (1977, S. 84).

Die Zahl der erfolgreichen Probanden bezeichneten die Peers als wichtiger als die Familie, und dies signifikant häufiger als die erfolglosen Probanden. Falls Yablonskys (1963, S. 196) Prinzip auch auf erfolgreiche Probanden anwendbar ist, könnte es eine Erklärung sein, warum erfolgreiche Probanden (bis zu ihrem 14. Lebensjahr) ihre Peers im Vergleich zu den erfolglosen Probanden als wichtiger als die Familie bezeichnen. Möglicherweise haben diese erfolgreichen Probanden gelernt, wie man Beziehungen außerhalb der Familie herstellt, die einem später (z.B. während der Bewährungszeit) nützlich sein können. Andere Resultate, die diese Feststellung bekräftigen, wären die, daß erfolgreiche Probanden stärkere persönliche Ressourcen zur Verfügung hatten, häufiger Kontakte mit Mitgliedern aller Spacerounds aufwiesen und in einer geringeren emotionalen Abhängigkeit zu ihrer Familie, ihrem Arbeitsplatz und der Gemeinschaft standen.

Die nächste und vielleicht wichtigste These zur Spaceround-Integration wurde in fünf Unterhypothesen unterteilt, je eine für jede getestete Interaktionsbedingung. Die Null-Hypothese wurde für alle Unterhypothesen angenommen, außer für die Hypothese der Häufigkeit der Kontakte. Rückblickend erwies es sich als ungeeignet, Hypothesen über alle Spacerounds hinweg aufzustellen, da jeder Spaceround unterschiedliche Ergebnisse für die gleichen Interaktionsbedingungen produzierte. Diese Erkenntnis ist besonders für den Spaceround Peers wahr.

Eine später aufgestellte Hypothese beschäftigt sich mit den signifikanten Beziehungen und, obwohl die Null-Hypothese angenommen wurde, erbrachten die Daten das interessante qualitative Ergebnis, daß die Reihenfolge der wichtigsten Beziehungen für erfolgreiche Probanden die folgende war: Mutter, Bruder, Schwester und Vater; im Vergleich dazu stellten die erfolglosen Probanden die folgende Reihenfolge auf: Vater, Mutter, Schwester und Großmutter. Während Hirschi (1969, S. 100-107) vermutete, daß in bezug auf den Einfluß von Vater oder Mutter kein Unterschied zwischen Delinquenten und Nicht-Delinquenten existiert, ist es schwierig, seine Ergebnisse auf unsere Resultate zum Erfolg/Mißerfolg der Probanden zu übertragen.

Ein weiteres wichtiges Ergebnis zum Modell der Spaceround-Integration und zum Unterschied zwischen erfolgreichen und erfolglosen Probanden, war das Ergebnis, das wir bei der Untersuchung der nächsten Hypothese erhielten. Diese Daten legen nahe, daß der Grad der Integration eines Probanden eine wichtige Determinante für den Erfolg oder Mißerfolg ist. Wenn wir die erfolgreiche Beendigung der Bewährung als Indikator für gesetzestreues Verhalten definieren und die nicht erfolgreiche Bewährung als Indikator für gesetzesbrecherisches Verhalten, dann würden frühere Untersuchungen der Kontrolltheorie, die Integration und Konformität gleichsetzten (Hirschi 1969; Friday u. Halsey 1977; Junger-Tas 1977), die vorliegenden Ergebnisse unterstützen.

Betrachtet man die Hypothesen zum Social Coping, findet man in jedem Fall signifikante Unterschiede zwischen Probanden, die ihre Bewährung erfolgreich beendeten, und Probanden, die dies nicht schafften. Die erste dieser Hypothesen beschäftigt sich mit Ressourcen. Tatsächlich werden alle Informationen der übrigen Hypothesen in dieser einen Hypothese zusammengefaßt. Benutzt man diese Ergebnisse, so kann man zwei Profile erstellen, die den typischen erfolgreichen Probanden und den typischen erfolglosen Probanden wiedergeben.

Diese Unterschiede deuten nicht nur auf unterschiedliche individuelle Charakteristika hin, sondern auch auf unterschiedliche Interaktionsmuster. Die erfolgreichen Probanden sind besser integriert, besonders über häufigeren und positiven Kontakte innerhalb konventioneller Spacerounds wie ihrer Herkunftsfamilie, Prokreationsfamilie, Arbeitsplatz, Peers ohne kriminelle Vergangenheit, Vertretern von Behörden und Schulen. Außerdem besitzen sie mehr Ressourcen, sind weniger hilflos und haben allgemein besser ausgebildete Coping-Fähigkeiten.

Die erfolglosen Probanden dagegen sind stärker von den traditionellen Spacerounds isoliert und haben hauptsächlich Kontakte zu Peers (darunter einige mit krimineller Vergangenheit), und in öffentlichen Treffpunkten wie Sportvereinen und Kneipen, die auch Spacerounds für Peers sind. Sie besitzen kaum ausreichende Ressourcen, sind hilfloser und haben schwächer ausgebildete Coping-Fähigkeiten.

Rückblickend scheinen die Hypothesen, die von den psychologischen Coping-Konzepten abgeleitet wurden, ergiebiger zu sein, was die Annahme oder Ablehnung der Null-Hypothese betrifft. Diese Schlußfolgerung kann nicht die Dominanz einer Disziplin über eine andere belegen. Sie stellt nur eine auffallende Beobachtung dar, die wahrscheinlich eher eine Kritik an unserem Erhebungsinstrument oder unseren Methoden ist als irgend etwas anderes.

Trotz der frustierend kleinen Stichprobe und den wenigen Antworten erfüllt diese Untersuchung insgesamt ihren primären Zweck, nämlich Unterschiede unter dem Aspekt der sozialen Kontrolle und des Social Coping zwischen Probanden aufzuzeigen, die ihre Bewährungszeit erfolgreich durchlaufen, und Probanden, die die Bewährung nicht bestehen, und zwar innerhalb des Rahmens vom Modell des Social Coping.

Schlußfolgerungen

Die folgenden Anmerkungen wurden den beiden Voruntersuchungen und den beiden Teiluntersuchungen entnommen: die Voruntersuchung der Bewährungshilfe-Zählkarten junger Probanden, die Voruntersuchung der Alltagsproblemen von Bewährungshilfeprobanden, die Untersuchung über Coping und Bewährungshilfe und die Untersuchung über Erfolg und Mißerfolg.

Zum Verfahren

Die meisten Anmerkungen in diesem Kapitel setzen die Validität des Modells des Social Coping voraus. Die allgemeine Anregung, die wir aus dieser Untersuchung ziehen wollen, ist die folgende: ein allumfassender Ansatz zur Betreuung und Kontrolle

Straffälliger, besonders solcher, die unter Bewährung stehen, sollte die Bedeutung der Interaktion zwischen situationsbedingten Variablen (im besonderen solche, die die Familie und den Bewährungshelfer betreffen) und individuellen Variablen (hier besonders jenen, die die lebensnahen Coping-Prozesse betreffen) berücksichtigen.

Die Untersuchung über Erfolg und Mißerfolg zeigte, daß die meisten der Probanden, die ihre Bewährungszeit nicht erfolgreich bestanden, nicht nur seltener in signifikante Spacerounds integriert sind, sondern darüber hinaus in den Spacerounds, in denen sie über Kontakte verfügen, auch weniger persönliche Kontakte als solche Probanden aufweisen, die die Bewährung erfolgreich beendeten; dies gilt besonders in Hinblick auf Familienmitglieder (sowohl in der Herkunfts- als auch in der Prokreationsfamilie), Behördenangestellte (Bewährungshilfe, Arbeitsamt und Wohnungsamt) und Peers.

Diese Ergebnisse deuten darauf hin, daß Isolation und erfolglose Bewährung Nebenprodukte eines gemeinsamen Faktors sind (eventuell einer mißlungenen Sozialisation, wie z.B. Yablonsky, 1963 vermutet) oder Isolation selbst ist die Ursache für den Mißerfolg (wie z.B. Friday u. Halsey, 1977 darstellten); möglicherweise ist beides zutreffend. Das Modell der Spaceround-Integration hebt die Bedeutung von Beziehungen für den Integrationprozeß hervor. Das Modell des Social Coping hebt die Bedeutung sozialer Ressourcen für den erfolgreichen Umgang mit Problemen hervor. Betrachtet man die empirischen und theoretischen Ergebnisse im Zusammenhang, erkennt man, daß Isolation (das Gegenteil von Integration in einen Spaceround) diejenigen Probanden, die ihre Bewährung erfolgreich beendeten, von denen trennt, die dies nicht schafften. Daher würde die logische Empfehlung an Bewährungshelfer sein, mehr Nachdruck auf die Verringerung der Isolation ihrer Klienten in allen traditionellen Spacerounds zu legen. Von besonderem Interesse sollten dabei die Interaktionsbedingungen Häufigkeit des Kontaktes in traditionellen Spacerounds und Ähnlichkeit von Normen im Spaceround Arbeitsplatz sein. Auch das Hinzuziehen von ausgebildeten freiwilligen Helfern ist zu empfehlen, um die Zahl der Interaktionen in den traditionellen Spacerounds zu erhöhen. Eine weitere Empfehlung wäre, spezielle Trainingsprogramme zur Entwicklung zwischenmenschlicher Fähigkeiten zu entwerfen, die in der Zeit kurz vor der Entlassung der Straffälligen eingesetzt werden, um die Eingliederung nach der Entlassung zu erleichtern und die Herstellung bedeutender Beziehungen zu ermöglichen.

Die beiden Untersuchungen zum Thema Coping und Bewährungsaufsicht und zum Thema Erfolg und Mißerfolg legen eine Anzahl von Folgerungen hinsichtlich des Coping nahe. Die Untersuchung über Erfolg und Mißerfolg ergab, daß erfolgreiche Probanden ein signifikant besseres Problemlösungsverhalten haben als erfolglose Probanden. Der Spaceround, der die höchsten und signifikantesten Coping-Scores für erfolgreiche Probanden hervorbrachte, war der Arbeitsplatz mit den Antworten im Rollenspiel "Auseinandersetzung mit dem Chef". Dieses Beispiel wurde aus der Voruntersuchung über Probleme der Probanden abgeleitet, wobei sich das Ergebnis früherer Untersuchungen bestätigte, daß Nicht-Straffällige und Bewährungshelfer den Arbeitsplatz als den problematischsten Lebensbereich bezeichneten. Wenn die jungen Probanden in dieser Untersuchung den Arbeitsplatz als den unproblematischsten Lebensbereich beschreiben (vgl. Abb. 17), kann man daraus wohl schließen, daß es für junge Bewährungshilfeprobanden eine wichtige (wenn nicht kritische) Rolle spielt, Probleme am Arbeitsplatz zu erkennen und sie lösen zu lernen, um ihre Bewährung erfolgreich zu beenden.

Auch eine der fünf Fragen im Fragebogen beschäftigte sich mit dem Spaceround Arbeitsplatz. Die Frage lautete: "Wenn ich mit meinen Kollegen am Arbeitsplatz zusammen bin, gibt es nie/selten/manchmal/häufig/immer Probleme". Die Ergebnisse zeigten, daß beiden Gruppen der ehemaligen Probanden sehr ähnliche Aussagen dazu machten, indem sie antworteten, sie würden <u>selten</u> Probleme haben. Die Ergebnisse dieser Voruntersuchung ließen ebenfalls erkennen, daß unter Bewährung stehende Probanden den Arbeitsplatz nicht als ernsthaften Problembereich ansahen. Betrachtet man diese beiden Ergebnisse, die wir unabhängig voneinander erhielten, so scheint es, als wenn junge Straffällige unter Bewährung und kurz nach Beendigung der Bewährungszeit sich der Probleme der Arbeitssituation relativ unbewußt wären. Unter diesen befanden sich auch erfolgreiche Probanden, die, mit dem Problem am Arbeitsplatz konfrontiert, mit ihm deutlich besser umgehen konnten. Diese Ergebnisse machen deutlich, daß jede Art von Trainingsprogramm vor Beginn der Bewährungszeit <u>Problembewußtsein</u> am Arbeitsplatz und <u>Lösungsfähigkeit</u> einschließen sollte. Zusätzlich sollten Bewährungshelfer eine Ausbildung zur Krisenintervention für Probleme am Arbeitsplatz erhalten. Die Rolle, die Bewährungshelfer im Leben ihrer Klienten spielen, sollte sich idealerweise mit denjenigen Lebensbereichen beschäftigen, die sich beim Prozeß des "Erfolgreich-Werdens" am Arbeitsplatz und in der Familie als kritisch erwiesen haben; dafür sollte der Bewährungshelfer gut ausgebildet und vorbereitet sein.

<u>Zur Forschung</u>

Da dieses Projekt nicht in erster Linie darauf ausgerichtet war, das Modell zur Spaceround-Integration und zum Social Coping zu validieren (beide Modelle wurden erst im Verlauf der Untersuchung entwickelt), ist es notwendig, für beide Modelle noch strengere theoretische Aussagen zu formulieren, die dann besser empirisch getestet werden könnten. Die Teile des Modells der Spaceround-Integration, denen es besondere Aufmerksamkeit zu schenken gilt, sind die folgenden: das Ausmaß, in dem die Interaktionsbedingungen die Bedeutung von Beziehungen bestimmen, die relative Bedeutung dieser Bedingungen, und die Frage, welche Bedingung den höchsten Varianzanteil der individuellen Integration erklärt.

Es scheint eine Binsenweisheit der Forschung zu sein, die besagt, daß das, was am schwierigsten durchzuführen ist, normalerweise als letztes erledigt wird, aber am dringendsten benötigt wird. In der Kontrolltheorie ist bei der Mehrzahl der Untersuchungen eine Querschnittsanalyse angewandt worden; die Natur der meisten theoretischen Aussagen umreißt jedoch Kausalaussagen über einen beträchtlichen Zeitraum hinweg. Einige der Hauptanliegen behandeln z.B. den Sozialisationsprozeß, die wechselnden Prioritäten bedeutender Beziehungen über die Zeit hinweg sowie die Funktion der Interaktionsbedingungen im Laufe der Zeit. Das wirft die Frage auf: Sind Langzeituntersuchungen die einzig logische Methode, um diese Fragen genauer beantworten zu können? Caplan gab in seiner umfangreichen Neugestaltung und Anwendung von Hirschis Kontrolltheorie die gleichen Empfehlungen, als er die größere Aussagekraft von Längsschnittuntersuchungen hervorhob, um den zeitlichen Ablauf zwischen unabhängigen und abhängigen Variablen überzeugend abzusichern (1978, S. 373).

Ein anderer Bereich in der Kriminologie, der sich den Forschern mehr und mehr entzieht, ist die Rolle der Peers in bezug auf die Kriminalität. Die Gluecks (1950, S. 164) konstatierten, daß Delinquenz bereits auftritt, bevor Freunde ausgewählt werden, während Reckless (1961, S. 311) feststellte, daß Freundschaften einer der wichtigsten allgemeingültigen Ursachen für Kriminalität bei Männern ist. Während der letzten dreißig Jahre behandelten Kontrolltheoretiker wie Hirschi (1969), Hindelang (1973), Thibauld (1974), Tiemann (1976), Junger-Tas (1977), Friday u. Hage (1976), Caplan (1978) und Dixon (1981) dieses Thema und erhielten sehr unterschiedliche Ergebnisse. Die vorliegende Untersuchung ergab, daß die erfolgreichen Probanden aussagten, der Spaceround Peers wäre der wichtigste Lebensbereich für sie. Die jungen Männer sagten außerdem aus, daß Peers die unproblematischsten Leute seien, mit denen sie in Kontakt ständen; die nicht-straffälligen Jugendlichen sagten dagegen, Peers wären etwas problematisch für sie. Trotz der häufigeren Kontakte hatten die erfolgreichen Probanden eine geringere Ähnlichkeit bei den Normen, schätzten die Beziehungen weniger bedeutsam ein, unter den Peers befanden sich <u>keine</u> kriminellen Freunde, ganz im Gegensatz zu den Probanden, die ihre Bewährung nicht erfolgreich beendeten. Sowohl erfolgreiche als auch erfolglose Erwachsene stuften die Peers als einen Spaceround von geringer Bedeutung ein, verglichen mit Arbeitsplatz, Gemeinschaft und Familie. So scheint es, daß die Vielfalt von Variablen, die zwischen Probanden unterscheiden, die besser integriert sind, oder denen, die Erfolg haben, oder sogar denen, die nicht kriminell werden, durch eine Menge undurchschaubarer Komplexitäten bestimmt werden, die in der relativ kurzen Zeit vom Jugendalter zum Erwachsenenalter darüber hinaus offensichtlich erheblichen Veränderungen unterzogen sind. Eigentlich ergibt es sich von selbst, daß dieser Bereich menschlichen Verhaltens hervorragend von einer ausführlichen, aber eng angelegten Langzeituntersuchung profitieren könnte, wobei am besten noch eine ganze Kohorte vor dem Hintergrund eines weiterentwickelten Modells der Kontrolltheorie als Untersuchungseinheit dienen sollte.

Vom theoretischen Standpunkt aus stellt die Eingliederung in Spacerounds das Bindeglied zwischen Coping und individueller Integration dar. Weil dieses Bindeglied in beiden theoretischen Modellen angenommen wurde, wurde es auch nicht konkret überprüft. Eingliederung meint hier die allgemeine Anpassung an einen gegebenen Lebensbereich. Der Prozeß der Eingliederung durch zahlreiche Coping-Ereignisse und deren Beziehung zur sozialen Kontrolle würde eine logische Erweiterung der vorliegenden Untersuchung sein. Es ist die Überzeugung des Autors, daß wir nur durch die Einbeziehung, sowohl der "Trait"- als auch der "State"-Dimensionen im Coping-Verhalten innerhalb eines sozialpsychologischen Rahmens vollständig verstehen können, wie eine Bewährungszeit erfolgreich beendet wird. Ich empfehle ein umfassendes und interdisziplinäres Modell, das einen breiteren Ansatz bieten kann, als gewöhnlich in einer einzigen Theorie zu finden ist. Wenn man anstrebt, die gesamte Varianz eines bestimmten Phänomens aufzuklären - und dies ist schließlich eines der Hauptziele wissenschaftlicher Bemühungen - so würde uns die Offenheit für mehr Beschreibungen der Realität diesem Ziel ein Stück näher bringen.

General Bibliography*

ABRAMOWITZ, S.I.: Locus of Control and Self-reported Depression among College Students. (In: Psychological Reports 25, 1969, 149-150).

ABRAMSON, L.: Universal versus Personal Helplessness: An Experimental Test of the Reformutated Theory of Learned Helplessness and Depression. (Unpublished doctoral Dissertation, University of Pennsylvania, 1977).

ABRAMSON, L.Y.; SELIGMAN, M.E.P.; TEASDALE, J.D.: Learned Helplessness in Humans: Critique and Reformulation. (In: Journal of Abnormal Psychology 87, 1978, 49-74).

AKERS, R.: Deviant Behavior: A Social Learning Approach. (Belmont, California: Wadsworth, 1973).

AMERICAN CORRECTIONAL ASSOCIATION: Manual of Correctional Standards. (Washington, D.C., 1966).

ANDREWS, J.: Recovery from Surgery, with and without Preparatory Instruction, for three Coping Styles. (In: Journal of Personality and Social Psychology 15, 1970, 223-226).

ANTONOVSKY, A.: Health, Stress, and Coping. (San Francisco: Jossey-Bass Publishers, 1981).

APSLER, R.; FRIEDMAN, H.: Chance Outcomes and the Just World: A Comparison of Observers and Recipients. (In: Journal of Personality and Social Psychology 31, 1975).

ARNDT-PAGE, B.; GEIGER, E.; KOEPPEN, M.; KÜNZEL, R.: Klassifizierung von Copingverhalten. (In: Diagnostica, Band XXIX, 1983, 2, 183-189).

ARNOLD, M.: Perennial Problems in the Field of Emotion. (In: M. Arnold (Ed.): The Loyola Symposium: Feelings Emotion, New York: Academic Press, 1970).

ARNOLD, W.R.: Juveniles on Parole: A Sociological Perspective. (New York: Random House, 1970).

AVERILL, J.R.; ROSENN, M.: Vigilant and Nonvigilant Coping Strategies and Psychophysiological Stress Reaction During the Anticipation of Electric Shock. (In: Journal of Personality and Social Psychology 23, 1972).

---

* This bibliography includes all references used directly and indirectly.

AX, A.: Goals and Methods of Psychophysiology. (In: Psychophysiology 1, 1964).

BAMBER, J.H.: Adolescent Marginality. A Further Step. (In: Genetic Psychology Monographs 88, 1973, 3-21).

BANDURA, A.; WALTERS, R.H.: Adolescent Aggression. (New York: Ronald, 1959).

BARTOLLAS, C.; MILLER, S.J.: The Juvenile Offender: Control, Correction and Treatment. (Boston: Allyn & Bacon, Inc., 1978).

BATTLE, E.S.; ROTTER, J.B.: Children's Feelings of Personal Control as Related to Social Class and Ethnic Group. (In: Journal of Personality 31, 1963).

BECKER, H.: Outsiders: Studies in the Sociology of Deviance. (New York: The Free Press, 1963).

BECKER, S.: Die Role Relationships Theory - mit besonderer Betonung des empirischen Beleges. (Unveröffentlichte Diplomarbeit, 1980).

BECKER, S.: Jugendgerichtshilfe am Beispiel eines Einzelfalles in der Stadt Mönchengladbach. (Unveröffentlichte Hausarbeit zur Erlangung der staatlichen Anerkennung, 1981).

BENEDICT, R.: Continuities and discontinuities in cultural conditioning. (In: Psychiatry 2, 1938, 161-170).

BENSON, J.S.; KENELLY, K.J.: Learned Helplessness: The Result of Uncontrollable Reinforcements or Uncontrollable Aversive Stimuli. (In: Journal of Personality and Social Psychology 34, 1976).

BEROCOCHEA, J.E.; HIMELSON, A.N.; MILLER, D.E.: The Risk of Failure During the Early Parole Period: A Methodological Note. (In: Journal of Criminal Law, Criminology and Police Science 63, 1972, 93-97).

BIDDLE, B.J.; THOMAS, E.: Role Theory: Concepts and Research. (New York, 1966).

BIRON, L.: Famille et delinquance. (Thése de maitrise inedite en criminologie, Université de Montreal, 1974).

BLATH, R.; DILLIG, P.; FREY, H.-P.: Arbeit und Resozialisation. (Weinheim: Beltz Verlag, 1980).

BLOCH, H.A.; NIEDERHOFER, A.: The Gang: A Study of Adolescent Behavior. (New York: Philosophical Library, 1958).

BLOOM, L.J.; HOUSTON, B.K.; HOLMES, D.S.; BURISH, T.G.: The Effectiveness of Attentional Diversion and situational Redefinition for reducing Stress due to a Nonambiguous Threat. (In: Journal of Research in Personality 11, 1977).

BLUMER, H.: Sociological Analysis and the "Variable". (In: American Sociological Review 21, 1956, 6, 683-690).

BLUMER, H.: Symbolic Interactionism. Perspective and Method. (Englewood Cliffs, N.J., 1969).

BREITKOPF, L.: Strategien und damit assoziierte Belastungen von Kandidaten in mündlichen Prüfungen - die Theorie der gelernten Hilflosigkeit übertragen auf das Verhaltensmuster der Prüfungsangst. (Unveröffentlichte Dissertation, Bochum, 1980).

BRESNITZ, S.: A Study of Worrying. (In: British Journal of Social and Clinical Psychology, 1971).

BRIAR, S.; PILIAVIN, I.: Delinquency, Situational Inducements, and Commitment to Conformity. (In: Social Problems 13, 1965, 1, 35-45).

BRUNNER, R.: Jugendschutzgesetz. Kommentar. 4. Aufl. (Berlin: de Gruyter, 1975).

BRUSTEN, M.: Soziale Schichtung, selbstberichtete Delinquenz und Prozesse der Stigmatisierung in der Schule. (In: Kriminologisches Journal 6, 1974, 1, 29-46).

BUCHWALD, A.M.; COYNE, J.C.; COLE, Ch.S.: A Critical Evaluation of the Learned Helplessness Model of Depression. (In: Journal of Abnormal Psychology 87, 1978, 180-193).

BULMAN, R.J.; WORTMAN, C.B.: Attributions of Blame and Coping in the "Real World": Severe Accident Victims React to their Lot. (In: Journal of Personality and Social Psychology 35, 1977).

BULCZAK, G.: Richtlinien und Orientierungshilfen. (Hameln, 1979).

BURGESS, R.L.; AKERS, R.L.: A Differential Association-Reinforcement Theory of Criminal Behavior. (In: Social Problems 14, 1966, 2, 128-147).

BURGESS, R.L.; BUSHNELL, D.: Behavioral Sociology: The Experimental Analysis of Social Process. (New York: Columbia Univ. Press, 1969).

BURISH, T.G.; BLOMM, L.J.; HOUSTON, B.K.; HOLMES, D.S.: Effectiveness of Avoidant Thinking and Redefinition in Coping with Stress. Paper presented at the meeting of the American Psychological Association. (Chicago, 1975).

BURKHARDT, W.R.: The Great Parole Experiment. (In: E.E. Miller, M.R. Montilla (Eds.): In Corrections and in the Community. Reston, Va.: Reston, 1977).

BURSTEIN, S.; MEICHENBAUM, D.: The Work of Worrying in Children Undergoing Surgery. (Unpublished Manuscript, Univ. of Waterloo, 1974).

BUTTERFIELD, E.C.: Locus of Control, Test Anxiety, Reactions to Frustration and Achievement Attitudes. (In: Journal of Personality 32, 1964).

CAPLAN, A.: A Formal Statement and Extension of Hirschi's Theory of Social Coping. (Thèse de Philosophiae Doctor de Ecole de Criminologie enedite, Universite de Montreal, 1978).

CHAIKEN, A.L.; DARLEY, J.M.: Victim or Perpetrator? Defensive Attribution of Responsibility and the Need for Order and Justice. (In: Journal of Personality and Social Psychology 25, 1973).

CHEIN, J.: The Environment as a Determinant of Behavior. (In: N.S. Endler, E. Magnusson (Eds.): Interactional Psychology and Personality. New Jersey: Lawrence, 1976).

CHODOFF, P.; FRIEDMAN, S.; HAMBURG, D.: Stress, Defences, and Coping Behavior: Observations in Parents of Children with Malignant Disease. (In: American Journal of Psychiatry, 1964).

CITIZENS' INQUIRY ON PAROLE AND CRIMINAL JUSTICE: Parole in Crisis: A Report on New York Parole. (In: Criminal Law Bulletin 11, 1975).

CLAUSEN, J. (Ed.): Socialization and Society. (Boston: Little Brown and Company, 1968).

CLAUSS, G. et al.: Wörterbuch der Psychologie. (Köln, 1976).

CLINARD, M.B.: Urbanization and Crime. (In: C.B. Vedder (Ed.): Criminology: A Book of Readings. New York: Dryden, D.J. Abbott, 1953).

CLINARD, M.B.: Crime in Developing Countries. (New York: John Wiley, 1973).

CLOWARD, R.A.; OHLIN, L.E.: Delinquency and Opportunity. (New York: Free Press, 1960).

COEHLO, G.V.; HAMBURG, D.A.; ADAMS, J.E. (Eds.): Social Structure and Personal Adaptation: Some Neglected Dimensions. Coping and Adaptation. (New York: Basic Books, 1974).

COHEN, A.K.: Delinquent Boys: The Culture of the Gang. (New York: Free Press, 1955).

COHEN, A.K.: Deviance and Control. (Englewood Cliffs, N.J.: Prentice-Hall, 1966).

COHEN, A.K.; SHORT, J.F.Jr.: Research in Delinquent Subcultures. (In: The Journal of Social Issues 14, 1958, 3, 20-37).

COHEN, F.; LAZARUS, R.: Active Coping Processes, Soping Dispositions, and Recovery from Surgery. (In: Psychosomatic Medicine 35, 1973).

COHEN, S.; ROTHBART, M.; PHILLIPS, S.: Locus of Control and the Generality of Learned Helplessness in Humans. (In: Journal of Personality and Social Psychology 34, 1976).

COLE, C.S.; COYNE, J.C.: Situational Specificity of Laboratory-Induced Learned Helplessness. (In: Journal of Abnormal Psychology 86, 1977, 6, 615-623).

COLEMAN, J.: Adolescent Society. (New York: Free Press, 1961).

CONGER, R.D.: Social Control and Social Learning Models of Delinquent Behavior. (In: Criminology 14, 1976, 1, 17-40).

COOLEY, C.H.: Human Nature and the Social Order. (New York: Charles Scribner's Sons, 1902).

COOPER, C.L.: The Stress Check: Coping with the Stress of Life and Work. (Englewood Cliffs, N.J.: Prentice-Hall, 1981).

COSTELLO, C.G.: A Critical Review of Seligman's Laboratory Experiments on Learned Helplessness and Depression in Humans. (In: Journal of Abnormal Psychology 87, 1978, 21-31).

CRESSEY, D.R.; IRWIN, J.: Thieves, Convicts and the Inmate Culture. (In: Social Problems 10, 1962, 2, 142-155).

DAVIES-OSTERKAMP, S.; SALM, A.: Ansätze zur Erfassung psychischer Adaptionsprozesse in medizinischen Belastungssituationen. (In: Medizinische Psychologie 6, 1980).

DAVIS, W.L.; PHARES, E.J.: Internal-external Control as a Determinant of Information Seeking in a Social Influence Situation. (In: Journal of Personality 35, 1967).

DAWSON, R.O.: The Decision to Grant or Deny Parole: A Study of Parole Criteria in Law and Practice. (Washington, University Law Quarterly, 1966).

DEPUE, R.A.; MONROE, S.M.: Learned Helplessness in the Perspective of the Depressive Disorders: Conceptual and Defitional Issues. (In: Journal of Abnormal Psychology 87, 1978, 3-20).

DEWEY, J.: Human Nature and Conduct. (New York: Modern Library, 1930).

DIWITT, D. et al.: A Study of Case Movement, Personality Change, Critical Situations, and Revocation Decisions in the Parole Process. (Diss., University of Wisconsin, 1966).

DIZON, D.: Jugendkriminalität in den Philippinen. Die RRT und ihre empirische Überprüfung. (In: C. Kirchhoff; G.F. Kirchhoff (Eds.): Das erste Internationale Mönchengladbacher Seminar für vergleichende Strafrechtspflege. Bochum: Brockmeyer, 1979, 153-176).

DIZON, D.: Role Relationship Theory: A Framework for the Planning and Evaluation of Delinquency Prevention Programs. Paper Presented for the International Symposium on "Sociological Perspectives on Delinquency Prevention". (Wuppertal 1981).

DÖRMANN U.: Sozialer Wandel und Jugendkriminalität in der Bundesrepublik Deutschland. (In: Kriminalistik 31, 1977, 2, 49-57).

DOUGLAS, D.; ANISMAN, H.: Helplessness or Expectation Incongruency: Effects of Aversive Stimulation on Subsequent Performance. (In: Journal of Experimental Psychology: Human Perception and Performance 1, 1975).

DOWNESS, D.: The Delinquent Solution. (New York: Free Press, 1966).

DURKHEIM, E.: The Rules of Sociological Method. (New York: Free Press, 1938).

DURKHEIM, E.: Suicide. (New York: Free Press, 1951).

DURKHEIM, E.: Education and Sociology. (New York: Free Press, 1963).

DURKHEIM, E.: On Morality and Society. (Chicago: Univ. of Chicago, 1973).

DUSSICH, J.P.J.: A Study of Life Coping Repertoires of Young Parolees. (Unveröffentlichter Forschungsplan des Kriminologischen Forschungsinstitutes Niedersachsen e.V. (KFN). Hannover, 1981a).

DUSSICH, J.P.J.: Some General and Specific Considerations on Parole. (In: H. Kury (Ed.): Perspektiven und Probleme kriminologischer Forschung. Köln, Berlin, Bonn, München: Carl Heymanns Verlag, 1981b, 614-631).

DUSSICH, J.P.J.: Social Coping of Young Parolees. An Interim Report. (In: H. Kury (Ed.): Prävention abweichenden Verhaltens. Maßnahmen der Vorbeugung und Nachbetreuung. Köln, Berlin, Bonn, München: Carl Heymanns Verlag, 1982, 516-570).

DUSSICH, J.P.J.; JACOBSEN, H.-F.: Social Coping: Eine Theorie zur Erklärung problemlösenden Verhaltens. (Social Coping: A Theory to Clarify Problem Solving Behavior). (In: H. Kury (Ed.): Prävention abweichenden Verhaltens: Maßnahmen der Vorbeugung und Nachbetreuung. Köln, Berlin, Bonn, München: Carl Heymanns Verlag, 1982, 663-712).

DUSSICH, J.P.J.; JACOBSEN, H.-F.; IWANNEK, U.: Aktuelle Probleme von Probanden der Bewährungshilfe. (Actual Problems of Parole Clients). (In: Bewährungshilfe, 30, 1983, 4, 315-330).

DWECK, C.S.: The Role of Expectations and Attributions in the Alleviation of Learned Helplessness. (In: Journal of Personality and Social Psychology 31, 1975).

DWECK, C.S.: Children's Interpretation of Evaluative Feedback: The Effect of Social Cues on Learned Helplessness. (In: C.S. Dweck, K.T. Hill, W.H. Reed, W.M. Steihman, R.D. Parke (Eds.): The Impact of Social Cues on Children's Behavior. Merrill-Palmer Quarterly 22, 1976).

DWECK, C.S.; REPUCCI, N.D.: Learned Helplessness and Reinforcement Responsibility in Children. (In: Journal of Personality and Social Psychology 25, 1973).

DWECK, C.S.; WORTMAN, C.B.: Learned Helplessness: Cognitions and Coping Strategies. (In: H.W. Krohne, L. Laux (Eds.): Achievement, Stress and Anxiety. Washington, D.C.: Hemisphere, 1981).

DWECK, C.S.; GOETZ, T.; STRAUSS, N.: Sex Differences in Learned Helplessness: IV. An Experimental and Naturalistic Study of Failure Generalization and its Mediators. (Unpublished Manuscript, University of Illinois at Urbana-Champaign, 1977).

DWECK, C.S.; DAVIDSON, W.; NELSON, S.; ENNA, B.: Sex Differences in Learned Helplessness: (II) The Contingencies of evaluative Feedback in the Classroom (III). An experimental Analysis. (Unpublished Manuscript, Illinois at Urbana-Champaign, 1976).

DYCK, D.G.; BREEN, L.H.: Learned Helplessness, Immunization and Task Importance in Humans. (Unpublished Manuscript, University of Manitoba, 1976).

EISENBERGER, R.; MAURIELLO, J.; CARLSON, J.; FRANK, M.; PARK, D.C.: Learned Helplessness and Industriousness Produced by Positive Reinforcement. (Unpublished Manuscript, State University of New York at Albany, 1976).

ELLIOTT, D.S.; AGETON, S.S.; CANTER, R.J.: An Integrated Theoretical Perspective on Delinquent Behavior. (In: Journal of Research in Crime and Delinquency 16, 1979, 3-27).

ENGLISH, H.; ENGLISH, A.: A Comprehensive Dictionary of Psychological and Psychoanalytical Terms. (New York: David McKay Company, Inc., 1958).

ERICKSON, R.; CROW, W.; ZURCHER, L.; CONNET, A.: Paroled But Not Free. (New York: Behavior Publications, 1973).

ERIKSON, E.H.: Identität und Lebensmythos. (Frankfurt/M., 1966a).

ERIKSON, E.H.: Identifikation und Identität. (In: L.v. Friedeburg (Hrsg.): Jugend in der modernen Gesellschaft. 3. Auflage. Köln, Berlin: Kiepenheuer u. Witsch, 1966b, 277-278).

ERIKSON, E.H.: Jugend und Krise. Die Psychodynamik im sozialen Wandel. (Stuttgart, 1970).

EYSENCK, H.J.: Dimensions of Personality. (London: Kegan Paul, 1947).

FAIRCHILD, H.P.: Dictionary of Sociology. (Totowa, N.J.: Littlefield, Adams and Company, 1968).

FAIRWEATHER, J.S.: Parole and the Return to Crime: The Effects of Prerelease and Postrelease Factors. (Diss., Stanford University, 1980).

FARRELL, R.A.; HARDIN, C.W.: Legal Stigma and Homosexual Career Deviance. (In: M. Riedel, T. P. Thornberry (Eds.): Crime and Delinquency: Dimensions of Deviance. New York: Praeger, 1974).

FARRINGTON, D.P.: Delinquency Begins at Home. (New Society, 1972).

FELTES, T.: Jugend, Konflikt und Recht. (Diss., Bielefeld, 1979).

FOLKMAN, S.; SCHAEFER, C., LAZARUS, R.S.: Cognitive Processes as Mediators of Stress and Coping. (In: V. Hamilton, D.M. Warburton (Eds.): Human Stress and Cognition: An Information Processing Approach. New York et al.: Wiley, 1979, 265-298).

FRIDAY, P.C.: Changing Theory and Research in Criminology. (In: International Journal of Criminology and Penology, 5, 1977, 159-170).

FRIDAY, P.C.: International Review of Youth Crime and Delinquency. Ch. 5. (In: G.R. Newman (Ed.): Crime and Deviance. Comparative Perspective. Beverly Hills, Cal.: Sage, 1980a, 100-129).

FRIDAY, P.C.: Patterns of Role Relationships and Crime. Paper presented at the Third Mönchengladbacher Seminar in Comparative Criminal Justice, July. (Mönchengladbach, 1980b).

FRIDAY, P.C.: Theoretical Issues in the Study of Deviance and Social Control. (In: H. Kury (Ed.): Perspektiven und Probleme kriminologischer Forschung. Köln, Berlin, Bonn, München: Carl Heymanns Verlag, 1981a, 187-223).

FRIDAY, P.C.: Delinquency Prevention Through Alternative Education. Presented at the International Symposium on Sociological Perspectives on Delinquency Prevention. (International Document and Study Centre for Conflicts of Youth (IDSC), University of Wuppertal, 1981b).

FRIDAY, P.C.; HAGE, J.: Youth Crime in Postindustrial Societies: An Integrated Perspective. (In: Criminology 14, 1976, 3, 347-368).

FRIDAY, P.C.; HALSEY, J.: Patterns of Social Relationships and Youth Crime. (In: P.C. Friday, V.L. Steward (Eds.): Youth Crime and Juvenile Justice: International Perspectives. New York: Praeger, 1977, 142-159).

FRIEDENBERG, C.Z.: The Vanishing Adolescent. (New York: Dell, 1959).

FUCHS, C.Z.; REHM, L.P.: A Self-Control Behavior Therapy Program for Depression. (In: Journal of Consulting and Clinical Psychology 45, 1977).

GARBER, J.; MILLER, W.R.; SEAMAN, S.F.: Learned Helplessness, Stress, and the Depressive Disorders. (In: R.A. Depue (Ed.): The Psychobiology of the Depressive Disorders: Implications for the Effects of Stress. New York: Academic Press, 1981).

GATCHEL, R.J.; PROCTOR, J.D.: Psychological Correlates of Learned Helplessness in Man. (In: Journal of Abnormal Psychology 85, 1976, 27-34).

GATCHEL, R.J.; McKINNEY, M.E.; KOEBERNIK, L.F.: Learned Helplessness, Depression and Physiological Responding. (In: Psychophysiology 14, 1977).

GATCHEL, R.J.; PAULUS, P.B.; MAPLES, C.W.: Learned Helplessness and Self-reported Affect. (In: Journal of Abnormal Psychology 84, 1975, 732-734).

GIARDINI, G.I.: The Parole Process. (Springfield, Illinois: Charles C. Thomas Publisher, 1959).

GLASER, D.: The Effectiveness of a Prison and Parole System. (Indianapolis: Bobbs-Merill Company. Original Ed., 1964. Abridged Ed., 1969).

GLASER, D.: Adult Crime and Social Policy. (Englewood Cliffs, N.J.: Prentice-Hall, 1972).

GLASS, D.; SINGER, J.: Urban Stress: Experiments in Noise and Social Stressors. (New York: Academic Press, 1972).

GLUECK, S.; GLUECK, E.: Unraveling Juvenile Delinquency. (New York: Commonwealth Fund, 1950).

GOLD, M.: Status Forces in Delinquent Boys. (Ann Arbor: Univ. of Michigan Institute of Social Research, 1963).

GOLDFRIED, M.R.; KENT, R.N.: Traditional versus Behavioral Personality Assessment: A Comparison of Methodological and Theoretical Assumptions. (In: Psychological Bulletin 77, 1972, 409-420).

GOODKIN, F.: Rats Learn the Relationship between Responding and Environmental Events: An Expansion of the Learned Helplessness. (In: Learning and Motivation 7, 1976).

GORE, P.M.; ROTTER, J.B.: A Personality Correlate of Social Action. (In: Journal of Personality 31, 1963).

GOTTFREDSON, D.M.: The Base Expectancy Approach. (In: N. Johnston, L. Savitz, M.E. Wolfgang (Eds.): The Sociology of Punishment and Correction, 2nd edition. New York: John Wiley and Sons, Inc., 1970).

GOUGH, H.G.; WENK, E.A.; ROZYNKO, V.V.: Parole Outcome as Predicted by the CPI, MMPI and A Base Expectancy Table. (In: Journal of Abnormal Psychology 70, 1965, 432-441).

GROTH, H.: Sozialdienst in der Niedersächsischen Strafrechtspflege. (In: Bewährungshilfe 27, 1980, 1, 86-94).

HAAN, N.: Coping and Defending: Processes of Self-Environment Organization. (New York: Academic Press, 1977).

HABERMAS, J.: Thesen zur Theorie der Sozialisation. Stichworte und Literatur zur Vorlesung im Sommersemester 1968. (Frankfurt/M., 1968).

HACKLER, J.C.: A Development Theory of Delinquency. (In: The Canadian Review of Sociology and Anthropology 8, 1971).

HAGE, J.: Techniques and Problems of Theory Construction. (New York, 1972).

HAGE, J.; MARWELL, G.: Toward the Development of an Empirically Based Theory of Role-Relationships. (In: Sociometry 31, 1968, 200-212).

HAHN, P.M.: Community Based Corrections and the Criminal Justice System. (Santa Cruz, Calif.: Davis Publishing Company, Inc., 1976).

HAMBURG, D.: Adaptive Problems and Mechanisms in Severely Burned Patients. (In: Psychiatry 16, 1953).

HAMBURG, D.A.; COELHO, G.V.; ADAMS, J.E.: Coping and Adaptation: Steps Forward a Synthesis of Biological and Social Perspectives. (In: G.V. Coelho, D.A. Hamburg, J.E. Adams (Eds.): Coping and Adaptation. New York: Basic Books, Inc., 1974, 403-440).

HANUSA, B.H.; SCHULZ, R.: Attributional Mediators of Learned Helplessness. (In: Journal of Personality and Social Psychology 35, 1977).

HARGREARES, D.H.: Social Relations in a Secondary School. (London: Rontledge and Keagan, Paul, 1967).

HASENPUSCH, B.: Prediction Techniques for Probation and Parole in Crime and/et Justice. (1977).

HASTORF, A.H.: The "Reinforcement" of individual Actions in a Group Situation. (In: L. Krasner, L.P. Ullmann (Eds.): Research in Behavior Modification. New York: Holt, Rinehart & Winston, 1965).

HEIM, E.: Coping und Anpassungsvorgänge in der psychosomatischen Medizin. (In: Zeitschrift für psychosomatische Medizin und Psychoanalyse 3, 1979).

HENKER, B.A.: The Effect of Adult Model Relationship on Children's Play and Task Imitation. (In: Dissertation Abstracts 24, 1964).

HINDELANG, M.J.: Causes of Delinquency: A Partial Replication and Extension. (In: Social Problems 20, 1973, 4, 471-487).

HIROTO, D.S.: Locus of Control and Learned Helplessness. (In: Journal of Experimental Psychology 102, 1974).

HIROTO, D.S.; SELIGMAN, M.E.P.: Generality of Learned Helplessness in Man. (In: Journal of Personality and Social Psychology 31, 1975).

HIRSCH, A. v.; HANRAHAN, K.J.: The Question of Parole. (Cambridge, Massachusetts: Ballinger, 1979).

HIRSCH, K.A.: An Extension of the Learned Helplessness Phenomenon to Potentially Negatively Punishing and Potentially Positively Reinforcing Stimuli Noncontingent upon Behavior. (Unpublished Manuscript, available from K.A. Hirsch, Galesburg-Mental Health Center, Galesburg, Illinois, 1976).

HIRSCHI, T.: Causes of Delinquency. (Berkeley: University of California Press, 1969).

HOMANS, G.: The Human Group. (New York: Harcort, Brace, 1950).

HORNEY, K.: Finding the Real Self. (In: American Journal of Psychoanalysis 9, 1949, 3-7).

HOUSTON, B.K.: Viability of Coping Strategies, Denial, and Response to Stress. (In: Journal of Personality 41, 1973).

HOUSTON, B.K.: Dispositional Anxiety and the Effectiveness of Cognitive Coping Strategies in Stressful Laboratory and Classroom Situations. (In: C.D. Spielberger, I.G. Sarason (Eds.): Stress and Anxiety 4. New York: John Wiley and Sons, 1977a, 205-226).

HOUSTON, B.K.: Open Ended and Structured Questionnaires to Elicit Information Concerning Coping Behavior. (Unpublished Manuscript, Psychological Clinic, University of Kansas, (Lawrence, Kansas 66045, USA), 1977b).

HOUSTON, B.K.; HOLMES, D.S.: Effects of Avoident Thinking and Reappraisal for Coping with Threat Involving Temporal Uncertainty. (In: Journal of Personality and Social Psychology 30, 1974).

HUNTER, I.M.L.: The Influence of Mental Set on Problem Solving. (In: British Journal of Psychology 47, 1956).

HUSSEY, F.A.; DUFFEE, D.E.: Probation, Parole and Community Field Services: Policy, Structure and Process. (New York: Harper & Row, Publishers, 1980).

ILFELD, F.W.: Coping Styles of Chicago Adults: Description. (In: Journal of Human Stress 4, 1980).

IRWIN, J.: The Felon. (Englewood Cliffs, N.J.: Prentice-Hall, 1970).

IRWIN, J.: Adaptation to Being Corrected: Corrections from the Convict's Perspective. (In: D. Glaser (Ed.): Handbook of Criminology. Chicago: Rand-McNally, 1974, 971-993).

JACKSON, E.F.: Status Consistency and Symptoms of Stress. (In: American Sociological Review 27, 1962, 4, 469-480).

JACOBSEN, H.-F.: Analyse der Nürnberger Zentralstelle für Strafentlassenenhilfe. (Unveröffentlichter Bericht, Nürnberg, 1980).

JACOBSEN, H.-F.: Research Plan. (Unveröffentlichter Bericht des Kriminologischen Forschungsinstituts Niedersachsen e.V. (KFN), Hannover, 1981a).

JACOBSEN, H.-F.: Die Kompetenz zur Auseinandersetzung (coping-competence) bei Probanden der Führungsaufsicht. (Unveröffentlichter Forschungsplan des Kriminologischen Forschungsinstitutes Niedersachsen e.V. (KFN), Hannover, 1981b).

JACOBSEN, H.-F.: Führungsaufsicht und Social Coping: Ein Institut der Strafvollstreckung unter sozialisationstheoretischer Perspektive. (In: H. Kury (Ed.): Prävention abweichenden Verhaltens. Maßnahmen der Vorbeugung und Nachbetreuung. Köln, Berlin, Bonn, München: Carl Heymanns Verlag, 1982, 717-785).

JACOBSEN, H.-F.; DUSSICH, J.P.J.: Zur Messung komplexer und dynamischer Phänomene auf der Verhaltensebene. (In: H. Kury (Ed.): Methodologische Probleme in der Kriminologischen Forschungspraxis. Köln, Berlin, Bonn, München: Carl Heymanns Verlag, 1983, 453-490).

JAMISON, B.M.; GUTTMANN, E.S.: An Analysis of Post-Discharge Criminal Behavior. (Sacramento: State of California, Department of the Youth Authority, 1966).

JAMISON, C.; JOHNSON, B.M.; GUTTMANN, E.S.: An Analysis of Post-Discharged Criminal Behavior. (Sacramento, Calif.: Department of the Youth Authority, 1966).

JANIS, I.: Psychological Stress. (New York: John Wiley and Sons, 1958).

JANIS, I.: Psychodynamic Aspects of Stress Tolerance. (In: S. Klausner (Ed.): The Quest for Self-control. New York: Free Press, 1965).

JANIS, I.: Vigilance and Decision Making in Personal Crisis. (In: G.V. Coelho, D.A. Hamburg, J.E. Adams (Eds.): Coping and Adaptation. New York: Basic Books, 1974, 139-175.)

JANIS, I.; MANN, L.: Emergency Decision Making: A Theoretical Analysis of Responses of Disaster Warnings. (In: Journal of Human Stress 3, 1977).

JENKINS, W.O.; SANFORD, W.L.: A Manual for the Use of the Environmental Deprivation Scale (EDS) in Corrections: The Prediction of Criminal Behavior. (Montgomery, Alabama: Rehabilitation Research Foundation, 1972).

JENSEN, G.F.: Parents, Peers, and Delinquent Action: A Test of the Differential Association Perspective. (In: American Journal of Sociology 78, 1972, 3, 562-575).

JOHNSON, B.: An Analysis of Predictions of Parole Performance and Judgement of Supervision in the Parole Research Project: Research Report No. 32. (California Youth Authority, 1962).

JOHNSON, G.; BIRD, T.; LITTLE, J.W.: Delinquency Prevention: Theories and Strategies. (The Office of Juvenile Justice and Delinquency Prevention, Washington, D.C.,1979).

JOURARD, S.M.; LASAKOW, P.: Some Factors in Self-Disclosure. (In: Journal of Abnormal and Social Psychology 56, 1958, 91-98).

JUNGER-TAS, J.: Verborgen Jeugddelinkwentie en Gerechtlijke Selektie. (Brüssel, 1976).

JUNGER-TAS, J.: Hidden Delinquency and Judical Selection. (In: F. Steward (Ed.): Youth Crime and Juvenile Justice. New York: Praeger, 1977).

JUST, B.: Das kognitive Defizit in der Erlernten Hilflosigkeit - Verfügen Hilflose im Fluency-Test über eine geringere Anzahl relevanter Items. (Unveröffentlichte Diplomarbeit, Bochum, 1980).

KARACKI, L.; TOBY, J.: The Uncommitted Adolescent: Candidate for Gang Socialization. (In: Sociological Inquiry 32, 1962).

KARMEL, M.: Thank you Dr. Lamaze. (New York: Doubleday, 1965).

KILLINGER, G.G.: The Federal Government's Parole Program. (In: Federal Probation 14, 1950, 2, 56-64).

KINGSNORTH, R.: Decision-Making in a Parole Bureaucracy. (In: Journal of Research in Crime and Delinquency 6, 1969, 2, 210-218).

KIRCHHOFF, C.; KIRCHHOFF, G.F.; JANSSEN, H.: Jugendgerichtshilfe und Strafvollzug - Überlegungen und Erfahrungen. (In: Sozialpädagogische Blätter, 1977).

KLEIN, D.C.; SELIGMAN, M.E.P.: Reversal of Performance Deficits and Perceptual Deficits in Learned Helplessness and Depression. (In: Journal of Abnormal Psychology 85, 1976, 1, 11-26).

KLEIN, D.C.; FENCIL-MORSE, E.; SELIGMAN, M.E.P.: Learned Helplessness, Depression, and the Attribution of Failure. (In: Journal of Personality and Social Psychology 33, 1976).

KLEINING, G.; MOORE, H.: Soziale Selbsteinstufung (SSE): Ein Instrument zur Messung sozialer Schichten. (In: Kölner Zeitschrift für Soziologie und Sozialpsychologie 20, 1968, 502-552).

KORNHAUSER, R.: Social Sources of Delinquency. (University of Chicago, Press, 1973).

KRANTZ, D.S.; GLASS, D.C.; SNYDER, M.L.: Helplessness, Stress level, and the Coronary Prone Behavior Pattern. (In: Journal of Experimental Social Psychology 10, 1974).

KROHNE, H.W.: Individual Differences in Coping with Stress and Anxiety. (In: C.D. Spielberger, I.G. Sarason (Eds.): Stress and Anxiety. Vol. 5. New York: Wiley, 1978).

KROHNE, H.W.: Parental Child-rearing Behavior and the Development of Anxiety and Coping Strategies in Children. (In: I.G. Sarason, C.D. Spielberger (Eds.): Stress and Anxiety. Vol. 7. Washington, D.C.: Hemesphere, 1980).

LAMONT, J.: Depression, Locus of Control, and Mood Response Set. (In: Journal of Clinical Psychology, 1972).

LAZARUS, R.S.: Psychological Stress and the Coping Process. (New York: McGraw-Hill, 1966).

LAZARUS, R.S.: The Concepts of Stress and Disease, (In: L. Levi (Ed.): Society, Stress and Disease. Vol. 1, London: Oxford University Press, 1971).

LAZARUS, R.S.; COHEN, J.B.: Environmental Stress. (In: J. Altman, J.F. Wohlwill (Eds.): Human Behavior and Environment. Vol. 1. New York: Plenum, 1978).

LAZARUS, R.S.; LAUNIER, R.: Stress-related Transaction Between Person and Environment. (In: L.A. Perövin, M. Lewis (Eds.): Perspectives in Interactional Psychology. New York: Plenum, 1979).

LAZARUS, R.S.; AVERILL, J.; OPTON, E.: The Psychology of Coping: Issues of Research and Assessment. (In: G.V. Coelho, D.A. Hamburg, J.E. Adams (Hrsg.): Coping and Adaptation. New York: Basic Books, 1974).

LAZARUS, R.S.; DEESE, J.; OSLER, S.F.: The Effects of Psychological Stress upon Performance. (In: Psychological Bulletin 49, 1952).

LAZARUS, R.S.; COHEN, J.B.; FOLKMAN, S.; KANNER, A.; SCHAEFER, C.: Psychological Stress and Adaptation: some unresolved Issues. (In: H. Selye (Ed.): Guide to Stress Research. New York: Van Nostand, 1980).

LAZARUS, R.S.; OPTON, E.M.; NOMIKOS, M.S.; RANKIN, N.O.: The Principle of Short-circuiting of Threat: Further Evidence. (In: Journal of Personality 33, 1965).

LEMERT, E.M.: Social Pathology: A Systematic Approach to the Theory of Sociopathic Behavior. /New York: McGraw-Hill, 1951).

LEMERT, E.M.: Beyond Mead: The Societal Reaction to Deviance. (In: Social Problems 21, 1974, 4, 457-468).

LENSKI, G.: Status Crystallization: A Non-Vertical Dimension of Social Status. (In: American Sociological Review, 19, 1954, 4, 405-413).

LERNER, M.J.: Observer's Evaluation of a Victim: Justice, Guilt, and Verdical Perception. (In: Journal of Personality and Social Psychology 20, 1971).

LERNER, M.J.; SIMMONS, C.H.: Observer's Reaction to the "Innocent Victim": Compassion or Rejection? (In: Journal of Personality and Social Psychology 4, 1966).

LEWIS, D.J.: Learned Helplessness: A Reply and an Alternative S-R Interpretation. (In: Journal of Experimental Psychology: General 105, 1976).

LEWIN, K.: Resolving social conflicts. (New York, 1948).

LEWIN, K.: Field Theory in the Social Sciences. (New York: Harper, 1951).

LIEBERMAN, M.A.; BORMAN, L. (Eds.): Self-help Groups. (Special Issue of The Journal of Applied Behavioral Science, 1976).

LIPTON, D.; MARTINSON, R.; WILKS, J.: The Effectiveness of Correctional Treatment: A Survey of Treatment Evaluation Studies. (New York: Praeger Publishers, 1975).

LOFLAND, J.: Deviance and Identity. (Englewood Cliffs, N.J.: Prentice-Hall, 1969).

LUMSDEN, D.P.: Towards a System Model of Stress. (In: I.G. Sarason, C.D. Spielberger (Eds.): Stress and Anxiety., Vol. 2. Washington: Hemisphere, 1975, 191-228).

MAIER, S.F.; SELIGMAN, M.E.P.: Learned Helplessness - Theory and Evidence. (In: Journal of Experimental Psychology: General 105, 1976).

MAIER, S.F.; SELIGMAN, M.E.P.; SOLOMON, R.L.: Pavlovian Fear Conditioning and Learned Helplessness. (In: B.A. Campbell, R.M. Church (Eds.): Punishment. New York: Appleton-Century-Crofts, 1969).

MANDLER, G.: Emotion. (In: R. Brown (Ed.): New Directions in Psychology. New York: Holt, Rinehardt & Winston, 1962).

MANN, J.W.: Adolescent Marginality. (In: Journal of Genetic Psychology 106, 1965, 221-235).

MARMOR, J.: The Psychodynamics of Realistic Worry. (In: Psychoanalysis and Social Science 5, 1958).

MARTINSON, R.M.: A Critique of Research in Parole. (In: R.M. Carter, L.T. Witkins (Eds.): Probation and Parole. New York: John Wiley & Sons, Inc., 1970).

MARTINSON, R.M.: What works? - Questions and Answers about Prison Reform. (In: Public Interest 35, 1974).

MARTINSON, R.M.; WILKS, J.: Save Parole Supervision. (In: Federal Probation 41, 1977, 3, 23-27).

MARTINSON, R.M.; KASSEBAUM, G.G.; WARD, D.A.: A Critique of Research in Parole. (In: Federal Probation 28, 1964, 3, 34-38).

MARWELL, G.: Adolescent Powerlessness and Delinquent Behavior. (In: Social Problems 14, 1966, 1, 34-47).

MARWELL, G.; HAGE, J.: The Organization of Role-Relationships. A Systematic Description. (In: American Sociological Review 35, 1970, 5, 884-900).

MASON, J.W.: A Historical Review of the Field of Stress. Part 2. (In: Human Stress 2, 1975).

MATZA, D.: Delinquency and Drift. (New York: John Wiley, 1964).

McCLEARLY, R.: How Structural Variables Constrain the Parole Officer's Use of Discretionary Powers. (In: Social Problems 23, 1975, 2, 209-225).

McCLEARLY, R.: How Parole Officer's Use Records. (In: Social Problems 24, 1977, 5, 576-589).

McGRATH, J.E.: A Conceptual Formulation for Research on Stress. (In: J.E. McGrath (Ed.): Social and Psychological Factors in Stress. New York: Holt, 1970).

MEAD, G.H.: The Genesis of the Self and Social Control. (In: International Journal of Ethics XXXV, 1925).

MEAD, G.H.: Mind, Self and Society.(Chicago: University of Chicago Press, 1934).

MEICHENBAUM, D.H.: Cognitive Factors in Behavior Modification: What Clients Say to Themselves. Paper Presented at the Association for Advancement of Behavior Therapy. (Washington, D.C., 1971).

MEICHENBAUM, D.H.: Therapist Manual for Cognitive Behavior Modification. (Unpublished Manuscript, University of Waterloo, 1973).

MEICHENBAUM, D.H.: A Self-instructional Approach to Stress Management: A Proposal for Stress Inoculation Training. (In: C.D. Spielberger, I.G. Sarason (Eds.): Stress and Anxiety Vol. 1 Washington, D.C.: Hemisphere, 1975, 137-263.)

MEICHENBAUM, D.H.; HENSHAW, D.; HIRNEL, N.: Coping with Stress as a Problem-solving Process. (In: H.W. Krohne, L. Laux (Eds.): Achievement, Stress and Anxiety. Washington, D.C.: Hemisphere, 1981).

MEICHENBAUM, D.H.; TURK, D.; BURSTEIN, S.: The Nature of Coping with Stress. (In: I.G. Sarason, C.D. Spielberger (Eds.): Stress and Anxiety. Vol. 2. New York: John Wiley and Sons, 1975, 337-360).

MERTON, R.K.: Social Structure and Anomie. (In: R.K. Merton (Ed.): Social Theory and Social Structure. 2nd Edition. Glencoe, Illinois: Free Press, 1957).

MILLER, E.E.: Furloughs as a Technique for Reintegration. (In: E.E. Miller, M.R. Montilla (Eds.): Corrections in the Community. 1977a).

MILLER, E.E.: Is Parole Necessary? (In: E.E. Miller, M.R. Montilla (Eds.): Corrections in the Community. 1977b).

MILLER, W.B.: Lower Class Culture as a Generating Milieu of Gang Delinquency. (In: Journal of Social Issues 14, 1958, 3, 5-19).

MILLER, W.R.: Learned Helplessness, Depression and the Perception of Reinforcement. (In: Behavior Research and Therapy 14, 1976).

MILLER, W.R.; SELIGMAN, M.E.P.: Depression and Learned Helplessness in man. (In: Journal of Abnormal Psychology 84, 1975, 3, 228-238).

MILLER, W.R.; SELIGMAN, M.E.P.; KURLANDER, H.M.: Learned Helplessness, Depression and Anxiety. (In: Journal of Nervous and Mental Deseases 161, 1975).

MINEKA, S.; KIHLSTROM, J.F.: Unpredictable and Uncontrollable Events: A New Perspective on Experimental Neurosis. (In: Journal for Abnormal Psychology 87, 1978, 2, 256-271).

MONAT, A.: Temporal Uncertainty, Anticipation Time and Cognitive Coping under Threat. (In: Journal of Human Stress 2, 1976).

MONAT, A.; AVERILL, J.R.; LAZARUS, R.S.: Anticipatory Stress and Coping Reactions under Various Conditions of Uncertainty. (In: Journal of Personality and Social Psychology 24, 1972).

MOOS, R.: Human Adaptation: Coping with Life Crisis. (Lexington: Heath, Mass., 1976).

MORRISSEY, R.F.: The Haan Model of Ego Functioning: An Assessment of Empirical Research. (In: N. Haan (Ed.): Coping and Defending: Processes of Self-environment Organisation. New York: Academic Press, 1977).

MOSCISKIER, A.: Delinquency in Regions under Intensified Industrialization and the Relation between the Dynamics of Delinquency and the Dynamics of Socioeconomic Processes (1958-1960 and 1964-1968). (In: Archives of Criminology 4, 1969).

MOSELEY, W.H.: Parole: How it is Working. (In: Journal of Criminal Justice 5, 1977, 185-203).

MOWRER, O.H.: Learning Theory and Behavior. (New York: Wiley, 1960).

MOWRER, O.H.; VIEK, P.: An Experimental Analogue of Fear from a Sense of Helplessness. (In: Journal of Abnormal and Social Psychology 43, 1948, 193-200).

MURPHY, L.: The Widening World of Childhood. (New York: Basic Books, 1962).

NATIONAL ADVISORY COMMISSION ON CRIMINAL JUSTICE STANDARDS AND GOALS: Correction. (U.S. Department of Justice, Washington, D.C.: U.S. Government Printing Office, 1973).

NEITHERCUTT, M.G.: Parole Violation Patterns and Commitment Offense. (In: Journal of Research in Crime and Delinquency 9, 1972, 87-98).

NEUPERT, G.: Jugendgerichtshilfe - Teil eines Sozialen Dienstes in der Justiz? (In: Zentralblatt für Jugendrecht und Jugendwohlfahrt 67, 1980, 8, 395-397).

NIEDERSÄCHSISCHER MINISTER DER JUSTIZ: Empfehlung zur Bewährungshilfe, Führungsaufsicht, Gerichtshilfe. (Hannover, 1979).

NUGENT, J.: Variations in Non-contingent Experiences and Test Tasks in the Generation of Learned Helplessness. (Unpublished Manuscript, University of Massachusetts, 1977).

NYE, I.F.: Family Relationships and Delinquent Behavior. (New York: MacMillian, 1958).

OHLIN, L.E.; PIVEN, H.; PAPPENFORT, D.M.: Major Dilemmas of the Social Worker in Probation and Parole. (In: National Probation and Parole Association Journal 2, 3, 1956).

O'LEARY, V.: Parole Theory and Outcomes Reexamined. (In: Criminal Law Bulletin 11, 3, 1975).

O'LEARY, V.; GLASER, D.: The Assessment of Risk in Parole Decision Making. (In: D.J. West (Ed.): The Future of Parole. London: Duckworth, 1972).

PARSONS, T.: The Social System. (New York: Free Press of Glencoe, 1951).

PEARLIN, L.I.; RADABAUGH, C.W.: Economic Strains and the Coping Functions of Alcohol. (In: American Journal of Sociology 82, 1976, 3, 652-663).

PEARLIN, L.I.; SCHOOLER, C.: The Structure of Coping. (In: Journal of Mental Health and Social Behavior 19, 1978).

PETRAGLIA, G.G.: Female Parole Violators: An Analysis of the Situational Aspects of Their Failure. (Ph.D. Dissertation, Fordham University, 1965).

PFEIFFER, C.: Jugendgerichtshilfe als Brücke zwischen Jugendhilfe und Jugendgerichtsbarkeit - Entwurf für ein Modellprojekt. (In: Zentralblatt für Jugendrecht und Jugendwohlfahrt, 67, 1980, 8, 384-395).

PHARES, E.J.; RITCHIE, D.E.; DAVIS, W.L.: Internal - External Control and Reaction to Threat. (In: Journal of Personality and Social Psychology 10, 1968).

POLK, K.; HALFERTY, D.S.: Adolescence, Commitment, and Delinquency. (In: Journal of Research in Crime and Delinquency 3, 1966, 2, 82-96).

PRICE, K.P.; TRYON, W.W.; RAPS, C.S.: Learned Helplessness and Depression in a Clinical Population: A Test of Two Behavioral Hypotheses. (In: Journal of Abnormal Psychology 87, 1978, 1, 113-121).

PRUS, R.C.; STRATTON, J.R.: Parol Revocation Decisionmaking: Private Typings and Official Designations. (In: Federal Probation 40, 1976, 1, 48-53).

PRYSTAV, G.: Die Bedeutung der Vorhersagbarkeit und Kontrollierbarkeit von Stressoren für Klassifikationen von Belastungssituationen. (In: Zeitschrift für klinische Psychologie 8, 1979, 283-301).

PRYSTAV, G.: Vorhersagbarkeit und Kontrollierbarkeit aversiver Reize als belastungsinduzierende Variablen. (In: Archiv für Psychologie 132, 1980).

PRYSTAV, G.: Probleme und Perspektiven der psychologischen Copingforschung. (In: W. Michaelis (Hrsg.): Bericht über den 32. Kongreß der Deutschen Gesellschaft für Psychologie in Zürich, 1980. Bd. 1. Göttingen: Hogrefe, 1981, 349-351).

QUINNEY, R.: Social Reality of Crime. (Boston: Little Brown, 1969).

RADLOFF, L.S.: Sex Differences in Helplessness - with Implication Center for Epidemiologie Studies. (Unpublished Manuscript, National Institute of Mental Health, 1976).

RECKLESS, W.C.: The Crime Problem. (Pacific Palisades: Goodyear Publisher, 1961).

RECKLESS, W.C.: The Prevention of Juvenile Delinquency. (Columbus, Ohio State, 1972).

RECKLESS, W.C.; DINITZ, S.; MURRAY, E.: Self Concept as an Insulator Against Delinquency. (In: American Sociological Review 21, 1956, 6, 744-746).

RECKLESS, W.C.; DINITZ, S.; MURRAY, E.: The 'Good Boy' in a High Delinquency Area. (In: Journal of Criminal Law, Criminology and Police Science 48, 1957, 1, 18-25).

REISS, A.J.: Delinquency as the Failure of Personal and Social Controls. (In: American Sociological Review 16, 1951, 2, 196-207).

REISS, A.J.: Occupations and Social Status. (The Free Press of Glencoe, 1961a).

REISS, A.J.: The Social Integration of Queers and Peers. (In: Social Problems 9, 1961b, 2, 102-120).

RENZEMA, M.W.: Coping With Freedom: A Study of Psychological Stress and Support in the Prison-to-Parole Transition. (Ph.D. Dissertation, State University of New York at Albany, 1980).

RIPPERE, V.: Comments on Seligman's Theory of Helplessness. (In: Behavior Research and Therapy 15, 1977).

RODMAN, H.; GRAMS, P.: Juvenile Delinquency and the Family: a Review and Discussion. U.S. Task Force Report: Juvenile Delinquency and Youth Crime. (Washington, D.C.: Government Printing Office, 1967).

ROGERS, M.F.: Instrumental and Infra-Resources: The Bases of Power. (In: American Journal of Sociology 79/2, 1974, 6, 1418-1433).

ROSKIES, R.; LAZARUS, R.S.: Coping Theory and Teaching of Coping Skills. (In: P. Davidson (Ed.): Behavioral Medicine: Changing Health Life Style. New York: Brunner/Mazel, 1979).

ROTH, S.: The Effects of Experimentally Induced Expectancies of Control: Facilitation of Controlling Behavior or Learned Helplessness? (Unpublished doctoral dissertation, Northwestern University, 1973).

ROTH, S.; BOOTZIN, R.R.: Effects of Experimentally Induced Expectancies of External Control: an Investigation of Learned Helplessness. (In: Journal of Personality and Social Psychology 29, 1974).

ROTH, S.; KUBAL, L.: Effects on Noncontinguent Reinforcement on Tasks of Differing Importance: Facilitation and Learned Helplessness. (In: Journal of Personality and Social Psychology 32, 1975).

ROTTER, J.B.: Generalized Expectancies for Internal Versus External Control of Reinforcement. (In: Psychological Monographs 80, 1966).

ROTTER, J.B.; SEEMAN, M.; LIVERANT, S.: Internal Versus External Control of Reinforcements: A Major Variable in Behavior Theory. (In: N.F. Washburne (Ed.): Decisions, Values and Groups. New York: MacMillan, 1962).

RUBIN, Z.; PEPLAU, L.A.: Who Believes in a Just World? (In: Journal of Social Issues 31, 1975, 3, 65-89).

SACK, F.; KÖNIG, R. (Hrsg.): Kriminalsoziologie. (Frankfurt/M., 1968).

SAGARIN, E.: Deviants and Deviance. (New York: Praeger Publications, 1975).

SARBIN, T.R.; ALLEN, V.L.: Rollentherapie. (In: H. Faulstich-Wieland (Hrsg.): Soziologie und Psychologie der Erziehung 1974).

SCHACHTER, S.: The Interaction of Cognitive and Physiological Determinants of Emotional State. (In: C.D. Spielberger (Ed.): Anxiety and Behavior. New York: Academic Press, 1966).

SCHMIDT, J.: Demystifying Parole. (Lexington, Mass. 1977).

SCHÜNEMANN, H.-W.: Bewährungshilfe bei Jugendlichen und Heranwachsenden. (Göttingen: Verlag Schwartz u. Co., 1971).

SCHUR, E.M.: Labeling Deviance Behavior: Its Sociological Implications. (New York: Harper and Row, 1971).

SELIGMAN, M.P.: Learned Helplessness. (In: Annual Review of Medicine 23, 1972).

SELIGMAN, M.P.: Fall into Helplessness. (In: Psychology today 7, 1973).

SELIGMAN, M.P.: Depression and Learned Helplessness. (In: R.J. Friedman, M.M. Katz (Eds.): The Psychology of Depression: Contemporary Theory and Research. Washington, D.C.: Winston-Wiley, 1974).

SELIGMAN, M.P.: Helplessness: On Depression, Development, and Death. (San Francisco: Freeman, 1975).

SELIGMAN, M.P.: Comment and Integration. (In: Journal of Abnormal Psychology 87, 1978, 1, 165-179).

SELIGMAN, M.P.; BEAGLEY, G.: Learned Helplessness in the Rat. (In: Journal of Comparative and Physiological Psychology 88, 1975, 534-541).

SELIGMAN, M.P; MAIER, S.F.: Failure to Escape Traumatic Shock. (In: Journal of Experimental Psychology 74, 1967).

SELIGMAN, M.P.; SOLOMON, R.L.: Unpredictable und Uncontrollable Aversive Events. (In: F.R. Brush (Ed.): Aversive Conditioning and Learning. New York: Academic Press, 1971).

SELIGMAN, M.P.; MAIER, S.F.; GEER, J.H.: Alleviation of Learned Helplessness in the Dog. (In: Journal of Abnormal Psychology 73, 1968, 3, 256-262).

SELIGMAN, M.P.; ROSELLINI, R.A.; KOZAK, M.: Learned Helplessness in the Rat: Reversibility, Time Course, and Immunization. (In: Journal of Comparative and Physiological Psychology 88, 1975).

SELLIN, T.: Culture and Crime. (New York: Social Science Research Council, 1938).

SHERROD, D.R.; HAGE, J.N.; HALPERN, P.L.; MOORE, B.S.: Effects of Personal Causation and Perceived Control on Responses to an Aversive Environment: The more Control, the Better. (In: Journal of Experimental Social Psychology 13, 1977).

SHOVER, N.: A Sociology of American Corrections. (Homewood, Illinois: The Dorsey Press, 1979).

SIGLER, M.H.: Abolish Parole? (In: Federal Probation 39, 1975, 2, 42-48).

SIMMEL, G.: Conflict and the Web of Group Affiliations. (London, 1955).

SIMMONS, J.L.: Public Stereotypes of Deviants. (In: Social Problems 13, 1965, 2, 223-232).

SKINNER, B.F.: Contingencies of Reinforcement: A Theoretical Analysis. (New York: Appleton-Century-Crofts, 1969).

SKOLNICK, J.H.; WOODWORTH, J.R.: Bureaucracy, Information and Social Control: A Study of a Morals Detail. (In: D.J. Bordua (Ed.): The Police: Six Sociological Essays. New York: John Wiley, 1967).

SMELSER, N.J.: Theory of Collective Behavior. (New York: Free Press, 1962).

SMITH, R.E.: Changes in Locus of Control as a Function of Life Crisis Resolution. (In: Journal of Abnormal Psychology 75, 1970, 3, 328-332).

SOLOMON, R.W.; WAHLER, R.G.: Peer Reinforcement Control of Classroom Problem Behavior. (In: Journal of Applied Behavior Analysis 6, 1973).

SOROKIN, P.A.: Society, Culture, and Personality: Their Structure and Dynamics. (New York: Haper, 1947).

STANLEY, D.T.: Prisoners Among Us. (Washington, D.C.: The Brooking Institution, 1976).

STATISTISCHES BUNDESAMT WIESBADEN (Ed.): Rechtspflege, Fachserie 10, Reihe 5: Bewährungshilfe. (Stuttgart, Mainz: W. Kohlhammer, 1979).

STOUFFER, S.A.: Analysis of Conflicting Social Norms. (In: American Sociological Review 14, 1949, 6, 707-717).

STUART, E.: Surveillance and Service in Parole. (Los Angeles: Institute of Government and Public Affairs, UCLA, 1972).

SUTHERLAND, E.H.: Principles of Criminology. 3rd Edition. (Philadelphia: Lippincott, 1939).

TAKAGI, P.; ROBISON, J.: The Parole Violator: An Organizational Reject. (In: Journal of Research in Crime and Delinquency 6, 1969, 1, 78-86).

TEASDALE, J.D.: Effects of Real and Recalled Success on Learned Helplessness and Depression. (In: Journal of Abnormal Psychology 87, 1978, 1, 155-164).

TENNEN, H.: Learned Helplessness and the Perceptions of Reinforcement in Depression: A Case of Investigator Missattribution. (Unpublished Manuscript, State University of New York, 1977).

TENNEN, H.; ELLER, S.J.: Attributional Components of Learned Helplessness and Facilitation. (In: Journal of Personality and Social Psychology 35, 1977).

TERRACE, H.S.: Classical Conditioning. (In: J.A. Nevin, G.S. Reynolds (Eds.): The Study of Behavior. Glenview, Ill.: Scott, Foresman, 1973).

THIBAULD, L.: Le groupe des pairs et la delinquance chez les adolescents. Thése de maitrise inedite en criminologie, Université de Montreal, 1974).

THIBAUT, J.W.; KELLY, H.H.: The Social Psychology of Groups. (New York: Wiley, 1959).

THOMAS, W.I.: The Problem of Personality in the Urban Environment. (In: E.W. Burgess (Ed.): The Urban Community. Chicago: University of Chicago Press, 1926).

THOMAS, W.I.: The Unadjusted Girl. (Boston: Little Brown, 1937).

THORNTON, J.W.; JACOBS, P.D.: Learned Helplessness in Human Subjects. (In: Journal of Experimental Psychology 87, 1971).

THORNTON, J.W.; POWELL, G.D.: Immunization and Alleviation of Learned Helplessness in Man. (In: American Journal of Psychology 87, 1974).

TIEMAN, Ch.R.: Social Control and Delinquent Behavior. (Unpublished Dissertation, Kentucky, 1976).

TILLNER, W.: Zur Trennung von kognitivem und motivationalem Defizit in Untersuchungen zur Gelernten Hilflosigkeit - Eine Untersuchung über Prozesse beim Anagrammlösen. (Unveröffentlichte Diplomarbeit, Bochum, 1980).

TYLER, B.B.: Expectancy for Eventual Success as a Factor in Problem-Solving Behavior. (In: Journal of Educational Psychology 49, 1958).

UNITED STATES: The President Commission on Law Enforcement and the Administration of Justice. Task Force Report: Corrections. (Washington, D.C.: U.S. Government Printing Office, 1967).

VAN COUVERING, N.: One-to-One Project Final Report. A Demonstration Program Sponsored by Stiles Hall. (Berkeley, Calif., 1966).

VOLD, G.: Prediction Methods and Parole. (Hanover, New Hampshire: The Sociological Press, 1931).

WALLER, I.: Men Released from Prison. (Toronto: University of Toronto Press, 1974).

WEINER, B.; HECKHAUSEN, H.; MEYER, W.; COOK, R.: Causal Ascriptions and Achievement Behavior: A Conceptual Analysis of Locus of Control. (In: Journal of Personality and Social Pschology 21, 1972).

WEISS, J.M.: Effects of Coping Behavior in Different Warning Signal Conditions on Stress Pathology in Rats. (In: Journal of Comparative and Physiological Psychology 77, 1971).

WEISS, J.M.; GLAZER, H.I.; POHORECKY, L.A.: Coping Behavior and Neurochemical Changes: An Alternative Explanation for the Original "Learned Helplessness" Experiments. (In: G. Serban (Ed.): Psychopathology of Human Adaptation. New York: Plenum Press, 1981).

WEISSMAN, A.D.: Coping With Untimely Death. (In: R.H. Moos (Ed.): Human Adaptation. Lexington, Mass.: Heath, 1976).

WEITEKAMP, E.: Kontrolltheorien seit Travis Hirschi - Causes of Delinquency - Unter besonderer Berücksichtigung des empirischen Beleges. (Unveröffentlichte Diplomarbeit, 1980).

WEST, D.J.; FARRINGTON, D.P.: Who Becomes Delinquent? (London: Heinemann, 1973).

WEST, D.J.; FARRINGTON, D.P.: The Delinquent Way of Life. (London: Heinemann, 1977).

WHITE, R.W.: Strategies of Adaptation: an Attempt at Systematic Description. (In: G.V. Coelho, D.A. Hamburg, J.E. Adams (Eds.): Coping and Adaptation. New York: Basic Books, 1974, 47-68).

WILLIS, M.H.; BLANEY, P.H.: Three Tests of the Learned Helplessness Model of Depression. (In: Journal of Abnormal Psychology 87, 1978, 1, 131-136).

WORTMAN, C.B.: Some Determinants of Perceived Control. (In: Journal of Personality and Social Psychology 31, 1975).

WORTMAN, C.B.; BREHM, J.W.: Responses to Uncontrollable Outcomes: An Integration of reactance Theory and the Learned Helplessness Model. (In: L. Berkowitz (Ed.): Advances in Experimental Social Psychology 8, 1975).

WORTMAN, C.B.; COATES, D.: Reactions to Victimization: A Social Psychological Analysis. (In: I. Frieze, D. Bartel, J. Carroll (Eds.): Applications of Attribution Theory. New York: Jossey-Bass, 1981).

WORTMAN, C.B.; DINTZER, L.: Is the Attributional Analysis of the Learned Helplessness Phenomenon Viable? A Critique on the Abramson-Seligman-Teasdale Reformulation. (In: Journal of Abnormal Psychology, 1978).

WORTMAN, C.B.; SILVER, R.: Coping With Undesirable Life Events. (In: M.E.P. Seligman, J. Garber (Eds.): Theory and Applications. New York: Academic Press, 1981).

WORTMAN, C.B.; PANCIERA, L.; SHUTERMAN, L.; HIBSCHER, J.: Attributions of Causalities and Reactions to Uncontrollable Outcomes. (In: Journal of Experimental and Social Psychology 12, 1976).

YABLONSKY, L.: The Violent Gang. (New York: MacMillian, 1963).

ZBOROWSKI, M.: People in Pain. (San Francisco: Jossey-Bass, 1969).

APPENDIX

TEXT OF SKITS

Figure 36:   SKIT: "Argument at the Dinner Table"

Announcer   : You will now see a short film about a family-situation. It is in the evening. Your parents just started to eat.

The film is recorded as though you were the camera. You just phoned a friend to make an appointment for the night.

(Dish noises in the background)

P.   : (telephone conversation) Yeah, yeah, you're gonna call Bernie, too? Yeah, that would be great, if he could come. About eight o'clock. At the Roxy. Sure, I'll be there. No problem. Hey, don't worry about it, I'll be there. Yeah, I know, that's what Charly said. Hey, talking about Charly, I gotta tell you something about him. O.K. about eight o'clock, I'll come. Hm.

Mother   : (Opening the kitchen door) Dinner is ready. Stop talking on the telephone. You can do that later. Come on now, before dinner gets cold.

P.   : O.K., I'll be there in a minute. (into the telephone) O.K., about eight o'clock then at the Roxy. See you later. Bye.

(P. enters the kitchen)

Mother   : Now sit down.
Father   : You should sit down when your mother tells you to!

(P. sits down)

Father :So how is school going? Don't you have anything to write?

P. :What do you mean, the mathematics things? Yeah, I flunked it. But I got a C-grade in English.

Father :So you flunked it. Typical. Big mouth and no brains. God. Just keep it up boy. But I'll tell you one thing: Don't fool around with me, is that clear? Now, I'll tell you another thing. If you don't graduate, then something's gonna happen.

P. :Like what?

Father :What will happen? I'll tell you what will happen: I'll kick you right out of this house. Is that clear? Right out on your ass. The thing is, as long as you are living on the money I earn, the least I expect of you is to graduate with decent grades and at the same time learn some kind of trade. We have enough wise guys around here. Being a wise guy will not support your family.

Mother :Dad!

P. :What are you getting upset about? Mathematics isn't the only thing in the world. And anyway, in the other classes I'm not so terrible. To be perfectly honest, I do not give a shit about school anyway.

Mother :Now try to be sensible. As soon as you finish eating you're going to your room to study. Now hurry up and eat so that I can wash the dishes. Tonight, I wanna watch Kojak.

P. :But tonight I wanted to go out with Charly and .....

Father	:.... do you mean to tell me, you wanted to go out tonight with those two friends of yours. I know, I know. Mother just told me. But this Charly and this - what's the other guy's name - this ....
Mother	:Bernie!
Father	:.... yeah that's it, this Bernie. They are just gonna have to go without your company tonight. Not to mention the future! Those two lousy hoods are the last people you need to hang around with! I wouldn't be surprised at all if they turn out to be nothings!
P.	:But you don't even know them!
Father	:To hell if I don't know them! I see them everyday driving up and down the streets with those motor cycles. They are both out of work and haven't got the <u>faintest</u> idea, what to do with their time. If they'd taken their time to learn some decent trade, they would have jobs now. And not to mention how they look!
Mother	:I have to admit, your father is right there! From those kind of boys you will never learn anything. They, for sure, will land in the gutter someday.
Father	:That's where they came from!
P.	:How do you know?
Mother	:It's plain as the nose on your face; you can see it!
P.	:See, see, what do you know about seeing. Those are my friends and they suit me just fine. I'm not going to let you tell me who my friends are gonna be or ain't gonna be. That's my problem, let me worry about it. They are more important to me than school is. At least you can rely on them.

- VII -

Father :Friends! Nice friends those two! They don't have any job, drinking alcohol all day, and bugging the people. I know. What I'd like to know is where the hell they get all the things: if you go out and meet these friends of yours tonight, then it's over, is that clear? Your pocket money then is cut off!

P. :But I already did my homework! Shit, I'll even wash the dishes if you want me to. All we're gonna do is go to the movies.

Mother :Now let's try to be sensible. And don't disappoint your father. He doesn't mean it like that.

Figure 37:   SKIT: "The Neighbor-Lady"

Announcer   : You will now see a short film dealing with a situation in the house where you have been living in for a few months. It is in the late afternoon and you just arrived home.

                    The film has been recorded as though you were the camera. It begins with the neighbor-lady ringing your bell.

Neighbor-Lady   : Tell me Mr. ......, is this your garbage-bag or do you know who it belongs to?
P.   : Good evening, I don't know who it belongs to. Sure doesn't belong to me.
N.L.   : Really Mr. ..... You know exactly that there are only three tenants living on this floor: you, humble person, and Mrs. .... So I .....
P.   : I don't really care, who lives here. All that I know is that it's not my garbage-bag.
N.L.   : But really Mr. ......you know exactly that Mrs. .....has been on vacation for two weeks. So it can only be your bag.
P.   : Now keep it cool.
N.L.   : What's that suppose to mean? Mr. .... remember the house-rules! Who would believe it, he simply threw his garbage in the hallway.
P.   : I've just told you that it is not my garbage-bag. Where did you get the big idea anyway that I'm the one who did it? Somebody else could have done it, couldn't they?

N.L.	:Mr. ..., the little elves, maybe, hm? Really, Mr. ...., this is a well run house, and you have exactly the same duty as all the other tenants here in this apartment-building. And that is to fit in with the house-community. So it has come that far already, puts the garbage in the hallway, shuts the door and thinks somebody else will clean up his mess for him. Mr. ......, that's not the way things go around here!
P.	:Could you please stop gaping about this stupid garbage-bag. What's going on here, anyway?
N.L.	:Well, Mr. ......, I don't want to get personal or anything, but for example your drapes, I bet you, they've never been washed. Mr. ..., you've got to pay more attention to things like that. What are the neighbors gonna think of you. Or what about the picture-window! Mr. ......, that really is so filthy, you can hardly look through it. You know, Mr. ......, they have invented something, understand, sprayed on, you wipe it off, works great. That's good, Mr. ...., you understand.
P.	:I think I know what I should do with my window.
N.L.	:Mr. ...., I would be glad to help you, to be a helping hand somehow. That's what neighbors are for, aren't they?
P.	:What I do in my apartment is my business, I'll do what I want to, and it's none of your business, anyway!
N.L.	:Mr. ......, you have to think about the reputation of this apartment-house! What this all have to do with me , you ask?

I'll tell you! Somebody here has got to take the responsibility of seeing that this place doesn't fall apart and seeing that it doesn't look like some pigsty and also seeing that people don't throw their garbage-bags in the hallway! Of course, Mr. ...., that has something to do with me. And you can also expect me to be on a look out in the future. And, Mr. ...., people who don't really care, who like to live in garbage, we can do without those kind of people, too. They can move out immediately. Believe me, Mr. ....., there are enough decent people who would gladly take your place. Don't you know that.

P. :I only know that I didn't put this god-damned garbage-bag in the hallway.

N.L. :What should a person do with people like you? Mr. ......, I'm offering you my help and what do I get for thanks? Mr. ......, that is not the way it works here. You cannot simply throw your garbage-bag in the hallway! Now clean up this garbage and take it downstairs and in the future, you ought to think a little more about the rules here. I have heard that the other tenants in this building talk about you.

Figure 38:   SKIT: "Poor Work"

Announcer   :You will now see a short film about a working place situation. After looking for a long time, you get a job. It is in the afternoon, in a short time work will be over.

The film is recorded as though you were the camera.
It starts with the boss looking at the work you spent a rather long time working on.

Boss   :Nick! Did you work on this part here?
P.   :Yeah, why?
B.   :I can tell you why, what did you do here? This is totally bungled up. The angles aren't right at all, tell me what this means.
P.   :I don't understand it either. I measured this piece exactly, before I put it into the machine.
B.   :Tell me another story. The angles in the front and the back do not fit at all. What do you think about that?
P.   :Boss, believe me, I really did it exactly the way you told us how to do it. But if it isn't exactly right, then it probably is because of the machine. The machine doesn't work anymore. You know the setting - the setting has a little play in it. In fact, the whole machine doesn't work very well. I think it's really too old.
B.   :What, the machine is too old? If it does have a little play in it, then you're sup-

	posed to hold your hand against it, exactly the way I showed you how to do it. And anyway, before you pass that piece along, you should have checked it over. That's quite normal isn't it?
P.	:Yeah, but it still doesn't work correctly.
B.	:Now he's gonna give me some lip, too.
P.	:Don't I have the right to say something?
B.	:Now I'm gonna tell <u>you</u> something: with your work attitude you're not gonna get very far here, you can count on that. Look what you've done, you completely bungled it up. And then you've got the nerve to try and open your big mouth.
P.	:I only meant that it's not my fault alone.
B.	:Yeah, perhaps it's mine?
P.	:That's not what I said.
1st colleague	:Just a moment, boss, about the machine: it's true what Nick said about the machine. This thing isn't a hundred percent right. The firm should have bought a new machine, then something like this would never have happened.
B.	:What a great idea! (to P.): What you've done here is wasted material at the firm's expense. Community work, complete indifference, and also bungled up. Completely bungled!
2nd colleague	:Now don't get yourself so excited. Everybody knows that the equipment isn't what it should be. And we, we are the ones who put up with it all.
P.	:It's not true, what you are saying. There is not much I can do about it, when the parts here can't be worked on more precisely. It's not possible anymore to set the machine exactly, and you know that as

- XIII -

	well as I do. In other companies machines have been put out of function years ago. That's what other colleagues told me.
B.	:That's about all I wanted to hear! Seem's that you don't like the whole company anymore. In that case, you can go. People like you, that sort we don't like having here! Why don't you go, find yourself another job? Stands around, everything bungled up and then starts giving me the lip. You probably would like to destroy the shop, wouldn't you?
P.	:Doesn't have anything to do with this!
B.	:I'd like to tell you what that has to do with this. These parts that are worked on, I'm responsible for them, they're needed, all right? And if they aren't correct, then the customers come to me and start bitching! Understand me? Then there are problems! But no, it doesn't make any difference to you! Main thing is that you get off work on time. You think, the faster you get home, the better. You would remember what I said, you can believe me.
P.	:Shouldn't think I'm gonna stand here and listen to all this shit ....
B.	:Hey, that's the end of it, all right? Now I want this work finished up. These parts have to go out today. All orders have to be filled. And that means, that every part is gonna be remade - remeasured and on that machine. And if you haven't finished in time, you gonna have the pleasure to work a little longer. After all you're to blame.
P.	:At four thirty, you can count on it, that I'm gonna go home.
B.	:We will see about that.

Figure 39: SKIT: "At the Employment Office"

Announcer : You will now see a short film about a situation at the employment office. You are out of work for some time already and are looking for a new job.

The film is recorded as though you were the camera. The film begins as you enter the officer's room.

Civil servant : Well, what can I do for you?
P. : Yeah, well, I'm looking for work.
C.S. : That's what I thought. What kind of work are you looking for?
P. : Yeah, well, I really don't know exactly. You know, I'm looking for work, that's not so boring, where I can have a little fun, that doesn't kill me so. I'd think I'd really like to .....
C.S. : .... what did you do last?
P. : Yeah, well, for the last three months I was working for Coca Cola. I worked part-time in the empties. I had to lift the empty bottle-cases on top of the convarse-belt. But that kind of a job, nobody can stand for very long. It's unbelievable the amount of noise there is in that place. You know from the empty bottles, smashing against each other, understand. And the pay, that wasn't that great, either.
C.S. : Oh, I see, part-time-worker, that's kind of what I thought. Being a part-time-worker you cannot expect to get any kind of fringe benefits. But with this job-market-situation, all these people out of

	work, I can imagine how many would be very happy to have a job like that, that's what you have to realize. You have to start being a little realistic and accept (your situation) the conditions.
P.	:Well, actually, what I'd really like to do is somehow work with cars. In the line of being a mechanic or something like that, you know, that's what I think I'd really like to do.

(Telephone rings)

C.S.	:(to the telephone) Hello? (laughs) Hey, it's you, don't have any time at the moment. Yeah, it's O.K. I'll call you back tonight, O.K.? Then we can talk in peace and quiet, alright? Yeah? Talk to you later! Well, bye then.
	(to P.) Could you tell me what qualifications you have and what's your school background?
P.	:Well, I've got my high-school diploma.
C.S.	:High-school diploma. Do you have any diploma in the area of mechanics?
P.	:No, perhaps I don't. I started a practical training course once, but that wasn't the right profession for me.
C.S.	:What kind of profession was it, by the way?
P.	:I started to be trained as a roofer.
C.S.	:Well, as far as working in the area of automotive, I'd have to say it looks kind of bad. I'm sorry, but I believe I don't have anything for you at the moment.
P.	:Yeah, that's what I nearly thought. Oh well, I can't do anything about it?

C.S.	:(turns over to the card-box) Oh wait, perhaps I do have something for you!
P.	:Yeah?
C.S.	:It is a job, working in a warehouse in a screw-factory.
P.	:Warehouse-worker in a screw-factory?
C.S.	:You could begin right away and the pay is not that bad.
P.	:I don't know - warehouse-worker in a screw-factory?
C.S.	:Well, at the moment that's all I can offer you. According to your qualifications, that's all considerable we can offer you right now. We have to orientate ourselves according to the job market, and at the moment there isn't anything else.
P.	:Isn't anything else, isn't anything else! Shit, I want a decent job. I'm sick of this part-time work at all the time!
C.S.	:I would be glad to help you further, but I don't have any influence on it. It would be best if you think the whole thing over once more and perhaps you can find something on your own.

- XVII -

Expamples of the Interview Interaction
According to Spacerounds

Figure 40: EXAMPLES OF THE INTERVIEW INTERACTION ACCORDING TO SPACEROUNDS: Family, Neighbor, Employment Office and Work

Spaceround: Family
1st interview:

Interviewer: How would you act in this situation?
Probationer: I'd go anyhow.
I. : In any case?
P. : Wouldn't say in any case, but I would behave the same way, just to get back at him.
I. : And what would you do if he would threaten to kick you out of the house?
P. : Then I'd go especially. Well, if he would have said it decently, I might have listened, but if he threatens to cut my money and things like that, I'd go.
I. : Couldn't you imagine another possibility?
P. : Of course, talking reasonably. But if he wants it that way, I'd act the same way, too. I'd have to find some sort of job just to get my money.

2nd interview:

Interviewer: How would you act in that situation?
Probationer: Think I'd find a way to get that money. Might be from grandma, if nothing else works. What else can I do? Can't force them to give me that money.
I. : Well, but what if he threatens to cut the money if you would leave.
P. : There's not much of a choice, if he's still a minor.
I. : And in this situation, would you go out with your friends?
P : In this case? Think so, just to get back at him.
I. : Do you see any other possibility?

P. : Sure, looking for some sort of job. Delivering newspapers or something like that. There is always something to do... It's always the same with parents, guess that's just family-life.

Spaceround: Neighbor
1st interview:

Interviewer: How would you act if you were Mr. .....?
Probationer: The neighbor-lady would get on my nerves. Anyhow, if I knew that it wasn't my garbage-bag, I wouldn't put up with that.
I. : What would you do?
P. : She should mind her own business. That's what I'd tell her.
I. : It wasn't your garbage-bag, etc.
P. : Could have been somebody else who put the bag there. Might be a tenant from upstairs or downstairs, that's what I would tell her, too. Not to mention that it isn't her business at all.
I. : But if she doesn't leave?
P. : I would close the door on her. That way I'd have my peace.
I. : And if she rings the bell again and again?
P. : Then I'd tell her a thing or two. I think she is really rude. First pretending as though she's helping and then telling everyone.

2nd interview:

Interviewer: How would you act in this situation?
Probationer: Would have sent her away. I mean .... can't tell her more than three times. If it was mine, I would have taken the garbage-bag away. But I wouldn't put up with this.
I. : What do you mean, you wouldn't put up with it?
P. : Slam the door and leave her outside. That's no way how to ......

I.   : What is no way?
P.   : How she started the thing with the garbage-bag. I mean if somebody gets on your nerves with a damned bag that doesn't belong to you, it's somehow funny, right? Had situations like that before .... "what you look like, how can you run around like that?"

Spaceround: Employment Office
1st interview:

Interviewer: Please try to picture yourself in that situation. You seriously need a job. How would you act?
Probationer: Well, if I really had to find a job, I would accept that one.
I.   : Besides this, are there any other possibilities?
P.   : Well, I could look for a job myself. I believe that if somebody seriously wants a job, he will find one. I found myself one as well, when I came out.
I.   : How did you manage that?
P.   : Well, I asked friends of mine, if they knew of some open truck driving job. One of them knew of a firm looking for truck drivers. I went there and introduced myself the way one should, so they hired me.
I.   : What other possibilities are there to react in this situation?
P.   : Well, accepting it or looking by yourself, that's all you can do, if one needs the money. Or you have to wait for some better job.

2nd interview:

Interviewer: How would you behave?
Probationer: Well, in his case I would take that job. I think he made a mistake. I would have taken that job first.

I. : But, of course, it didn't fit in with his plans.
P. : That's right, but nowadays you can not simply follow your own plans. That's my opinion. First I would go there, to find out what the job was like or maybe find another job on the way.
I. : And how would you manage that?
P. : Well, looking through the paper and the yellow pages, call firms, somehow I'd find a job. I would try at any rate. If there isn't any job, I can't help it, but I would try. Hanging around wouldn't help. I mean, some time ago I didn't care, but now my opinion changed.
I. : And what was your impression of the employment officer?
P. : Well, he wasn't seriously interested. He wanted to cut him short. That's what I noticed. Maybe it's not true, but it's the way I saw it.
I. : And how would you react to this behavior?
P. : First I would try to talk to him. If that wouldn't help, I would tell him to give me that job, and I'll see what is involved. He can't do anything else but to call the firms. What else should he do? He only got the offers in his card-index. I mean, I know that damned well.

Spaceround: Work
1st interview:

Interviewer: Imagine you are in the position of .... You got troubles with your foreman.
Probationer: What should I say? Didn't talk well to him, right?
I. : Right.
P. : Well, and then, it would have gotten worse, if he had given him more lip. I would have dropped that job and found another one. I wouldn't care.
I. : Well, that would be rather difficult, finding a new job.

P.	:	I wouldn't care. Even if I had to run around half a year. I wouldn't let him make a fool out of me.
I.	:	Wouldn't you work overtime or something like that?
P.	:	No. If he would have said seriously: "Will not happen again ..." and things like that, then it would be O.K. But if he talked on that way I would say: "Here you are, do that shit yourself!" I'm going! That's my opinion. I would have found another job, even as a road man. I wouldn't care. But not this way.

2nd interview:

Interviewer:	How would you react?
Probationer:	Well, there's not only the foreman, but also the grievance committee. That depends on the size of the firm. But the foreman isn't God himself. And if the other colleagues even say that the machine doesn't work right, and the foreman knows it himself and I really tried, but the machine bungles the piece, then I'll tell him that it's not my fault. And then I'd go one step further. One has to hold him responsible, if he knows that the machine doesn't work right.
I.	: Would you stay any longer in that firm?
P.	: Of course. (laughs) Wouldn't leave a firm because of one person.
I.	: But we are now talking about the objects he wants you to remake.
P.	: No, I wouldn't remake them. That's nearly extortion.
I.	: So you would contact the grievance committee?
P.	: Yes, or the foreman's boss. Don't know; but I think he is the training foreman, so there must be a top boss. I would contact the top boss and tell him how things are. Think I got support from my colleagues.

- XXIII -

COPING DIMENSIONS

Figure 41: COPING DIMENSIONS

1. CONSTRUCTIVE I (social)

Behavior is considered constructive when the client uses his or her social resources to fulfill the spaceround's normative expectation.

DESTRUCTIVE II (social)

This behavior is considered destructive when the client does not use his or her social resources and thus the normative spaceround expectations are not fulfilled.

2. CONSTRUCTIVE II (psychic)

Constructive behavior is that behavior that protects and strengthens the individual's sense of self worth. The sense of self worth is strengthened by striving to reduce the distance between real behavior and intended behavior.

DESTRUCTIVE II (psychic)

Destructive behavior is that behavior that does not protect or strengthen the individual's sense of self worth. In fact this behavior damages the individual's sense of self worth and renders it more vulnerable.

3. ACTIVE

This behavior shows that the person is self motivated and takes it upon himself or herself to activate existing resources.

PASSIVE

This behavior may manifest itself in either resignation, stubbornness, or helplessness. There is the expectation that others will take the necessary action.

4. GOAL ORIENTED

The client displays an intention to move toward a given destination.

FORTUITOUS

The client expects luck and is tentative and speculative in his behavior.

5. PROBLEM ORIENTED

Client is focused on the basic elements of the problem solving process.

NON PROBLEM ORIENTED

Client expresses behavior that has nothing to do with solving the problem.

6. PERSON ORIENTED

Client focuses on personalizing the problem, he or she reacts to the persons involved in the problem.

NON PERSON ORIENTED

This is behavior that abstracts the presence of other persons and does not acknowledge their presence.

7. SUCCESS ORIENTED

Client displays the expectation of achieving a goal, is confident and optimistic.

FAILURE ORIENTED

Client expects to fail, is not confident and displays pessimism.

8. RATIONAL

Behavior that is oriented toward long range and strategic action.

ACTIVISTIC

Behavior that is short ranged and spontaneous and based on feelings.

9. PEACEFUL

Behavior that binds a relationship and offers warmth and friendliness.

AGGRESSIVE

Behavior that injures a relationship and expresses coldness and hostility.

10. CREATIVE

Behavior that offers new ideas and develops previously non existing procedures for problem solving.

REACTIVE

Behavior which is limited only to responses from the interaction partner and offers nothing new.

11. LEGITIMATE

The client behaves within the formal rules, regulations, and laws. Negative sanctions do not follow this behavior.

NON LEGITIMATE

The client offers behavior that is outside the formal norms. Negative sanctions do follow this behavior.

12. TOGETHER

Behavior that includes at least one other person in the problem solving process.

ALONE

Behavior that excludes others in the problem solving process.

13. AUTHORITY IMMUNE

Behavior that identifies others on positions of authority as being on the same level as the client.

AUTHORITY FIXATED

Behavior that accepts another's power and permits himself or herself to be dominated.

INTERVIEW QUESTIONNAIRE

Figure 43: INTERVIEW QUESTIONNAIRE

1. How old are you?

   Date of birth: ....

2. How many years

   a) have you gone to school?   ....years
   b) have you been an apprentice
      or been in vocational training?   ....years

3. What is your marital status?

   ( ) single, but living together with my girlfriend/betrothed
   ( ) single
   ( ) married, living together
   ( ) married, living separately
   ( ) divorced
   ( ) widowed

   (show the answer pattern card and say "Maybe this card will help you find the answer")

4. What is your father's education?

   ( ) I don't know my father (***** then go on to question 7)
   ( ) I don't know
   ( ) no school diploma
   ( ) elementary school   ( ) with ( ) without graduation
   ( ) junior high school   ( ) with ( ) without graduation
   ( ) high school   ( ) with ( ) without graduation
   ( ) professional school   ( ) with ( ) without graduation
   ( ) specialty college/uni-   ( ) with ( ) without graduation
       versity

5. What is your father's profession?

   ....(Encourage client to describe clearly)

   (with retirees, as well as with those whose fathers are deceased, ask about their last activity)

6. What is his current profession?

   ....
   ( ) I don't know
   ( ) unemployed
   ( ) has been sick for a long time
   ( ) retired
   ( ) other ....

7. What is your mother's education?

   ( ) I don't know my mother (**** then go on to question 10)
   ( ) I don't know
   ( ) she didn't finish school
   ( ) elementary school   ( ) with ( ) without graduation
   ( ) junior high school   ( ) with ( ) without graduation
   ( ) high school   ( ) with ( ) without graduation
   ( ) professional school   ( ) with ( ) without graduation
   ( ) specialty college/uni-   ( ) with ( ) without graduation
       versity

8. What is your mother's profession?

   ....(Encourage client to describe clearly)

   (with retirees, as well as with those whose mothers are deceased, ask about their last activity)

9. What is her current profession?

   ....
   ( ) I don't know
   ( ) unemployed
   ( ) has been sick for a long time
   ( ) retired
   ( ) other ....

10. How much money do your parents earn together at present per month?

    ....before taxes   ....after taxes

    (with retirees, as well as with those whose parents are deceased, ask about their last income)

11. How large was your family, when you were 14 years old?

    ....(number of persons)
    ( ) I did not live at home then, but ....

12. If you are married: How many persons are in your own family today?

    ....(number of persons)

Instructions:

The term "important persons" refers to those persons in your past before your 14th year of life, who exerted the greatest impression on you or with whom you were often together.

13. Please, name the most important persons in your family, thus all persons to whom you are related before your 14th year of life?

    A..................rank ( )
    B..................rank ( )
    C..................rank ( )
    D..................rank ( )
    etc.

    "Of these persons, who was the most important for you?"
    "Was x more important than y?"

14. How often have you been together with your family members before your 14th birthday?

	never	monthly or less often	weekly or once every 14 days	2-3 times per week	4-6 times per week	daily
A	1	2	3	4	5	6
B	1	2	3	4	5	6
C	1	2	3	4	5	6
D	1	2	3	4	5	6

    etc.

    (show the answer pattern cards and say "Maybe this card will help you find the answer")

15. Who were the most important persons in your school before your 14th birthday? (if possible with names)

    A......................rank ( )
    B......................rank ( )
    C......................rank ( )
    D......................rank ( )
    etc.

    "Of these persons, who was the most important for you?"
    "Was x more important than y?"

16. How often had you been together with these persons before your 14th birthday?

	never	monthly or less often	weekly or once every 14 days	2-3 times per week	4-6 times per week	daily
A	1	2	3	4	5	6
B	1	2	3	4	5	6
C	1	2	3	4	5	6
D	1	2	3	4	5	6

etc.

(show the answer pattern card and say "Maybe this card will help you find the answer")

17. Who were the most important friends before you were 14 years old? (if possible with names)

A......................rank ( )
B......................rank ( )
C......................rank ( )
D......................rank ( )
etc.

"Of these persons, who was the most important for you?"
"Was x more important than y?"

18. How often were you together with these friends before your 14th birthday?

	never	monthly or less often	weekly or once every 14 days	2-3 times per week	4-6 times per week	daily
A	1	2	3	4	5	6
B	1	2	3	4	5	6
C	1	2	3	4	5	6
D	1	2	3	4	5	6

etc.

(show the answer pattern card and say "Maybe this card will help you find the answer")

19. Before your 14th birthday, what was more important for you, your family, the school or your peer group?

   ( ) family
   ( ) school
   ( ) peer group

Instruction:

The term "important person" refers to those persons that now have the largest influence on you or with whom you are often together.

20. Are your parents, brothers and sisters still important for you today?

   ( ) yes
   ( ) sometimes
   ( ) no (***** then go on to question 29)

21. Who are the persons in the family you come from (parents, brothers and sisters, grand parents, other relatives) who are currently important to you?

   A......................rank ( )
   B......................rank ( )
   C......................rank ( )
   D......................rank ( )
   etc.

   "Of these persons, who was the most important for you?
   "Was x more important than y?"

22. How often are you now together with these persons from your family?

	never	monthly or less often	weekly or once every 14 days	2-3 times per week	4-6 times per week	daily
A	1	2	3	4	5	6
B	1	2	3	4	5	6
C	1	2	3	4	5	6
D	1	2	3	4	5	6

etc.

(show the answer pattern card and say "Maybe this card will help you find the answer")

23. Do you regularly get money from your parents?

    ( ) yes   ( ) sometimes   ( ) no

24. Are you dependent on your family?

    ( ) yes ( ) mostly ( ) sometimes ( ) seldom ( ) never

25. Do the members of your family influence the way you think and the way you live?

    ( ) yes ( ) mostly ( ) sometimes ( ) seldom ( ) never

    (show the answer pattern card and say "Maybe this card will help you find the answer")

26. Are there persons in your family, to whom you can talk frankly about your problems?

    ( ) yes, with ....
                  ....
                  ....
    ( ) no

27. Do you and the members of your family, whom you just mentioned, have the same or similar ideas on how a person should live?

    ( ) yes   ( ) yes, somewhat   ( ) no

28. Are there persons today in your family, with whom you do things, go together to a bar or a movie, belong to the same sports club, or perhaps work together?

    ( ) yes, with ....
    ....
    ....

    ( ) no

29. Have you established your own family?

    ( ) yes   ( ) no

30. When yes, identify those persons who are the most important from your own family:

    A..............rank ( )
    B..............rank ( )
    C..............rank ( )
    D..............rank ( )
    etc.

    "Who is the most important one for you?"
    "Is x more important than y?"

31. (***** If "no" to question 29, then ask:)
    "Do you have a steady girlfriend/betrothed?"

    ( ) yes, but we are not yet living together
    ( ) yes
    ( ) no (***** then go on to question 40)

    (question about the girlfriend/betrothed should only be used as an alternative to the question about the family)

32. How would you judge the relationship between you and your wife/girlfriend/betrothed?

    ( ) very weak   ( ) weak   ( ) strong   ( ) very strong

    (show the answer pattern card and say "Maybe this card can help you find the answer")

33. Do you get money regularly from your wife/girlfriend/betrothed?

    ( ) yes   ( ) sometimes   ( ) no

34. Recently, how often have you been together with your wife/girlfriend/betrothed?

never	monthly or less often	weekly or once every 14 days	2-3 times per week	4-6 times per week	daily
1	2	3	4	5	6

    (show answer pattern card and say "Maybe this card can help you find the answer")

35. Do you always try to say what your wife/girlfriend/betrothed wants to hear from you?

    ( ) yes   ( ) mostly   ( ) sometimes   ( ) seldom   ( ) never

36. Before you do something, do you speak about it with your wife/girlfriend/betrothed?

    ( ) yes   ( ) mostly   ( ) sometimes   ( ) seldom   ( ) never

    (show answer pattern card and say "Maybe this card can help you find the answer")

37. Can you speak about your problems with your wife/girl-friend/betrothed?

    ( ) yes ( ) mostly ( ) sometimes ( ) seldom ( ) never

    (show answer pattern card and say "Maybe this card can help you find the answer")

38. Does your wife/girlfriend/betrothed have the same opinion as you about how people should live?

    ( ) yes ( ) yes, somewhat ( ) no

    ("How people should live, means: do you think that you share the same opinion with this person as to how one should behave, and what is right and wrong?")

39. Are you also together with your wife/girlfriend/betrothed in other places for example at work, during free time, or in the family you come from?

    ( ) yes, where................
    ....
    ....
    ( ) no

40. Are there persons at your place of work, who are currently important for you?

    ( ) yes   ( ) no
    ( ) no, I am unemployed
    ( ) no, I've been sick for some time
    (***** If no, then go on to question 48)

41. Who are the persons at work who are most important to you?

   A........................rank ( )
   B........................rank ( )
   C........................rank ( )
   D........................rank ( )
   etc.

   "Of these persons, who was the most important for you?"
   "Was x more important than y?"

42. How often have you been together with these persons away from your place of work?

	never	monthly or less often	weekly or once every 14 days	2-3 times per week	4-6 times per week	daily
A	1	2	3	4	5	6
B	1	2	3	4	5	6
C	1	2	3	4	5	6
D	1	2	3	4	5	6

   etc.

   (show the answer pattern card and say "Maybe this card can help you find the answer")

43. Do you have the same opinions about life as your colleagues?

   ( ) yes, with ....
                 ....
                 ....

   ( ) no

44. Can you speak frankly about your problems with your fellow workers?

    ( ) yes ( ) mostly ( ) sometimes ( ) seldom ( ) never

    (show the answer pattern card and say "Maybe this card can help you find the answer")

45. Do your fellow workers have an influence on what you think or the way you live?

    ( ) yes ( ) mostly ( ) sometimes ( ) seldom ( ) never

46. Do you try to say, what your fellow workers want to hear from you?

    ( ) yes ( ) mostly ( ) sometimes ( ) seldom ( ) never

    (show the answer pattern card and say "Maybe this card can help you find the answer")

47. Can you tell me, how important the work place is for you?

    ( ) unimportant
    ( ) rather unimportant
    ( ) rather important
    ( ) important

    (show the answer pattern card and say "Maybe this card can help you find the answer")

48. Do you belong to clubs or organizations, in the neighborhood, local bars or sports clubs?

    ( ) yes, where:..............
                   ....
                   ....
    ( ) no, why: ....
                   ....

    (***** If no, then go on to question 56)

49. Are there persons in the community that you consider very important? (if possible with names)

   A...................rank ( )
   B...................rank ( )
   C...................rank ( )
   D...................rank ( )
   etc.

   "Of these persons, who was the most important for you?"
   "Was x more important than y?"

50. How often were you together with these persons?

	never	monthly or less often	weekly or once every 14 days	2-3 times per week	4-6 times per week	daily
A	1	2	3	4	5	6
B	1	2	3	4	5	6
C	1	2	3	4	5	6
D	1	2	3	4	5	6

   etc.

   (show the answer pattern card and say "Maybe this card can help you find the answer")

51. Do any of these persons have contact with your family, or do they work with you, or belong to your peer group?

   ( ) yes, with ....
               ....
         in ....
               ....
   ( ) no

52. Do you have the same opinion as these persons about how one should live?

   ( ) yes, with ....
   ....
   ( ) yes, some, with ....
   ....
   ( ) no

   ("How people should live, means: do you think that you share the same opinion with this person as to how one should behave, and what is right and wrong?")

53. Can you speak frankly with these persons, that are neighbors, club colleagues or others about your problems?

   ( ) yes ( ) mostly ( ) sometimes ( ) seldom ( ) never

   (show the answer pattern card and say "Maybe this card can help you find the answer")

54. Do you always try to say what you think your neighbors, colleagues, etc. expect to hear from you?

   ( ) yes ( ) mostly ( ) sometimes ( ) seldom ( ) never

55. Are you influenced by these people in what you think and how you live?

   ( ) yes ( ) mostly ( ) sometimes ( ) seldom ( ) never

   (show the answer pattern card and say "Maybe this card can help you find the answer")

56. Today what is more important to you, your family, your work or the peer group?

   ( ) family
   ( ) work
   ( ) peer group

57. How important are people in your age to you?

   ( ) extremely important
   ( ) very important
   ( ) not more important than other people
   ( ) unimportant

   (show the answer pattern card and say "Maybe this card can help you find the answer")

58. Are there cliques or groups, that are especially important to you?

   ( ) yes, which ....
              ....
   ( ) no (***** then go on to question 67)

59. Identify the persons or groups in your age, who are <u>now</u> the most important to you?

   A......................rank ( )
   B......................rank ( )
   C......................rank ( )
   D......................rank ( )
   etc.

   "Of these persons, who was the most important for you?"
   "Was x more important than y?"

60. How often have you been together with these people recently?

	never	monthly or less often	weekly or once every 14 days	2-3 times per week	4-6 times per week	daily
A	1	2	3	4	5	6
B	1	2	3	4	5	6
C	1	2	3	4	5	6
D	1	2	3	4	5	6

etc.

(show the answer pattern card and say "Maybe this card can help you find the answer")

61. Are any of the people, in these cliques or groups, with you in other areas, for example at work or in a club (for example in a football team)?

    ( ) yes, with ....
          ....
          in ....
    ( ) no

62. Before you do something, do you talk about it with people of your group, clique etc.?

    ( ) yes   ( ) mostly   ( ) sometimes   ( ) seldom   ( ) never

63. Do you depend on people of your clique?

    ( ) yes   ( ) mostly   ( ) sometimes   ( ) seldom   ( ) never

(show the answer pattern card and say "Maybe this carc can help you find the answer")

64. Can you talk frankly about your problems with people of your clique or group?

   ( ) yes, with ....
      ....
   ( ) no

65. Do you believe that you have the same opinion as those in your group about the way one should live?

   ( ) yes   ( ) yes, surely   ( ) no

66. In these cliques or groups are there people who have been convicted of crimes?

   ( ) yes   ( ) no   ( ) I don't know

67. How often are you now in contact with civil servants?

never	monthly or less often	weekly or once every 14 days	2-3 times per week	4-6 times per week	daily
1	2	3	4	5	6

68. Are there government offices which are important to you? Name them please!

   A........................rank ( )
   B........................rank ( )
   C........................rank ( )
   D........................rank ( )
   etc.

69. Are there civil servants (like Parole officers, social workers) who are of importance to you?

   A......................rank ( )
   B......................rank ( )
   C......................rank ( )
   D......................rank ( )
   etc.

   (***** If no, then go on to question 75)
   "Of these persons, who was the most important for you?"
   "Was x more important than y?"

70. Do you always try to say what these civil servants want to hear from you?

   ( ) yes ( ) mostly ( ) sometimes ( ) seldom ( ) never

71. Are you dependent on these people?

   ( ) yes ( ) mostly ( ) sometimes ( ) seldom ( ) never

   (show the answer pattern card and say "Maybe this card can help you find the answer")

72. Do you have the same opinion as these people about how one should live?

   ( ) yes   ( ) yes, approximately   ( ) no

   ("How people should live, means: do you think that you share the same opinion with this person as to how one should behave, and what is right and wrong?")

73. Can you talk frankly about your problems with some of these civil servants with whom you have contact?

   ( ) yes, with ....
                 ....
              in ....
   ( ) no

74. Have you already been let down or disappointed by these civil servants?

   ( ) always
   ( ) often
   ( ) sometimes
   ( ) rarely
   ( ) not yet

Now we would like to know something about your <u>current</u> life.

75. Do you have a job?

   ( ) yes, a permanent job
   ( ) yes, a temporary job
   ( ) no (***** then go on to question 78)

76. If you have a permanent or temporary job, how long have you had it?

1-3 months	3-6 months	6-12 months	1-2 years	longer
1	2	3	4	5

77. Are you satisfied with your work?

   ( ) yes
   ( ) yes, mostly
   ( ) no, not particularly, but it's OK
   ( ) no, not at all
   (***** go on to question 80)

78. If you don't have a job, since when have you been unemployed?

1-3 months	3-6 months	6-12 months	1-2 years	never had one
1	2	3	4	5

79. Why did you loose your job?

    ( ) the company went out of business, many were fired
    ( ) due to your own fault (tardiness, lost interest, made too many mistakes
    ( ) I've not yet had a job

80. Where do you live now?

    ( ) with parents
    ( ) with your own family, with girlfriend/betrothed
    ( ) with friends
    ( ) alone

81. Do you get along with your neighbors?

    ( ) yes ( ) mostly ( ) sometimes ( ) seldom ( ) never

    (show the answer pattern card and say "Maybe this card can help you find the answer")

82. Can you cope with most of the things that happen to you in your life?

    ( ) yes ( ) mostly ( ) sometimes ( ) seldom ( ) never

    (show the answer pattern card and say "Maybe this card can help you find the answer")

83. When you have problems, do you give yourself encouragement?

    ( ) yes ( ) mostly ( ) sometimes ( ) seldom ( ) never

    (show the answer pattern card and say "Maybe this card can help you find the answer")

84. Do you have the feeling that in the future things will work out better for you?

    ( ) yes ( ) no

85. Can you usually persue your own interests?

   ( ) yes   ( ) no

86. How long were you in prison for the last conviction?

   ....months

87. When were you released?

   ....(Date)

88. Since being released from prison, how long did your parole last?

   ....months

THE INTEGRATION INSTRUMENT

Figure 44: THE INTEGRATION INSTRUMENT

I FAMILY OF ORIENTATION (parents, grandparents, siblings)

   ( ) no family of orientation

1. The relationship to my family of orientation is

   ( ) very good
   ( ) somewhat good
   ( ) average
   ( ) somewhat bad
   ( ) very bad
   ( ) no information

2. With regard to my family of orientation, I have the feeling that I belong

   ( ) very well
   ( ) somewhat well
   ( ) to some extent
   ( ) sometimes not
   ( ) never
   ( ) no information

3. The reactions of my family of orientation toward me are

   ( ) very positive
   ( ) somewhat positive
   ( ) average
   ( ) somewhat negative
   ( ) very negative
   ( ) no information

4. I'm involved with my family of orientation

   ( ) very often
   ( ) often
   ( ) sometimes
   ( ) hardly ever
   ( ) never
   ( ) no information

5. When I am with my family of orientation there are

   ( ) never any problems
   ( ) seldom problems
   ( ) sometimes problems
   ( ) frequent problems
   ( ) always problems
   ( ) no information

II FAMILY OF PROCREATION (wife, fiance, girl friend, children)

( ) no family of procreation

1. In my family of procreation I feel

   ( ) very well
   ( ) well
   ( ) average
   ( ) somewhat bad
   ( ) very bad
   ( ) no information

2. I have the feeling that I fit in with my family of procreation

   ( ) very well
   ( ) somewhat well
   ( ) average
   ( ) somewhat poorly
   ( ) not at all
   ( ) no information

3. The reactions of my own family toward me are

   ( ) very positve
   ( ) somewhat positive
   ( ) average
   ( ) somewhat negative
   ( ) very negative
   ( ) no information

4. I'm involved with my family of procreation

   ( ) very often
   ( ) often
   ( ) sometimes
   ( ) hardly ever
   ( ) never
   ( ) no information

5. When I am with my family of procreation there are

   ( ) never any problems
   ( ) seldom problems
   ( ) sometimes problems
   ( ) frequent problems
   ( ) always problems
   ( ) no information

V FRIENDS AND ACQUAINTANCES (peers, buddies, the gang, etc.)

( ) no friends or acquaintances

1. When I am with my friends and acquaintances, I feel
   ( ) very well
   ( ) well
   ( ) sometimes well
   ( ) hardly ever well
   ( ) never well
   ( ) no information

2. I have the feeling that I fit in with my friends
   ( ) very well
   ( ) well
   ( ) average
   ( ) somewhat bad
   ( ) very bad
   ( ) no information

3. The way my friends act toward me, tell me that I fit in
   ( ) completely
   ( ) considerably
   ( ) somewhat
   ( ) hardly
   ( ) not at all
   ( ) no information

4. When I am involved with my friends, then things go
   ( ) very well
   ( ) well
   ( ) average
   ( ) bad
   ( ) very bad
   ( ) no information

5. When I am together with my friends, there are
   ( ) never any problems
   ( ) seldom problems
   ( ) sometimes problems
   ( ) frequent problems
   ( ) always problems
   ( ) no information

*Interdisziplinäre Beiträge
zur kriminologischen Forschung*

Band 1
Perspektiven und Probleme kriminologischer Forschung
Herausgegeben von Dr. Helmut Kury
1981. 707 Seiten. Broschur 38,- DM. ISBN 3-452-19021-8

Band 2
Methodische Probleme der Behandlungsforschung
– insbesondere in der Sozialtherapie
Herausgegeben von Dr. Helmut Kury
1983. 287 Seiten. Broschur 24,- DM. ISBN 3-452-19540-6

Band 3
Prävention abweichenden Verhaltens
– Maßnahmen der Vorbeugung und Nachbetreuung
Herausgegeben von Dr. Helmut Kury
1982. 864 Seiten. Broschur 49,- DM. ISBN 3-452-19338-1

Band 4
Schule, psychische Probleme und sozialabweichendes Verhalten
– Situationsbeschreibung und Möglichkeiten der Prävention
Herausgegeben von Dr. Helmut Kury und Hedwig Lerchenmüller
1983. 590 Seiten. Broschur 39,- DM. ISBN 3-452-19451-5

Band 5
Methodologische Probleme in der kriminologischen Forschungspraxis
Herausgegeben von Dr. Helmut Kury
1984. 568 Seiten. Broschur 44,- DM. ISBN 3-452-19904-5

Band 6
Deutsche Forschungen zur Kriminalitätsentstehung und
Kriminalitätskontrolle
German Research on Crime and Crime Control
Herausgegeben von Prof. Dr. Hans-Jürgen Kerner,
Dr. Helmut Kury und Prof. Dr. Klaus Sessar
1983. 3 Teilbände 2.187 Seiten. Broschur 46,- DM je Teilband.
ISBN 3-452-19678-X

Band 7
Ambulante Maßnahmen zwischen Hilfe und Kontrolle
Herausgegeben von Dr. Helmut Kury
1984. 649 Seiten. Broschur 44,- DM. ISBN 3-452-20133-3

Carl Heymanns Verlag KG · Köln · Berlin · Bonn · München

Band 10
Kriminologische Forschung in der Diskussion:
Berichte, Standpunkte, Analysen
Herausgegeben von Dr. Helmut Kury
1985. 672 Seiten. Broschur 49,– DM. ISBN 3-452-20281-X

Band 11
New Perspectives in Control Theory:
Social Coping of Youth under Supervision
Von John P. J. Dussich
1985. 358 Seiten. Broschur 49,– DM. ISBN 3-452-20282-8

Band 16
Führungsaufsicht und ihre Klientel
– Intentionen und Realitäten einer Maßregel –
Von H.-Folke Jacobsen
1985. 264 Seiten. Broschur 45,– DM. ISBN 3-452-20461-8

Carl Heymanns Verlag KG · Köln · Berlin · Bonn · München